The Prosperous Translator
Advice from Fire Ant & Worker Bee

Compiled and edited by Chris Durban

The Prosperous Translator
Advice from Fire Ant & Worker Bee
Compiled and edited by Chris Durban

ISBN: 978-0-615-40403-5
First edition

www.prosperoustranslator.com

This book is published by FA&WB Press and is based on the original Fire Ant & Worker Bee columns that ran in Translation Journal from October 1998 through July 2010. Some content has been updated, and all information is believed to be correct at the time of printing.

Opinions expressed are the authors' own and are based on personal experience, which they are very happy to share. Feedback is welcome. Please send comments or corrections to fa&wb@translationjournal.net.

Book design: Mark Richardson

Index: Nicole Blakey

Dedicated to our endlessly fascinating correspondents and the many very generous expert colleagues who have allowed their brains to be picked over the years. There are some very skilled translators out there!

Contents

INTRODUCTION

My, how times have changed. Or have they?

The Fire Ant & Worker Bee column was launched in October 1998 by two translators who met on FLEFO, then one of the Web's very few watering holes for translation folk. The virtual ambiance was lively—at times rowdy—and infinitely stimulating.

Yet how success-averse many translators seemed in those days, even the articulate, skilled and manifestly dedicated ones. Combating a pervasive poverty-cult mentality was a noble cause, thought FA & WB, and we were proud to wade into battle.

A dozen years have gone by, and there are now countless sites and blogs and discussion lists dedicated to translation, many very insightful indeed. Yet myth, misinformation and the poverty cult still abound. Which explains our decision to review, tweak and publish this compilation of columns that originally ran from 1998 through 2010.

Warning: This volume is not an A-to-Z guide to translation; it gives no definitions, nor will it walk you through each of the steps involved in setting up and running your own translation business.

For a start, we opted from the beginning for a strict Q&A format, little imagining how very widely readers' questions would range. Second, these readers live around the globe, and the legal, tax and accounting environment varies enormously from one country to another. Third, at the core of the Fire Ant & Worker Bee credo is the conviction that if you want professional expertise on running your business, hey buddy, hire a professional. Read: lawyer, tax specialist, accountant.

We—the authors—are none of those. Who are we? Professional translators with decades of experience serving demanding clients who come back for more, plus an enduring fascination with the work itself—the best job in the world.

So here's the bottom line: regardless of whether you stride, blast or sidle your way into the market, professional translation requires a set of skills that take time and effort to develop and maintain. Happily—and quite rightly—there is a payback. Eugene and I sincerely hope our advice will help translator readers enjoy that payback, along with the texts that come their way.

Chris Durban

1
Is this a real option for me?

Some aspiring translators have visions of traveling the world or working from a beach house beneath palm fronds swaying in the Caribbean breeze. Others are seeking a path back into employment based on existing skills and semi-skills. Still others possess The Flame—a passion for words and language.

STUDIES

Q *The 27-year old daughter of an old friend is interested in pursuing translation studies. She grew up speaking both English and French, though English is really the language most spoken at home. Her father tells me she studied fashion design and spent some time as a wardrobe mistress in a theatre group, but her other pursuits sound not all that substantial ("other assorted B.S." is his term).*

He sounds modestly overjoyed that she has at last thought of doing something that could actually qualify as a career and wants to provide paternal encouragement. More specifically, he is wondering whether a degree program is absolutely necessary (vs. a certificate program), and whether there are places that do a particularly good job with teaching the skills of translation in a way that supersedes the particular language, or if the best programs are all within particular language departments. He is concerned also with the importance of developing a specialty. Any thoughts?

Roped In Expert

A Dear Roped,
Question 1: Is this young woman truly language sensitive? (Is she a rabid reader? Does she write for her own pleasure, or to be read by others?)

Bilingualism, while enormously impressive to monolinguals, is not on its own enough to guarantee a successful career as a translator.

Question 2: How rich is this family? A focused budding 27-year old translator may not need a two or three-year program to make the leap, but if she lacks discipline she must somehow acquire or polish her research and writing skills, and here a structured program might be just the ticket.

For details on specific courses, your best bet is your national translators' association. We are aware of quite a number of good certificate programs; she'd probably want to do her course in an English-speaking environment if that is to be her A language.

Re specialties, and to cite just one example, if she is interested in theater arts, she might apply for a place on a dubbing/subtitling course. But this is where money comes into it—can she afford a year or two in London, Manchester, Strasbourg or Lille?

Ultimately, beyond a certain age and level of job experience, a translation diploma is unlikely to make or break a career, although formal classes may be a good way to encourage a promising candidate to start creating the network s/he needs to hit the ground running.

A successful translator friend whose academic credentials are in a different field altogether remarked recently that his job satisfaction and business took off once he stopped "doing translations" to pay the bills and "became a translator," i.e., upped his intellectual investment and commitment.

That's the direction your friend's daughter should be headed in if she's going to make it.

FA & WB

Q *I'm fully bilingual, though I daresay a bit more fluent in English than any other language, Chinese being the other. I used to write poetry, and the most important thing I learned from that particular experience was that the translator's fluency in the target language was most important; while fluency in the original language is needed for picking up the nuances in the language, fluency in the target language was needed for expressing it. While I'm sure that's all old-hat to you, it was a revelation for me.*

I first noticed this when I started watching Chinese films and actually noticing the subtitles, and thinking to myself, "ugh, THAT was an awkward translation," or "THAT could have been done a lot better." I love the idea of seeing a graceful translation that mirrors the original language: using archaic English to express a passage in archaic Chinese, or using slang to show modern-day colloquialisms. It's gotten to be an obsessive habit, where I mentally try and translate every Chinese film I see. It seems like a plausible—and very appealing—career choice.

I'm currently undergoing my quarter-life crisis (I'm 19) and trying to figure out what, exactly, I'm going to do with my life. I'm studying at a university as a biochemistry major, though I've taken a few linguistic and cultural courses as well, as it strikes my fancy. But if I were to seriously pursue this translation-as-a-career idea, what should I do?

Are there any courses or paths of study I should look into? And lastly, any words of advice? (Things like, "Trust me, dear girl, you will regret becoming a translator" would be helpful about now, before I jump headfirst into it.)

May

A Dear May,
Do we all agree that it is far preferable to have a job one is passionate about? Good.

Successful, happy translators are, in our experience, all passionate about language and words, so you seem to be on the right track there. But to be successful, they also need outstanding writing skills and a specialization.

Why not use your remaining years in college to hone these skills—keeping in mind that a university specialization in biochemistry will get you off to a strong start in scientific translation, especially with your language combination. You can then branch out into film or other translation—texts that, like Heineken, reach the parts others don't.

FA & WB

PS: By the way, the late Federico Fellini agreed with you that film translation is not just translating words, rather the challenge of slipping humbly and discreetly into another culture. Bravo, maestro!

Q *I am an eighteen-year-old high school student in the US—ready to graduate, and thinking about majoring in Spanish, and possibly minoring in translation, in efforts to become an interpreter/translator in a hospital. Do a lot of people do this as a full time job? What is the pay? Qualifications? Demand?*

Any advice you could give me would be greatly appreciated.

Hospital Hopeful

A Dear Hopeful,
Interpreting and translation in health care are viewed as emerging fields in the US, but current demand depends entirely on where you live and whether you are willing to work by telephone.

Experts tell us that in some areas you can make a living as an in-person medical interpreter, while in others professionals mix medical interpreting with translation and interpreting in different venues, such as court and social service agencies. If, however, you are interested in working as a "telephonic interpreter," you can make a living (albeit not necessarily a good one) wherever you are, say these contacts.

For medical interpreting, you will need:

- Language skills, especially oral comprehension and production, including comprehension of regional dialects.
- Interpreting techniques and skills, especially in consecutive mode.
- Health care and social service vocabulary.
- Knowledge of anatomy, physiology, common medical conditions and common medical procedures.
- Awareness of health-care beliefs and practices of the communities for which you will be interpreting.
- All-important interpersonal skills.

To translate written documents in this field, you will still need specialist knowledge of medical procedures and social services, plus, of course, training in translation proper and excellent writing skills.

For more information on both areas and suggestions on training, check out the website of the National Council for Interpreting in Health Care at www.ncihc.org.

FA & WB

Q *I will soon be attending a university directly from high school. I love languages and dream of becoming a translator; French is my chosen foreign language, and I plan to major in it. Is this enough to work as a translator or is there a special school that I need to attend?*

If there is a special school, what is the amount of time to get the certification?

Is demand high for French/English translators in France? Do you think there is a large demand for French/English translators in the United States?

Language Student

A Dear Student,
We'll let the head of a premium US translation company answer this one:

"Forget about language schools. Professional translation is not about language, it is about ideas, mostly very technical or complex ones. Get a degree in mathematics or computer science. Go to law school. Learn how to assemble a lathe. Trade equities on a stock market. Above all, focus on how to write very well in your native language. When you learn your foreign language(s) of choice, go all the way—take courses taught in the language, live in-country for at least a year, fall in love with a native speaker, etc. But don't kid yourself: it will be your ability to write well in your native language combined with your technical knowledge of a specialty field that will determine your future in translation, not how cool French sounds to the novice ear on a fine spring afternoon. Also, get over the "certification" insecurity. Insecurity is very unattractive and you need to work on that if you hope to attract a young French woman (see "fall in love," above)."

This expert is in North America.

We are based in Europe and have precisely the same experience.

What the best translation programs can bring you is feedback on your work, and a chance to interact with other members of the profession. They can help you master key work processes and get your computer skills up to speed. The best teachers will also help you devise a strategy for internships—an essential means of positioning yourself for an enjoyable and lucrative career.

For information on translation programs in North America, contact the American Translators Association [atanet.org] for a copy of its *Guide to Translating and Interpreting Programs in North America.*

But don't lose sight of the fact that in professional translation you are judged by the quality of your work on the page, not the letters after your name.

FA & WB

Q *I am a university student in the US, halfway through my junior year. I'm a Spanish major, and am studying French on my own (successfully). I plan to study many languages as time goes by.*

The thing I value the most is being able to travel for extended periods of time in different countries. As I love the study of language, translation seems one of the very rare ways to support oneself and have total freedom of location. I would just like to know if I am pursuing an impossible dream, or if there really is a solid freelance translation market in which I could carry out my plans, even if I have to get a few clients here in the U.S. before going abroad.

World is My Oyster

A Dear Pearl,

Working as a language teacher or translator is a time-honored way of supporting yourself while visiting foreign countries. If you are just out of college, your financial needs are unlikely to be huge, which makes it all the more feasible. Enthusiasm—which you seem to have in abundance—is also a tremendous resource and will serve you in good stead.

But before you pack your bags, two comments:

• Immigration laws are increasingly restrictive, at least in the European Union. In general, Americans receive only a three-month tourist visa; work permits are almost impossible to get unless you work for a major corporation or are able to invest millions. So if you want to extend your stay in Europe, you may want to think about enrolling as a graduate student at a university. Unlike tourists, foreign students are allowed to work a certain number of hours every week in most EU countries.

• The real question is not whether a solid freelance market exists out there—don't worry, it does—but how solid your own skills are. While non-translators often view translation as a natural spin-off of fluency in foreign languages, successful practitioners know that it is first and foremost about writing smoothly and accurately in your native tongue.

Unless you're prepared to make a serious commitment to honing your writing skills (to a level far beyond what most people pick up in college) and specializing, you may find yourself stuck with low-prestige, low-paying jobs. Not that this need interfere with your enjoyment of an overseas experience. But it might—especially if you pick up a spouse, mortgage and kids en route, as sometimes happens.

Our advice? Define your priorities. If you want to delay your choice of a career while you indulge in the freedom of travel, set yourself a time limit. The streets of Europe are littered with expatriates who drift into a kind of limbo they find difficult to escape.

Oh, and—bon voyage!

FA & WB

Q *I am Colombian-Australian. I am going to finish high school by the end of this year, if everything goes all right. I intend to become a translator and wonder if you could advise me on a university in the USA, where I could study, as I tried in Australia, and they seem to focus on Asian languages rather than Spanish.*

Heading North

A Dear North,
Sounds like you need *Park's Guide to Translating and Interpreting Programs in North America*, published by the American Translators Association and touted as "the best source of comprehensive information on translating and interpreting education in the United States, Mexico, and Canada." You can order it online at www.atanet.org/bin/view.fpl/13761.html.

FA & WB

Q *I am about to embark upon a gap year in Latin America and am looking for ways of financing my plans. I can speak Spanish reasonably but not fluently, and, being an English student, can write English well, and have a good turn of phrase and sense of idiom. I recognise that I would not be able to command such high prices as professional translators, and that no translation agencies would be willing to take me on, but is there any work out there for young amateur translators? Nothing would be too boring or too badly paid for me. Any suggestions would be welcome.*

Gapster

A Dear Gap,
Ah, timing.

Your letter came in just after the last issue went to press, and we bet anything you're reading this in a cybercafé in downtown Quito with your non-refundable, non-exchangeable plane ticket home next March 30 stashed in the bureau drawer of the hostal you're staying at. There you are, sipping a batido de naranjilla, with a few rush assignments from Traducciones Acme in your bag.

Our advice: reconsider. Not the gap year, of course—taking a year off to see the world before starting university is a terrific idea. But your prime aim at this stage in your life and education should be to immerse yourself in a foreign culture and language 24/7. Which means hanging out with locals of all ages, speaking Spanish only, and acquiring life experience that will serve you later at university and out in the rat race.

The only way to achieve this is to avoid expats, and you are sure to stumble into their clutches if you venture across the threshold of even the humblest translation establishment.

You need money? Look around: if you like kids, apply for childcare positions (a great way to hone foreign language skills). Wait on tables. Flip the local equivalent of burgers. Pick grapes. Pump iron and sign up as a bouncer at a salsa club. But whatever you do, live and talk in Spanish—only Spanish.

If we've got this wrong and you're sleeping under a bridge, with no gainful employment in sight except trading on your mother tongue, consider conversation classes rather than dabbling in low-end translation. Direct oral exchanges will allow you to get mileage out of your laudable energy and early-gap-year confidence ("being an English student, [I] can write English well").

Best of all, conversations are by nature ephemeral, and thus entail less risk for clients, who deserve output several notches above student efforts even if they are shopping at the low end of the market.

FA & WB

Q *Hello, I stumbled across your website by accident and I have a question. I am a 19-year-old college student with no real direction. I have flip-flopped from business administration to carpentry to computer science to my present course of studies, languages, and am also taking an auto mechanics course for my own interest. I have above excellent control of my mother tongue, English, and I have an almost equal grasp of French because I was raised in both languages here in Quebec. I also have Spanish and German under my belt, but they are not as strong as my English and French.*

I have received several odd jobs doing translating for friends and family who know that I have a knack for writing and languages. I've even done some subcontracting work for a major automotive company, albeit through several middlemen. To put it bluntly, my interest has been piqued by translating and I would like to know how to get started in the industry. Canada is an ideal location because of the official bilingualism, but I would like to know if there are opportunities abroad or in the United States, seeing as I also have dual US-Canada citizenship.

I still have three semesters remaining in languages at my CÉGEP (the Québec version of junior college) and I don't know what, or if, I will study at university. There are translation programs here in Montréal, but I would like to hear your suggestions or counsel.

Need a Compass

A Dear Compass,
The sheer diversity of paths taken by practicing translators into the field makes it hard to give career-starting advice to someone as young as you. It's great that your interests are diverse, for this indicates curiosity, and burning curiosity is an essential prerequisite for becoming a translator.

Should you go on to university directly after CÉGEP or not?

If you are hell-bent on an academic career, our answer would be yes. But since you have already cut your teeth doing paid translation and enjoyed it, you may want to start working at least part time right after graduation. Become a translator? Before committing yourself, why not use your three remaining college semesters to look into your chances of finding "job satisfaction."

You might do it like this: pick a dozen French-English translators from the Yellow Pages and ask each one for an interview. Prepare a list of questions that interest you—how did they get started, how long have they been working in the field, do they work from home or rent an office, what subjects do they handle, how did they acquire specialist knowledge, what do they do to stay current, what equipment/software/books do they use, do they employ office help, what arrangements have they made for assuring quality (editing/proofreading/client review) and so on.

Not everybody will be immediately comfortable answering these questions; be sure to tell them that you will treat their information in strict confidence. Generally, though, people are flattered to be interviewed about their work. You should be able to get an idea of the diversity of translators and whether some of them lead the kind of life that you can imagine for yourself, too.

With some help from your academic adviser, you might even be able to turn this project into a for-credit paper, but make sure you preserve your respondents' confidentiality.

Whatever you decide, keep up the carpentry and car-repair work. Not only can you fix things for yourself, family and friends, but they provide an excellent counterbalance to a cerebral (and sometimes lonely) pursuit like translation!

FA & WB

Q *Dear Fire Aunt, Can I call you that just this once? I am a final-year French medical student aged 22 and have fallen like the proverbial ton of bricks for a free-lance translator who lives near Paris. Although this man is 63 years old and comes from a vastly different culture, I have decided, against the advice of my family and well-wishers, to wed my destiny to his and build a future with him, so much so that I have now made up my mind to give up my plans to be a healer of persons and instead become a translator (a "healer of words" as my sweetheart calls himself).*

As you must realize, this is a big step for me, practically a leap into the unknown, and so I have three questions for you, dear Fire Aunt.

Firstly, what is the success/failure rate for translator couples? I have been told that male translators, especially of the free-lance persuasion, are not always easy to live with, that they develop strange quirks and need to be humoured on a regular basis. Is this true?

Secondly, what is the tax situation for a free-lance translator couple in France? I know little about money matters but my sweetheart lays great store by them. Would you advise us to set ourselves up as a company? I am sure (and so indeed is my sweetheart) that I could persuade my father to finance us in this area even if he is still in his "tantrum" phase at the present time.

9

Thirdly, how would you suggest I set about getting work? My sweetheart is vague on this point, he says the market is "down" right now but I am sure you can help.

Madly in Love

A **Fire Ant rasps:** So sweetie "sets great store by money matters." An appeal to your father for funding is the cherry on the cake. Give this bounder the gate and get back to something serious.

Worker Bee advises: Fire Ant has a point. But there is also something that doesn't quite square in your own account (age 22, final year medical student?).

Assuming that was simply a typo—but worrying nonetheless: translators who make typos on essential issues don't last long in a competitive market—here's a stab at answering your questions.

1. Successful, happy translator couples are pretty thick on the ground, and depending on their language combination have a leg up on meeting the four-eyes revision criteria of the CEN standard on translation services.

2. The tax situation of translator couples in France is identical to that of other freelance professions (that's freelance without a hyphen, by the way). How were you planning to work as a medical doctor—self-employed or salaried? A skilled and market-savvy translator can, through specialization, earn as much as a medical doctor in France, but as yet we (and you, let's face it) know little about your skills.

3. As for suggestions on getting work, consult back issues of this column and the website of the French translators' association (www.sft.fr) for training courses, in particular a very focused one entitled *Réussir son installation et se constituer une clientèle.* This is offered three or four times a year, in Paris and in regional capitals.

This may be going a bit beyond our brief, but the suggestion that your dad might finance a company is unsettling. You should definitely run a credit check on your sweetheart (useful experience for checking out future agency and direct clients should you head down that road).

Q *I am a Syrian and am studying translation from English to Arabic and vice versa. I have a big problem: I do not know how to use the tenses in my translating. Would you please help me?*

Thanks at any way.

Would If I Could

A Dear Would,
Your question raises another one: how well do you have to know languages

in order to translate?

The answer, as always, is "it depends." Not just on the complexity of the text, but on the purpose of your translation—are you helping a friend out, studying resources on the Internet, drafting a brochure, or preparing evidence for a court case?

With that in mind, let's return to your query. We may be wrong, but the translating you refer to seems designed to demonstrate to your teacher that you have mastered certain structures in a foreign language. Fair enough—this translation-as-testing-device is certainly common in the foreign-language classroom. But genuine translation (for clients, bless their hearts) comes only after you have learned each language thoroughly. And that includes the verb systems. (Tell your teacher we said so.)

Note, too, that professional translators work only into their native language.

We are not familiar with works in Arabic—perhaps some of our readers might have suggestions?—but in English an extremely useful book for students in your situation is Michael Swan's classic "Practical English Usage" (Oxford University Press). It's well-written and insightful, with entries that explain a lot about English verbs and many of the other pitfalls teachers love to test.

FA & WB

CAREER CHANGE

Q*I am currently working as an ESL instructor in Japan teaching English. However I do not want to do this forever and I am thinking of entering translation. I am particularly interested in entering the video or film industry and subtitling foreign films. My second languages are Italian and French, and I am studying Japanese.*
1. How does one break into this field?
2. Do you know of any organizations where I can obtain information? Are there any institutions that train film/video translators in North America or Europe?
I Think I Cannes

A Dear Cannes,
You break into subtitling by being the right person in the right place at the right time.

So you start by developing the skills, then the network.

Like most types of translation, subtitling is much much harder than it looks. As our local expert Nigel Palmer says, you'll need "flair, practice, perseverance, a real interest in film as a medium, an amenable temperament and a crossword puzzle (problem-solving) mentality." And that's just for starters.

Subtitling is as much about reading the picture and the situation and knowing what does *not* need to be translated as it is about encapsulating everything said. For that reason, many good movie subtitlers are also film buffs/critics/scriptwriters, have been to film school, etc.

Nigel's hands-on suggestion: test your skills/potential by renting foreign films and trying to improve the subtitles without lengthening them. Focus on expressing ideas in the most concise and unambiguous way possible. Collect short words. Don't even think of applying for—much less taking on—a job until you have some mentored experience, since deadlines can be tight enough to drive even an experienced subtitler to despair. As a career choice, it is not particularly compatible with family life for precisely that reason.

Once you think you are on the right track skill-wise, get yourself into the right place: consult the trade press and professional sources to find out where films are being subtitled in your language combination/direction. Go there and find a mentor—someone whose work you admire. Establish contact, and be prepared to invest the time needed to hone your skills until your Big Break comes along.

Some universities offer courses in foreign-language subtitling. These may be useful (a few are excellent), but are by no means a passport to a living in subtitling. We also have a sneaking suspicion that some well-meaning academics launch and promote subtitling courses for no other reason than that these sound sexier than grammar and literature (oh, and that they like films). In a worst-case scenario, such programs will be staffed by failed subtitlers—the successful ones are busy producing subtitles! Steer well clear of them.

An Internet search will give you useful addresses, including this one: ec.europa.eu/culture/media/programme/index_en.htm

FA & WB

Q *I was head of human resources in a company that went broke and I'm thinking of going into business as a translator when my unemployment benefits end in June. I've already prepared a business plan and begun a correspondence course in translation. The instructors give me useful feedback, but I'm wondering if my work is really going to be good enough. How do I find out?*

Wondering in Wales

A Dear Wondering,
Seek out other translators. You can often attend several meetings of your local translators' association as a guest, even if you are not yet a member. Introduce yourself and talk to people.

But don't stop there.

Scrutinize the trade papers and business press for translations that give you the feeling the translator knew what he or she was doing and did it well. Contact the publication or author for the translator's name, and write to compliment them on their work. If you are really lucky, they may be willing to act as a mentor, taking time to review and critique your translations in exchange for input from you (proofreading texts, for example). Even if this is not possible, an established translator can often put you in touch with other translators in your position. Networking always pays off sooner or later.

Since you are in the UK, you might also look into the Peer Support Group (PSG) program run by ITI [Institute of Translation and Interpreting]. Run annually by a team of experienced translators, the course attracts about 20 translators each year from all over the UK and beyond, and gives ITI members planning a freelance career guidance in getting their business under way.

Above all, don't hide—get out and meet people, because some of them will become valuable professional contacts. And view your experience in a field outside translation as a plus: it has brought you subject-matter knowledge as well as insights into what end-users of translations expect and need. That will be priceless as you head into the market.

FA & WB

Q *I am a 28-year-old American and have little time due to my financial responsibilities. But I am working hard to reduce my cost of living, going as far as selling my house, to be able to accomplish the things I want in life.*

I studied French, German, Spanish and Latin in high school as well as Russian as an exchange student and for the one year of college I have completed.

Events in my life postponed further college education and I am now attempting to find a way to continue my education in languages. At this time however, I would not be able to attend a course of study with large weekly time requirements.

So here is my question: how might I be able to study for a job as a translator with the limited time I possess, given the need of a full-time job and a lack of additional income?

Are there certain programs that are better recognized in the translation community for their excellence? Is there a specific certification program for translation that is best recognized outside of the USA?

My goals are to live and work in Europe in a field I enjoy.

Many thanks,

Bobby in Pa.

A Dear Bobby,

Here's what we think: the deck is stacked against you as things currently stand.

You want to (1) live in Europe and (2) practice a profession you enjoy, both objectives that we wholeheartedly endorse.

Yet even a cursory attempt at drawing up a game plan to make this happen as a translator reveals a few gaping holes:

(+) You've dipped into the study of languages and enjoyed it—that's great.

(-) Your current foreign-language skills are not strong enough to build a career on.

(+) You realize that you need further training.

(-) You have neither time nor money to pursue such training right now.

Professional translators work in a tremendously exciting field with lots of opportunities, but these are only open to those who enter with a strong hand right up front. High-school level French isn't enough, and audio tapes and "learn Spanish while you sleep" methods do not scratch the surface of what a professional translator must know to set up in business and build up a clientele.

For that, you'll need outstanding writing skills in your native language; excellent foreign-language skills in your source language(s); an initial specialization in a field or two where demand is heading up; and a very good grasp of technology.

Most specialists also insist that the general knowledge picked up in a college-level education is a strict minimum. We tend to agree, even as we admire a few passionate autodidacts.

So if you want to learn more about the profession, contact the American Translators Association at atanet.org. If you want to build up your language skills but are not free to take classes, by all means hunker down with a teach-yourself method, watch satellite TV in your foreign languages, and join a salsa or tango club to meet some native speakers.

But if what you really want to do is live in Europe, get a plan B.

You don't mention what your present job is, but is an overseas posting with your current employer an option? Keep in mind that you will need to get your papers in order in any case. As we advised a student correspondent in January 2000 (see World is My Oyster, page 5), "The streets of Europe are littered with expatriates who drift into a kind of limbo." With visas and work permits now required Europe-wide for non-EU citizens, it is unlikely that you'll get even that far.

FA & WB

Q *I graduated ten years ago in History, but am only now trying to return to the job market (I am 41).*

My language skills were really gained at school level where I got some good grades (German Grade B, French C), but as you can see from my age, that was some time ago.

Yet I have recently brushed up my skills, mainly through reading, and I would say I can now read general texts fairly fluently in German. I would also say I can write well in English.

I would like to know where I stand with my present level of competence, and how far I need to improve to reach the level required of a professional translator.

I would really like some way of gauging my current German language competence and, should it not be adequate to the task, how I can make it so, and how long that would take.

Finally, in your professional opinion, is it realistic for me to consider this career option, given my age and background, as I really can't afford to waste time on unrealistic dreams at this stage?

Late Learner in London

A Dear Learner,

Accuracy, speed and style are generally what clients look for in a translator, although not necessarily in that order. Different market segments have different priorities—ideally you will seek one where demand is on the rise and you can maximize your special strengths.

If you write well in your native English, you are one step up. But reading general texts in your foreign language "fairly fluently" is below the bare-bones minimum; increasingly, translation buyers seek suppliers offering total fluency in their foreign language as well as in-depth knowledge of one or more specialized fields. Most successful translators will also have spent at least some

15

time living in the country where their source language is spoken.

So—if you are seriously contemplating a career in translation, you've got some very hard work ahead.

Concrete steps?

You don't say what you've been up to since leaving school, but you might analyze your work and life experience to date to see what specialist knowledge you've picked up en route and consider building on this as a focus for your language learning.

You might also try translating a few passages and submitting these to a practicing translator for an opinion. Where do you find one of these? Being in the UK, you should visit the website of the Institute of Translation and Interpreting (iti.org.uk).

You might also go along to one of the increasing number of universities offering short translation courses and ask for an opinion. Here too, ITI can help put you in touch.

Join online translator forums and lurk or participate actively to gain insights into issues affecting professionals and their language skills.

A final thought: most of the successful professional translators we know have a genuine fascination—even passion—for language. The Flame. This may be what makes many of them so eccentric, er, creative. Whether or not you've got that is something only you know, but its presence or absence may also help you decide whether to pursue this career option further.

FA & WB

Q*I am a Russian lady living in Florida for 8 years by now. I would like to obtain information about employment opportunity translating Russian into English and English into Russian. I am fluent in both languages. Please, let me know if you can help me. I appreciate your time. Thank you.*

Rimma

A Dear Rimma,
The golden rule in translation is that professionals work into their native language only. Full stop. Be sure to keep that in mind as you investigate career options; there are some awkwardnesses in your letter that underscore the risk of translating into a non-native language.

One option might be to team up with a native English-speaking translator working out of Russian. You could then reread each other's work, acting as safety nets. But this is only possible if the numbers add up.

The best place to find information about the profession is your national association of translators—in the US, that's ATA (www.atanet.org). Give them a call, then dip your toe in the surf by attending local meetings and talking with translators who have already set up.

Желаем удачи!

FA & WB

Q *I would be extremely appreciative if you could help me evaluate whether my current plan makes sense and deserves investment of time.*

I am in a serious financial bind right now, and I need to increase my family's income by $400 US per month. I can devote about 20 hours per week to this project, but if this will take months to start then I need to do something else.

To give you some background, I am from the United States and presently living in Mexico. My Spanish is fairly good but I do not yet understand the culture or the economy here. I have almost finished a Master's degree in Community Counseling back in the US. I have worked as an interpreter but have no training in translation.

My plan is to do literary, legal, or business translations. I prefer to translate from Spanish to English, but for less than US $4.00/hour I can employ good writers of Spanish to help me produce high quality translations from English to Spanish.

My immediate problem is that I have no customers.

I would also like to do editing of academic writing here, if I can attract customers. I am leaving flyers at local universities for proofreading or editing of English language academic writings.

I have been trying to find customers through personal contacts. Right now I am working to enhance my website. My next step may be to do some unsolicited literary translations and give them to the authors in hopes of getting some attention.

Another option is to go to the United States for a week to try to drum up some business among attorneys and professors I know. I don't have any international business leads, but suppose I could visit companies in hopes of connecting with a need.

The advantage I have to offer is a much lower price than other high-quality Internet translation services, and my service can also be customized to the client's needs.

Can you give any suggestions to help me evaluate what aspects of my plan might be most realistic for helping my family out of our immediate financial crisis? Do you know about the market for thesis editing in Mexico?

By the way, I respect good translators and their work, and while the urgency of my situation makes me bold to presume I am one, I intend to keep learning and to

17

become increasingly worthy of the profession!

South of the Border

A Fire Ant rasps: Do something else.
Worker Bee buzzes: Better invest your time and effort elsewhere, South, for this is a dead one. There are simply too many competitors trying to do something along the lines of what you've got in mind, but with a huge head start on you. I.e., they already understand the local culture and the economy, and already speak and write excellent Spanish. Many are under less financial pressure, and can invest the time needed to build their business: unless you are extremely well connected and have a portfolio of successful projects to show prospects, "going to the US for a week" ain't gonna secure you a client base there.

Many of your competitors will also be able to judge the quality of what the $4.00-an-hour "good writers" are handing in (from your letter, we're not sure how you were planning to cover that one, which—admit it—is essential). Which is why many of them will have given this supplier group a miss.

In short, your perceived advantage—"a much lower price than other high-quality Internet translation services, and my service can also be customized to the client's needs"—may look good on paper to people who know nothing about how translation is performed and sold, but is desperately hollow in real life.

Moving right along, do you know anything about law and legal translation?

In addition, bare-bones minimal market research will show you that academics are notorious skinflints (and yes, many of our best friends are academics) and that literary translators all have day jobs.

Finally, even if you plan to work through translation agencies, your pricing is wrong: a translation company owner comments that he might be tempted to try out a translator out if he or she is 10 to 20% cheaper than the going rate, but says that if the rate is way below that, "it betrays the novice who doesn't know how much to charge or is insecure regarding his or her competence." Just like being offered a car for less than half of its fair market value leaves the impression that either it's stolen or there's something fundamentally wrong with it.

Nope, back to the drawing board.

Q *YES!! I HAVE THE FLAME!!! (jumping up and down, high fives all around!!!!!) Ding dong!!! (rap rap rap) Let me in dearies, I'm home!!! (fluttering of eyelashes, beseeching look)*

Thank you for the hard work you have obviously invested in this website. I delight in the reading of it. And I was genuinely thrilled to read the words (paraphrase) "Most of the successful professional translators we know have a genuine fascination—even passion—for language. The Flame. Whether or not you've got that is something only you know, but its presence or absence may also help you decide whether to pursue this career option further."

HOLY COW, I am not a freak after all. (mouth agape)

I am so happy and relieved to know my "malady" has a name and face. And you call it "The Flame", yes? My, but you are a SMART fire ant and worker bee. Because it truly does feel just like a flame. I nearly burn up just thinking of where a word originated from, and what necessitated that invention, and then I am overcome by a desperately greedy wish to be immersed in every culture so that I may KNOW the answers to ALL "Mysteries of the Word"!! Unearthing secret treasures like this, manipulating the language however you fancy—isn't it so exciting??!! (deep sigh) Pure bliss, I tell you. Rapture.

I thought I was just plain weird. Thanks to you, I now see there was a perfectly reasonable explanation behind my obsessive behavior, and that I am NOT weird. (okay, maybe a little eccentric—you got me!) But now, dear fire ant and worker bee: Could you advise me how best to go about using my "flame"??

Having never been, I want to go to college NOW. But, alas, I will have to wait a couple of years (when time constraints have lessened, i.e., work and children) for this greatly anticipated event. But I am 36—isn't it too late for me?? Will I really have a future in this field "at my age"?? I have to do SOMETHING—my friends, and family, and acquaintances, and strangers are sick to death of receiving 15 page (typewritten) letters from me every few days!!!! (yes, I write to strangers, too. You would not BELIEVE some of the reactions I've gotten) I'm not exaggerating about 15 pages, either—hear me now and believe me later!!!

I have been doing that since I was about eight, and I can't help it, the words simply spew out of me. Please, could you just take a peek at some of my below listed "obsessions", and would you then be kind enough to impart your sage counsel??? (if you merely write back to say "hi" I'll be happy)

1. I am fascinated by writing. I love to write and can't STOP (nothing of true substance, very sophomoronic as you can see—my writing skill was unfortunately stunted in high school)

2. I am fascinated by words. (if I see a word I don't know the meaning of, I will mentally dissect it until I can ascertain the required information. Or, as I like to call it, "The Jackpot")

3. I am fascinated by the dream of reading, writing, and speaking in foreign languages. (Latin, Farsi, French, Italian, Spanish, German, and Japanese especially—but I'm a glutton for more. Told you I was greedy)

19

4. I am fascinated by the idea of learning everything about different cultures (but not simply book learning, I want to behave precisely as the natives do)
5. I am fascinated by manners, and believe that ETIQUETTE RULES. Miss Manners is my hero. (well that has to help me somehow, right? Particularly in regard to Japanese culture!)

So what do you think? There are two really great universities near me:

Southeastern University in Hammond, La., and Louisiana State University In Baton Rouge. If I want to become a translator, should I get four years majoring in foreign language, with a minor in (fill in the blank) and then get specialized "translator" training elsewhere, or what?? I'm unsure how to go about this, and so I really need the benefit of YOUR advice via personal experience.

Thanks so much for reading this far. (ha!) I appreciate your time and attention!!!
Sherri, of the Grossly Talkative Clan

Fire Ant buzzes: Confirmation: to be a translator, you must master at least one foreign language. That is the first step in FA & WB's "10 steps to success as a translator" program. Come back when you've got it under your belt and we'll tell you about steps two to ten.

Worker Bee hums: Your enthusiasm is heart-warming, Sherri, but (pursed lips, furrowed brow) to make it as a translator you need the Flame + the Skills and a whole lot more. So go to college, major in a foreign language and minor in communications and technical writing. But keep your day job.

Q *I am currently a German teacher in New York State. I studied at a German university for two years and then worked for a US luxury retailer in Frankfurt for a year. I've now been back in New York for three years and am totally bored and uninterested in teaching. I am looking to begin translating but have no experience. I know that if given a sample translation I could do a good job but how do I get agencies to even give me the time of day?*

I have filled out many online applications but without result because I have no work experience. I have just discovered a program at New York University that offers a translation certificate. Would this help my chances? I just don't know how or where to begin. My teaching job runs through June and I would hate to start a new school year in September.

Classroom Blues

A Dear Blues,
Well, what's to stop you from sitting down and producing some sample

work? Translation, like writing, is one of those activities where the conviction that you've got it in you will only get you so far: at some point you have to sit down at the keyboard and produce.

Feedback from qualified critics will let you know if your work has promise, while tracking time spent and calculating after-tax income will let you know if this new career is one you might be able to live with and through. For your first efforts, select texts in an area you know well—luxury goods? Retailing? But watch the business press for mention of hot subjects and industries, areas where German companies are negotiating with their US counterparts. Read up on these and try translating related material to limber up in fields where demand may take off.

For feedback and practical advice, link up with the professional translation community in your area. The local chapter of the American Translators Association is the New York Circle of Translators at www.nyctranslators.org; NYCT, P.O. Box 4051, Grand Central Station, New York, NY 10163-4051. You might also join some of the online translator forums and email lists for discussions of the issues and challenges experienced practitioners face.

Thumbs up for the translation certificate at NYU, which will bring you structured input and feedback on your fledgling attempts.

Above all, get yourself out of teaching: life is too short and kids too vulnerable for anybody to engage in this professional activity if it no longer appeals or—worse—bores them.

FA & WB

Q *I've decided to quit my day job and become a translator. Can you give me any pointers on how to find clients? Please note that I haven't got a fax machine or a computer yet, I will buy these later once I've made enough money.*
Thrifty in Trieste

A Dear Pound Foolish,
You have got to be kidding. What do you think this is, Earn Money from Needlepoint in Your Spare Time, Send No Money Now? Get real.

If you aren't ready to invest in a bare minimum set-up—which includes, among other essentials, a computer and a high-speed Internet connection—then you are not being serious.

Like every other business, translation means investing money and taking risks. You can't dip one toe in the water and expect the fish to bite.

Come back when you've bought a rod, some tackle and bait.

FA & WB

2
Getting started

Beginners seeking reliable information on the business of translation turn to blogs, discussion lists and professional associations. Yet myth and misinformation abound, perhaps because many candidates (and practitioners) are more at home with words than with numbers. Or is it simply that the translation industry is so very diverse?

NUTS & BOLTS

Q *I am, I admit it, a near-amateur translator. I know you serious professionals not infrequently scorn those in my category as interlopers and charlatans. As I sidle into the profession, I would like to do my best to be neither. I would like your advice on how best to do so.*

I am trying to gain experience and sharpen my skills without undercutting professional translators. I have been directly soliciting badly-translated ("We are second-rate hotel situated in tranquil bowels of green....") and untranslated Italian web sites. I identify myself as a student, and I charge about 60% of the rates suggested by the association of Italian translators.

Am I thereby devaluing the market and ruining the lives of Italian translators around the globe? It seems hardly fair to charge full rate when I've been translating part-time for about three months. I try very hard to deliver the best possible translations. I carefully research all jobs and I turn to a listserve of Italian translators for help on difficult points. Yet, I am not a true professional, do not have the latest equipment and dictionaries, and cannot meet tight deadlines. Eventually, I would like to be such a translator.

For now, how can I best proceed without stepping on toes or cheating clients?
Non-Charlatan Near-Amateur

A Dear Charly,
What price level should a translator starting out in business choose?

If "too high", then (a) you may not get the business, or (b) you may overcharge customers for what they get. If "too low", (c) you may step on toes by undercutting professionals, and (d) you may lose money and go broke.

We respect your concern about (b) and (c), but would suggest giving at least equal attention to (a) and (d).

Being dedicated and hardworking, you are going to deliver translations that will at the very least be competent, so you won't be ripping off your customers.

On the other hand, highly paid translation assignments usually come through referrals based on reputation, and you haven't had time to build a reputation yet.

As a broad outline, starting with lower rates to gain experience, both as a wordsmith and a business person, and then replacing your clientele as you raise your rates over the years sounds like a good plan, but the devil's in the details. You have to develop a gut feeling for what the market will bear, and that comes from a combination of experience—otherwise known as paying your dues or the school of hard knocks—plus the terrible pressure of having to succeed because there is no safety net.

Anyone lacking either of these elements is an amateur. There's nothing wrong with that; as you know, the word "amateur" is not a derogatory term. Some of the best work in many fields has been done by amateurs: Heinrich Schliemann excavated the city of Troy, and the Hale-Bopp comet was discovered by hobbyist astronomers. Nor should you let professionals make you feel guilty for undercharging—most of them started out that way themselves.

So go ahead and charge 40 percent less than the rate suggested by a translators' association (which will in any case be an arbitrary figure and lower than what discerning clients are willing to pay), or 40 percent more, or the same. Whatever you feel comfortable with is fine. But remember, the game starts in earnest only when you play for keeps. Regardless of whether you are sidling or blasting your way into the market, the work you produce must be good enough to serve as a reference for the next job, and the next, and the next.

FA & WB

Q *Good evening. I have a few questions about working in the translation industry.*

I have recently earned my MA in classics, but have decided that modern languages are more my style. For now, I'm focusing on Italian, but later I would like to become fluent in at least two other languages.

My difficulty lies in not knowing exactly how to become a professional translator. I know I need to spend time in Italy, which I plan to do beginning in February, but as for other requirements, I'm at a loss. Is schooling required? If so, how much? If one wants to translate fiction, is it necessary to work for a huge publishing house? As you can see, I truly am a novice at this. I would greatly appreciate it if you could help me with these questions and other general information. It seems everything I read is general and vague, and not much help. Thank you for your time.

Starting Out

P.S. Just so you know, this is not meant for the column.

A Dear Still Out,
Start by getting your web search skills up to speed—if you think there is no concrete information out there, something is seriously wrong.

For general information on how to become a translator, both the ITI (www.iti.org.uk) and ATA (www.atanet.org) sites are helpful (not to mention back issues of Translation Journal). For literary translation, see our comments to Eager to Study (pages 37-38) and consult the websites mentioned there.

That said, if you are intent on translating fiction our first question is: have you got an independent income, sir? So little foreign fiction is translated into English—and generally at such appallingly low rates—that this is simply not a full-time career option. Insiders tell us there are only one or two people in all of the UK in this position. Everyone else has a day job.

By the same token, a postgraduate degree in literary translation will help train you technique-wise, but will not guarantee you work. Experts speak highly of the UEA at Norwich or Middlesex University, North London... even as they suggest you might be better off focusing on one language rather than two or three.

In any case, note that publishing houses do not "employ" translators. They use freelancers.

For more information, contact the Society of Authors (Translators' Association) at +44 207 373 6642, www.societyofauthors.org/translators-association. Good luck!

FA & WB

P.S. We know you were just kidding about demanding a private reply, but just in case you weren't, remember Rule 59 of the Ferengi Rules of Acquisition: Free advice is seldom cheap.

Q *Channel 9 News recently ran a story about the FBI needing people who can speak Arabic, Persian, and Mandarin Chinese. I gave them a call, and they sent me an application for their language division. I sent it in a few weeks ago, and just yesterday received a call. They want me to come in next Tuesday and do a language test, part of which includes a written translation test. They allow the use of a dictionary. However, I am sure the test will be timed.*

Do you have any general suggestions that may help? For example, should I read through the whole exercise (maybe it is a sentence, paragraph, or a whole page, who knows) first in order to get the general meaning and then go back and look up any words I do not know?

Pencil Chewer

A Dear Pencil,
It would be a good idea to contact the FBI and find out as much as you can beforehand. Will they give you a newspaper article, an engineering text, legal matter? How many words, and how much time? Then do a few practice runs at home. If possible, ask a professional translator to review your results.

Don't try to think too much about the examiner's supposed preferences. Just do the very best job that you can, emphasizing quality over quantity. Better to turn in a sterling translation and stop short of translating everything than to complete every paragraph and put junk on the page. A basketball coach can make a tall player run faster, but he can't make a short, fast player taller.

Good luck!

FA & WB

Q *I was born in Medellin, Colombia. I have lived in Venezuela, Puerto Rico, and am currently living in the United States. Throughout all this change, I have kept my native language (Spanish) very alive.*

I currently work with Hispanic youth for my church. For this, I have to constantly speak in Spanish and produce documents and letters in Spanish. I translate into Spanish every week at the church services and I also teach at my denomination's Bible Institute in Spanish.

I am an architect by profession. I would like to start using the skills I already have, and begin translating part-time, voice or written.

Where should I start?

Jumping In

A Dear Jumping,
Visit the American Translators Association (www.atanet.org) for concrete information on how to get started and contact details for your local ATA chapter. Go along to meetings, start participating on translator e-lists, and ask practicing translators you meet about training opportunities in your area. You might even consider attending the ATA's annual conference or signing up for one of its professional development courses.

Rest assured that many professional translators and interpreters have followed the path you describe, applying language proficiency acquired through studies, travel and life experience to volunteer projects, then honing their skills and moving up into language services as a professional.

We see no better recipe for job satisfaction than finding something you love to do, then figuring out a way to get paid to do it.

Best of luck as you enter this fascinating profession.

FA & WB

Q *I live in Maine in the US. I am about to graduate with a B.A. in English and I'm interested in translation or interpretation for graduate studies or a future profession.*

I have reading fluency in Mandarin and speaking fluency in Cantonese, as well as average reading ability in Portuguese, French, and Spanish. I am extremely passionate about learning languages but know that I may not qualify for a translator yet.

Could you give me some advice as to how I may begin a path toward a profession as a translator? Could you also tell me what range of translators there are? I am extremely interested in literary translation, for example, but know that this has not been an easy field to enter. What are the best ways and places, whether online or not, to meet other translators?

Sincerely,

Faithfully Curious

A Dear Curious,
It sounds like you're ready for some face-to-face exchanges with people already in the business. Which means you might consider attending the New England Translator Association's annual conference and other events (www.netaweb.org) or some of the many educational seminars offered by the American Translators Association (www.atanet.org).

But do some background reading first:

- ATA will send on request its start-up kit for beginners, along with its client education brochure "Translation, Getting it Right."
- The US Department of Labor has written up a fairly comprehensive overview of the different types of careers possible in translation. You can download it at www.bls.gov/oco/ocos175.htm.
- If you are interested in literary translation—and you're right, it's a difficult field to crack—contact the American Literary Translators Association directly at www.literarytranslators.org.
- For advice from a panel of practicing translators on skills needed, read "Bridging the Gap" in Translation Journal on line at accurapid.com/journal/23roundtablea.htm

For remote exchanges with practicing translators, there are a host of forums and discussion lists, ranging from commercial platforms (translatorscafe.com, proz.com and others) to specialized private lists (free in many cases) and association lists, although many of the latter are open only to members.

Whence a request: readers, which of these are the most useful?

FA & WB

Q *I am looking to get into translating business.*
I was born in Seoul, Korea and currently reside in Southeast region of U.S.
I was lost as to what I should be doing with my life until recently, when I ran into an opportunity to translate a whole service for my wife's church. I was able to translate it okay without problems. Now, I'd like to make it my career. Where do I start? I only have some college education. However I am very fluent in American English and Korean speaking and writing, as well as idiom.

Was Lost Now Found

A Dear Now,
The sites and articles in our response to Faithfully Curious should be of some help, although as an immigrant you face a particular challenge.

Translation is traditionally one of the first "intellectual" jobs people move into on arrival in a new country. (Teaching one's native language is a close second, with documented cases going back to the French Huguenots in England and earlier.)

This is no doubt due to the widespread misperception that both translating and language teaching require no particular skills aside from speaking and writing one's native language, something most people—rightly or wrongly—feel they can handle. Which, in turn, is one explanation for translators' low pay and low status in many market segments: a steady flow of new potential suppliers steps off every boat, many untrained and most prepared to put up with a lot as they find their feet in a new land.

We are not blaming anyone here, incidentally—except translators who fail to explain to the general public that the work delivered by an experienced professional is substantially different from most of these well-meaning ad hoc efforts.

But as an immigrant you will probably find yourself in the front line battling this popular misconception about skills, pricing and expertise. Hey, ask Daughter in Law (page 237).

If you want to develop a translation practice, you will have to work very hard to differentiate yourself from the hundreds of thousands of other Korean-Americans who are your competitors.

The best way to do this is to link up with professional translators in your area, perhaps through the ATA online directory. Work only into your native Korean (that's rule number one for professionals), or with a skilled native-English speaking editor if you try going the other direction. Specialize. Find a mentor. And network like the devil.

Good luck!

FA & WB

Q *I have an undergraduate degree in French and Spanish and am working as an English teacher in Spain while preparing for the Institute of Linguists' Diploma in Translation (French/Spanish - English).*

However I am unsure how to proceed; should I start looking for an in-house position now since I am unsure of the business side of translation, or is it better to wait until I get the diploma and set up as a freelance? Also, how do I go about looking for an in-house position if this is the best way forward? I intend to stay in Spain in the long term.

Thank you,

Preoccupied

A Dear Preoccupied,
You're off to a good start, if only through your decision to spend some serious time in your source language country. Classroom learning is fine, but immersion is essential for anyone planning a career in translation, and the best time to do it is during or immediately after your studies, before you acquire a spouse, a mortgage and children.

• Job-wise: In our experience there are very few in-house positions going anywhere these days, and even fewer for people just starting out. So should one come your way, grab it and use the opportunity to get your work revised by real live users or colleagues. But don't hold your breath.

• Contact your country or region's professional association now and see if there are any courses on offer on "how to set up in business." If not, suggest one and/or start attending association events to network with experienced practitioners today. You might also ask if you could shadow an experienced colleague for a few days or weeks to get a feel for the ebb and flow of translation in the real world.

Whence an observation.

It is true that many translation courses provide no information at all about the environment in which graduates will find themselves. Understandably so, say some: your teachers are helping you refine the skills needed to craft text on screen or page, and there are only so many hours in the day. It is also entirely possible that the teachers have no direct experience of real-world translation, in which case it is probably just as good that they not relay common misperceptions.

On the other hand, many observers (including FA & WB) are wary of courses in which there is little or no input on how to hook up with buyers of the skills you are busy honing. The reason goes beyond paying the rent: interacting with buyers from the very start is how you pull together the attitude and information you need to produce outstanding work.

Teachers should be aware of this (in the best schools some are) and make sure that it is part of the translation assignments they dole out.

Good luck with your exam!

FA & WB

INTERNSHIPS & MENTORS

Q *I am a student at a European translation school and, if all goes well, will graduate in June this year. If you had just one piece of advice to give me and my classmates, what would it be?*

Advice Seeker

A Dear Seeker,
Find a mentor and put in an apprenticeship before you strike out on your own. An expert translator can teach you far more than you would learn by churning out work for low-end agencies to get the one million or more words you need under your belt.

To locate your mentor, sit down right now and think about your dream job: the kind of texts you want to be working on a few years down the road. Find a few. Analyze them. Find out who translated them, and approach that person for tips. Do not become a pest, but do ask for other references/contacts/suggested reading in the field. Fan the flames of any correspondence that may ensue. Try to meet up in person if possible. Offer to work as an intern. This will give you first-hand experience while honing the many skills required in translation—proofreading, software, administration and general drudgery.

Good luck with your final exams!

FA & WB

Q *Young translators are often advised to look for internships to train and break into the profession. Yet in my experience the number of internships offered by big companies is relatively small compared to the number of candidates. It was suggested to me that experienced translators should stop relying on big companies to train new recruits and do it themselves. After all, most other professions have some form of compulsory on-the-job training provided by experienced professionals (e.g., lawyers, chartered accountants and doctors).*

Do you think that there is a way this could work? Isn't it something that translators' associations could look into?

Young One

A Dear Young One,
Some already have. For more information on ITI's mentoring scheme in the UK visit iti.org.uk and look for "PSG." In the US, ATA's mentoring program is well under way.

And hallelujah, this seems to be one of those issues with broad appeal: most students and young graduates claim to be actively seeking internships, while nearly all experienced translators deplore the dearth of mentored in-house positions for junior staff members—a direct consequence of the downsizing of big in-house translation departments.

Unfortunately, even for practitioners dedicated to promoting professional development, interns are often uneconomic. This is particularly true in a freelance structure.

These freelancers have a point: depending on the sector, it can take two or more years for young graduates' output to be marketable, and editing along the way is extraordinarily time-consuming. Interns themselves may be lukewarm on the prospect of providing input less noble than translation proper (making coffee, clipping news items), which is not helpful.

One solution is for both sides (translators and interns) to focus on young graduates' immediately useable skills—in terminology and technology, for example. They can be assigned to compiling glossaries or proofreading (not editing), data mining and more.

Likewise, while a full-time intern might be impractical, freelancers (or translation companies) might consider banding together to share a promising candidate.

If FA & WB headed a student outplacement association in a translation school, we'd begin by kick-starting a few high-profile alliances—contacting prominent translators/translation companies and matching them up with outstanding candidates, then writing these experiences up in association magazines to encourage other mentors to sign on. There are a lot of well-disposed translation professionals out there, many vaguely guilty about not playing a more active role in shaping the industry's future. Successful case studies and a how-to fact sheet would lure more into mentoring—to everyone's advantage!

FA & WB

Q *What is the best way to go about finding internships without a degree in translation or any real practice, so to speak? I don't want to be too much of a burden on a firm or an individual, but I do believe that I could learn quickly and become an asset rather than a handicap to the translation staff at a given office.*

Ground Floor

A Dear Ground,
Grab the bull by the horns. Identify firms or individuals who produce the type of work you'd like to produce, in markets you'd like to work in, and actively seek opportunities to meet them face to face. When you finally meet up, no need to hide The Flame, but do avoid excessive displays of eccentricity (plenty of time for that later).

Professional association get-togethers are one good venue, regional and local translator networks another.

Don't become a pest, but do be prepared to suggest a "free trial offer." If accepted, use that time to wow them with your energy and efficiency. Don't be a clock-watcher. Be cheerful. And yes, be prepared to do non-translation work if asked, but be sure to use at least part of your internship to produce translations, too, or at the very least to solicit feedback on your work.

A successful internship is the number-one way to net job offers and/or stellar references for future work, so investing time and energy at this critical stage is one of the very best things you can do to get your career off to a strong start.

FA & WB

Q *I'm from Argentina. I'm studying translation in my home city, Rosario, in the second year of a three-year program. I'd like to start working now, since I've discovered that there are a lot of working "translators" who actually don't even have a degree. But my problem is that I don't know where to begin. Have you got any tips? I'd prefer to work via the Internet.*

Southern Tip

A Dear Southern,
We're surprised that you're surprised that many working translators don't have degrees in translation. The nature of the translation market is such that many excellent practitioners do enter the field from prior careers.

Not to downplay the importance of higher education, but none of our direct clients have ever asked for copies of diplomas or paper qualifications. What they look for in potential freelance suppliers is in-depth knowledge of their sector and the ability to craft translations that work, which makes compiling a portfolio of your very best work a good move.

That's tip number 1: start building a portfolio now, and be sure to update it regularly.

Where your diploma will come in handy is in applications for salaried positions, or, perhaps, mailings to translation agencies.

Does your study program require internships? In our opinion, that's where you should be investing your time at this stage, since relevant in-house stints and the contacts they foster can make or break a translator's CV and prospects on completing a degree course.

One recommended tactic is to locate some translations that you admire, with luck in a sector that is expanding (and that you can imagine specializing in). Find out who produced them, and devise a way to meet the person or team responsible. You then cultivate that contact, without becoming a pain in the neck, and try to leverage it into an internship.

Finally, we're not sure what you mean by a preference for working via the Internet. That's how virtually all freelance translators receive and deliver their work these days. But do keep the proximity mantra in mind: if you are working for clients far away, you must figure out a way to meet them in person at some point. Become a known face and quantity; build on a personal relationship. No serious business is going to send high-paying, mission-critical work to somebody they don't even know.

FA & WB

TRAINING

Q *I am a native French speaker and I'll be taking entrance exams for translation schools this year.*

Some of the courses I'm interested in look very good (e.g., Université Denis Diderot in Paris, Université Marc Bloch in Strasbourg, and City University in London) but these schools are not CIUTI members.

Should I focus instead on CIUTI-member schools like ESIT (Paris), ETI (Geneva) or ISTI (Brussels)? I dream of working as a translator for the European Commission or another international organization, and I want to be sure to make the right choice now so as to get a crack at one of those elite jobs.

Career Path

A Dear Career,
Let's reword your question: are all the juicy jobs in the international organizations sewn up by an old-boys'/old-girls' network?

Your query gave us a chance to poll experts in our ambit, and the results, while revealing, are hardly surprising.

• CIUTI (Conférence Internationale des Instituts Universitaires de Traduction et d'Interprétation)-member administrators, teachers, and graduates assured us, with unnervingly wide eyes, that the reason CIUTI graduates are well-represented in international organizations is that the teaching is outstanding.

• Non-CIUTI folk polled were either reassuringly neutral (choose the school that seems the best match for you and your skills, work like crazy, and you'll do fine when the exam comes) or unnervingly narrow-eyed—hinting and sometimes stating outright that the teaching at CIUTI schools is so far behind the times you'd be better off elsewhere.

So we trundled along to the European Commission, where insiders' off-the-cuff, behind-the-scenes comments include:

Fact No. 1: recruitment to all EU language services is by competition. You don't even have to have had formal training in translating, although it does help. An example quoted by one respondent: a competition is now open for English (only). Candidate must offer either French and German into English, or either French or German plus one other official language into English; some institutions will accept only candidates from the second category. Neither experience nor a translation degree is required this time. For upcoming competitions, visit www.eu-careers.eu.

Fact No. 2: Brussels—and Luxembourg—may be full of French-language translators, but many are not French. Lots are Belgian (and many are not over-impressed by French university and grande école translation courses, it would appear).

Fact No. 3: Whether or not juries show any preference for graduates of particular schools, the double-blind anonymity of candidates and test markers "ought to rule it out."

The jury's main aims, once the candidates' identities are known, are to ensure that any additional languages skills claimed on the application forms are genuine, to pick the best of the bunch, and to take care that they don't let any real misfits through. There are quite enough weirdoes in the language world already, says one contact. People who express willingness to be posted to Luxembourg may well get a bonus point.

These experts' specific advice to you: check the terms of the current English competition in the expectation that a future French competition will resemble it. Search archives of the JOCE for previous French competitions. Do your utmost to ensure that your paper qualifications match what is needed. If you have not got a Bac+4 you will need to cross that hurdle first, but unless you have good reason to believe that a translation diploma (from a CIUTI member or any other establishment) will improve your skills, put your time into getting practical experience. This will also be more lucrative: you don't get paid for coursework done, no matter how good it is. If you have contacts with EU freelance contracts, try to get some work from them—even at slave rates or through a free internship—for experience with the genre.

They—and we—wish you the best of luck!

FA & WB

PS: As this book goes to press (late 2010) the first generation of European Commission linguists is easing into retirement, and the Commission's Directorate-General for Translations is conducting an aggressive campaign to recruit new staff translators and interpreters. See http://ec.europa.eu/dgs/translation/index_en.htm

There has rarely been a better time for European students with outstanding language skills to set their sights on a career in languages with the EC.

Q *For the past ten years I've been an engineer, but left my job in the UK in February to follow my husband and live in the US for a couple of years. Having worked for a German company for the last 5 years (and lived and worked in Munich for 6 months in 2000), I plan to use my time in the US to change my career path and become a technical translator.*

I want to do some sort of formal translator training before embarking in the world of freelance translation, but find the options bewildering. Many courses in the UK focus exclusively on language skills, and as an engineering graduate I wonder if I qualify. The only distance course in German that I see is very literature-based and as a techie I'm not sure it is for me. Another course is oral-based—good practice, no doubt, but do I really need oral skills for translating written German?

In the US, several universities offer distance-learning courses for German but there is no qualification at the end. To get onto the NYU Translation certificate course, the administrator said that I didn't need a degree, just "be able to read a German newspaper."

What should I do? Take the UK structured approach? Or just improve my German reading skills by courses and self-study, and then take the NYU course? Would the latter path disadvantage me when I return to the UK, since my CV would feature no language qualifications as such, or are you only judged by your experience?

Confused in New Mexico

A Dear Confused,
Most professionals agree that subject-matter knowledge and writing skills in your native language are the keys to a successful career in technical translation. We agree, and recommend that you make them the core of your offer—in the US, the UK, or anywhere else.

A former translation company manager who read your letter agrees: "In the early part of your career, your c.v. should stress your engineering background and the skills you have acquired in industry (appreciation of management methods, quality assurance programs, etc.). These give you a real edge over other new translators, who essentially have a degree in languages and lots of youthful enthusiasm, but little knowledge of the real world."

Rest assured that you will be judged primarily on the quality of your work, which means keeping abreast of developments in your specialist field and honing your writing skills. We know plenty of subject-matter experts who can't write their way out of a paper bag, so if you have any doubts on this score, you might consider taking a technical writing course in English.

That said, a distance course in translation—with or without a formal qualification at the end—can provide good feedback, raising both your confidence and your awareness of pitfalls. Although undue emphasis on oral skills seems a bit odd, don't worry too much about content: no course will ever meet your needs 100%. Keep in mind that all training ultimately depends on the skills, preparation and organization of your teacher, input from classmates, and your own efforts.

Why not start now by spending an hour or two a day at any of the following sites:

www.zeit.de (Die Zeit)
www.faz.net (Frankfurter Allgemeine Zeitung)
www.dpa.de (DPA-Nachrichten)
www.ftdlatestnews.de (Financial Times Deutschland)
www.handelsblatt.com (Handelsblatt)
www.nzz.ch (Neue Zürcher Zeitung)
www.spiegel.de (Spiegel)

Good luck!

FA & WB

Q *You two emphasize the importance of client education, and in one way I agree. But if you think of translators en masse, there is also a great need for translator education. With so many working in isolation, many tend to find their own comfort zone and stay there regardless.*

As I get to talk to a lot of both young and old translators, I am constantly struck by how many lack the will to break out of their comfort zone—i.e., learn a new subject, offer different services, learn new things, invest in learning/equipment/dictionaries, etc.

Few universities equip students to really launch a career or run a small business (though perhaps this is getting better?), and with everything changing around us, there are few safe little islands. I'm confident many universities could run short courses or summer schools aimed at their newly hatched students or MAs, and others. Professional bodies have a problem in that they are dependent on hiring premises and finding people to run the courses, but surely this is not insurmountable. One of the great weaknesses in the translation industry is that so many translators have to invent the wheel all over again and find out things for themselves. There is a huge gap in the market here; it's about time somebody did something about it!

Scorpion

A Dear Scorpion,
You said it, not us. Although we, too, have noticed that some of the loudest moans and most abject hand-wringing in the translation community come from those trading on language skills acquired decades ago and applied—sometimes misapplied—for years in a vacuum. The market has long since headed elsewhere, and the more attractive options are open only to those willing to invest the time to investigate.

Fortunately there are a growing number of opportunities for anyone prepared to venture outside their comfort zone (nice expression, that).

National and regional translator associations always post upcoming events on their websites, but the truly energetic should cast a wider net. For those working into English, courses organized by the Society for Technical Communication (www.stc.org/) are good value, as are the often free programs offered by professional associations in areas you have specialized in or might want to specialize in. Not to mention Chamber of Commerce events. There is no time like the present to get out and stretch your world view.

FA & WB

Q *I recently graduated from Gadjah Mada University www.ucm.ac.id in Indonesia, and have worked for several months with the United Nations Development Program in Jakarta. I would like to become a professional translator, and am looking for a post-graduate course abroad (my languages are Indonesian and English). Do you have any information about institutions offering scholarships to study translation?*

Eager to Study

A Dear Eager,
The simple answer: no, with the exception of a few leads you might want to follow up directly (the American Foundation for Translation & Interpreting

(AFTI) via walter@atanet.org, and the training institutions listed on the ATA website at atanet.org).

Indeed, all our contacts indicate that there is only limited funding available for overseas students, which means that you should be prepared for fierce competition and plan on working at least part-time, since by all accounts your living costs will exceed the amount of any scholarship.

The most promising resources appear to be university networks and exchange programs, education advisers at local embassies, and, of course, the Web. So why not start with your former teachers at Gadjah Mada and move out to Internet forums, especially those specialized in the teaching of translation? But don't neglect the embassies/consulates of English-speaking countries in Jakarta, which may have advisers with information on exchange programs and scholarships.

Finally, don't limit yourself to training programs: at your level, any extended stay in an English-speaking country will be an excellent means of honing your language skills. So look into work options as well—perhaps through your current employer.

FA & WB

3
Doing the job

The backbone of any successful translator's practice is the ability to produce texts that work—day in, day out. It's as simple (or difficult) as that. Which means mastering language, cultural and technical issues, workflows, and interaction with partners.

BEST PRACTICE

Q*I went freelance a year ago and now work from an office in our home. But even without the commute I'm feeling less productive. The reason? Intrusive neighbors, friends and even family members who drop in any old time to chat. "I was just passing by and thought I'd say hi," is something I hear two or three times a day. I've tried telling them I'm busy, but they don't seem to take it in and I don't want to be unfriendly. Driinggg. There goes the doorbell now. What to say?*

Knock Knock

ADear Knock,
We say bite the bullet. Open door, nice smile, "Ah, great to see you—but I've got a client on the line. Can't talk, 'bye!" You then step back, wave, close door. You can always call them back or invite them over for a drink after your work is done.

If you don't think you can manage this, place a telephone next to the front door, pick up the receiver and hold it to your ear automatically as you answer the doorbell. Having a prop may help get you through.

The only other option we know of is to chitchat during the day and work at night—but do you really want to do that?

FA & WB

Q*I specialize in a lucrative field and have a small but loyal customer base. I love translating, but over the past six months I've found it harder and harder* *to sit down and actually do the work. I procrastinate until deadline and beyond, then sink my teeth in—and enjoy the work! I actually enjoy it once I start. My clients are loyal but they aren't going to put up with missed deadlines forever. How can I do this to them? Good God, how can I do this to myself? How can I get over my "translator's block"?*

Frazzled & Frozen

A Dear Frazzled,
How urgent is your query? If you have an overdue job staring you in the face this very moment, implement suggestions 1 and 2 immediately. Then have a cup of coffee and consider 3-8.
1. Clear the decks.

Get a cardboard box from your local supermarket and sweep all the clutter on your desktop into it. Everything. Keep only a keyboard, mousepad, mouse, one writing implement and your source text. Now sit down: you're ready to roll.
2. Ease into the job.

Try starting with an activity less stressful and more structured than translation per se. Example: terminology. Make a list of terms you will have to look up, and begin your working day with dictionary spadework and web searches. This should generate a lot of the raw material you'll need when you settle down to do the actual language transfer work.
3. Read through each new source text the day it arrives, regardless of the deadline.

You'll have a better idea of what awaits you, and your mind will already be processing information and linking up ideas.
4. Longer term, look into sharing an office.

Having a quiet, businesslike place where somebody else is hard at work at a keyboard can get you into work mode, too.
5. Tell people when you are busy on a job.

Especially fellow translators. And tell them how long you think it is likely to take. The more people who know you are occupied through Thursday afternoon, the more guilty you will feel about not being busy doing it (massive guilt can also backfire, but it's worth a try).
6. Establish a work routine.

The "freedom" of freelance life can become the freedom to push back the moment you head for the office until truly ridiculous hours, which is bad for your physical and mental health. Decide when you work best—crack of dawn? mid-morning? middle of night?—and reserve two 3-hour chunks of time at your computer around that window. Don't let yourself skip those working periods. Ever.

7. Get a good night's sleep.

Fatigue—mental and physical—saps energy and interferes with your ability to concentrate. Take up a sport, preferably one that leaves you physically exhausted. You'll sleep better.

8. As a last resort, look for a salaried position doing the same type of work, which you say you enjoy.

If you're cut out to be a freelance translator, six months back on the 9-to-5 circuit will remind you why you left in the first place. If not, perhaps you've reached a point in your life where you need an outside structure to keep you on track. Why not? People change. Good luck, and keep us posted.

FA & WB

Q *The work just keeps rolling in and I can't keep up! There are only so many hours in a day. It seems like a waste to let all those potential earnings fall by the wayside.*

Swamped

A Dear Swamped,
Yours is an enviable dilemma. Fortunately, there are many different strategies for coping with growth.

1. Defer it if you can...

Thank the caller for the inquiry and say, regretfully, that you would love to take on the assignment... if they can extend the deadline. This does two things: (1) it signals to the client that you are in demand, confirming their choice of you as a preferred supplier; (2) you come across as a woman of her word, someone who would rather turn down lucrative business than risk delivering late and wreaking havoc on a client's deadlines. You never know: a couple of in-house phone calls later, your client contact may be back in touch to tell you that as it turns out, the deadline can be pushed back after all!

2. ...Refer it if you can't.

Be prepared to make referrals to able colleagues. Yes, we have all met the colleague from hell who turned out to be a venomous snake, badmouthing you to the client and trying to steal your business. May she roast on a spit over an open fire for many millenniae. Learn from your mistake and next time pay attention to your gut instinct.

This is another reason why you should attend translator meetings and keep in touch with the expat community in your town. What is the ratio of translators you personally meet to translators you can safely refer your customers to? About 50 to 1, so get out of the house and start building up a stable of contacts! Make sure that everybody profits from the referral. Your clients will appreciate your advice when you refer them to another good translator instead of simply turning down work. If you head down this road, there are several options: some translators ask colleagues for a commission of, say, 15% (a common practice in the PR profession). Better yet in our opinion: barter your recommendation for a deposit in the "favor bank", to be withdrawn when you need it. If you want to simply park the client with your colleague temporarily, be upfront and clear about that; in this case, the colleague is doing you a favor so do not expect a commission.

3. Cash in on the bonanza.

When you ask the boss for a raise and are turned down, it's tough. But being in business for yourself means that you get as many chances to do this—and also try out different strategies—as there are clients. It's Economics 101, folks: the best—some say the only—time to up your rates is when you are so busy, you are turning down work.

Curiously (or perhaps not), many translators are squeamish about plunging in and charging what the market will bear. They claim that their clients will resent this and retaliate by not giving them business in leaner times when the client no longer needs them so badly. We beg to disagree. For one thing, when the cyclical downturn comes there will be less work anyway. You think clients will keep you busy then out of gratitude for your modesty?

Moreover, charging not one penny less than what the market will bear is the very essence of free enterprise, and as buyers of products and services we face it every day. If you can supply the quality to back up your high fee, you would be an idiot to surrender your chance to turn the principle to your advantage.

4. Farm out work.

Assign work to colleagues with spare capacity. But beware of the pitfalls: there is no swifter way to ruin your reputation than to deliver somebody else's sub-standard output under your good name. And make sure that you price the work high enough. You need to budget not only for what your contractors charge you, but also for the time you spend scheduling and tracking assignments and performing quality control: you must review each translation line by line and word by word to bring it up to your accustomed quality. In addition to dealing with your client, you need to communicate well with your colleagues and be ready to support them if they have queries. Turn down assignments if the client is unwilling to cover these costs.

5. Share the wealth.

Translators balk at the idea of hiring salaried workers. They cite the unpredictable nature of the business, the difficulty of reconciling the individualistic nature of translation with an office setting, and fear of losing clients to defecting staff.

Although these are valid concerns, the difficulties are not insurmountable. And consider the benefits:
- Year-round availability of your office even when you go on vacation
- Ability to control outcomes, since you and your staff can work practically shoulder-to-shoulder
- Intellectual stimulation from a collaborative environment
- Preserves your bonds with the human community and helps to keep you from turning into a filthy, muttering recluse.

Finally, let's be very clear on why you should make the most of this surplus demand: it's not a windfall. You earned it through hard work, and it won't last forever. The time to earn beyond your immediate needs—so that you can invest in your business and save for retirement—is now.

FA & WB

Q *I was interested to read the letter from a bank translation department complaining about unethical outside suppliers. A year ago I, too, was hired to head a bank translation department, but unlike your correspondent my gripe is in-house people.*

It's the long-time staffers who pose a problem: they seem to be positively proud of not knowing anything about banking. Almost more aggravating to me is the fact that despite their "literary" airs, their own writing is the most uninspired I have ever seen. They arrive late and leave early. Oh, and the head of human resources has just confirmed that there is no way on earth I can fire them and take on some new, more enthusiastic talent.

Any suggestions on how I can kick this team into shape?

No Dream Team

A Dear Coach,
You know and we know that the only way you are going to get a dream team together is by throwing these turkeys out on their ears. Since that is

impossible, you must revert to Plan B, which assumes that they have potential but have been allowed to slide into bad habits.

Remind yourself that some of these guys may not know how bad they are. Really.

Others may have a sneaking suspicion that they are not very good, but not know how to improve. It is far easier to slack off if your vision of your job stops at the edge of your desk, and if they knew little about banking when hired and were never encouraged to get interested in it—well, tuning out of professional life becomes more understandable.

In practical terms, staffers who have got into a rut for these reasons can be salvaged. We'll look at the no-hopers in a minute. But your own immediate aim must be to get some momentum going, making it clear that there are definite advantages ahead for those who take their job seriously.

Start by securing the support of your human resources manager or another higher-up for a 12-month program aimed at kicking the department into shape. Since many of our suggestions will cost nothing to implement, your proposals should fall on fertile ground.

The road to revival begins with ensuring that all staff members know what the documents they translate are supposed to achieve. The older (and "literary") ones will be pretty good at bluffing, so be sure to start with the basics and take a wide-ranging approach. It is amazing how many staffers (and freelancers, for that matter) view texts as matter that materializes at one end of their desk and disappears, transformed, into a black hole in space at the other. Your job is to change this mindset.

Specifically:

1. Organize a mini-training course for your team. Aim: ensure that everybody knows what each client department does. Have someone from each department come in and give a 20-minute presentation, then answer questions. Choose a schedule that will fit in with your unit's workload, and make it clear that this is an on-going series.

2. You have probably already compiled a list of translation requirements in each bank department. If not, have your team help you do this, pairing one more energetic translator with a slacker in each case.

3. Using a rotation system, bring a member of staff along with you each time you go out into the bank to discuss a text or project. The best antidote to translator isolation and ennui is contact with real live authors and readers.

4. Tackle quality head-on by instituting brown-bag lunches (you aren't in

France, are you?): once a week everybody lunches together informally in the office and each translator in turn submits a text for constructive criticism. You might start the ball rolling with an anonymous text from an outside supplier. It is usually easier to focus on terminology first—this will allow you to feed in some of the technical background needed—but be sure to hit a few style points each time, too. Be prepared to put your own work up for criticism, of course.

5. Track banking industry conferences on topical issues and send motivated translators along to events whenever possible.

6. Institute a fast track and a slow track, and at your annual performance reviews reward those who have progressed personally or provided input to the rest of the team to carry the whole unit forward. Use every incentive you can think of to encourage staff members to invest time and energy in their work.

Ultimately, training/outreach opportunities for the entire department give everybody a chance to tune back into the big picture. Those who subsequently choose to re-tune out are no-hopers and you can relegate them to the slow track with a clear conscience. No bonuses, no travel, least desirable offices. They have only themselves to blame.

FA & WB

Q *What do you do when the text you are given to translate is badly written? How much should you "tidy up" and how much should you leave as is? And how much should you say to the client?*

I am translating (French to English) a series of articles on a popular history topic. Although they seem to read well, on closer inspection the sentences fall apart: they are full of grammatical errors, mixed metaphors, and unclear ideas. I want to respect the style, of course, but I also want to make the articles clear and readable in English! In each article there is also a sprinkling of misspelled names, wrong dates, words used incorrectly, etc. I have been pointing out these errors to my contact person (the project manager—I'm not in contact with the writer) so they can be corrected before publication, but I don't think it's winning me any brownie points.

Advice?

Broom in Hand

A Dear Broom,
Forget the pundits who speak in hushed tones about respecting source-text style; for a start, how are you going to achieve equivalent bumpiness and spelling mistakes? More importantly, why on earth would anybody want you to?

If you translate for publication—with the sole (possible) exception of literature—identifying and fixing bits that don't work goes with the territory. Likewise flagging inconsistencies and factual errors.

Why? Because regardless of what is actually on the page, you can safely assume that the author's intent was to demonstrate mastery of his subject and communicate information while keeping as many readers as possible on board. In your case, the publisher no doubt wants to sell copies of his magazine, too.

This was the purpose of the original text/project. Your job is to achieve the same end in the target language. If, on the way, you produce a piece of work that represents an "improvement" on the original, you are just doing your job. Because the quality of your work should be driven by your sensitivity to reader expectations—that is the key to and core of your skill. Appropriate grammar, spelling, register and style are natural and inseparable aspects of this skill.

Not that you are taking all these decisions on your own: adjustments should be made in close collaboration with the author or coordinator. If your project manager discourages improvements/questions, something is definitely wrong, and we can think of at least two explanations:

• Your questions are not put clearly or efficiently. As experienced linguists know, virtually all texts benefit from interaction with the originator, but calling the project manager—or author, for that matter—every fifteen minutes with a new query is not an efficient way to go about it. Ideally your agency contacts will have a procedure in place for asking questions/resolving problems. This makes all the more sense if the text is being translated into several languages. Note how the procedure works before starting the job and follow it to the letter. Questions numbered, on a separate sheet? Footnotes? Color-coded in-text queries? Do it!

• S/he belongs to the line-'em-up, churn-'em-out school. If papering over cracks is the name of this agency's game, it is time to shift to more worthy clients. There are a lot more of them around than you'd think. They welcome input and comments—and generally pay a lot more, too.

FA & WB

Q *I am Language Services manager at a translation agency. Here's a poser we recently received from one of our freelancers:*

"In almost every order I work on there is something I need to ask the author. When I work for translation agencies like yours, any questions I have must

be filtered through your account manager as, despite my having signed an undertaking not to 'steal' your clients, you obviously don't trust the clients not to approach me (or other translators) direct. That means I sometimes don't get the answer I wanted and certainly can't probe any further when the answer isn't quite what I was looking for. Effectively you are preventing me from turning in my best performance and denying a loyal translator a fair measure of job satisfaction. Surely if so many customers are so keen to 'cut out the middleman' they can't be aware of the value you're adding to my translation. Can't you solve this by better marketing instead of building firewalls between two—relative— experts (the author and a specialist translator)?"

The problem is, I know she's right and on gut feeling I'd like to tear down the firewalls—but first I'd like to hear from someone who's been there and done that. Can you help?

Name Withheld

A Dear Withheld,
Your freelancer puts the question very clearly, and your own willingness to examine possible solutions speaks well for the climate of trust you are inclined to develop.

Before taking any action, we suggest you set out the logic behind your agency's current policy in equal detail.

For example, what your correspondent calls a firewall is not there solely to prevent freelancers from stealing clients. With multilingual projects, having a single contact point can be an essential means of handling product flow— nobody wants nine translators phoning the same client nine times for that fuzzy bit on page 17. Far better to centralize each project with one company representative.

But for many other products, it can make sense to set up a structure that allows direct translator/client interaction. This can also make good business sense: in Europe, some premium customers are beginning to insist that agencies allow them direct contact with translators for single-language assignments. In an on-going relationship, there is no better way to resolve form and content questions quickly and efficiently, they say.

Your company has already put in place one important protective measure by telling your translators clearly what they must not do—steal clients. Your terms and conditions with clients should be equally clear: you do not expect them to circumvent you. In the interest of transparency, insist that translators copy you in immediately on all relevant correspondence or notes from telephone conversations.

But we also urge you to look into opportunities to consolidate translator loyalty by explaining what your policies are and why. We know two translation agencies that organize annual retreats for their core team of freelancers to discuss corporate objectives and brainstorm on how service can be improved. Translator transport and accommodation is, of course, paid by the agencies—and seen by them as the cost of doing business. Participants emerge in a glow of loyalty and mutual respect, we are told.

Perhaps the best rule would be to include names and address details of your customer's contacts with each work assignment for certain subcontractors. Whenever you do not provide these, it is understood that translators should not attempt to make contact themselves. Remind your freelancers of your policy at regular intervals.

Good luck!

FA & WB

Q *I have been translating professionally for four years, from Spanish into my native English. I lived in Spain for a year and a half after college, and then spent six months in Mexico, so my Spanish is very good.*

I know that professional translators are supposed to work only into their native language, but I occasionally get a request in the other direction and rather than let the client flounder and perhaps place the job with an unreliable supplier, I generally accept and have my husband (who is Spanish) proofread my work. I think our joint efforts are in fact very good, and no client has ever complained.

But recently another translator told me this is not professional, as my husband is not a trained translator. Technically she's right; he's an accountant. But he has been to college and is a native speaker of Spanish, and is of course interested in me keeping all my clients, so he really puts his heart into it. What do you think?

Both Ways

A Dear Both,
We think you're on a slippery slope.

As professional associations intone with mind-numbing regularity, fluency in a foreign language does not, on its own, make someone a professional translator. Nor does bilingualism. Nor does a diploma, for that matter (your friend is wrong on that score).

But that's not all:

• Two years in a foreign country doesn't come close to building the expertise

48

you need to work into a non-native language.

• Don't kid yourself: unhappy clients hardly ever tell producers of sub-par translations how unsatisfactory these are. Instead inertia reigns—they slog along with their known under-performer until a better option comes along.

• And don't get us started on the writing skills of "college graduates."

But here's the real problem: by assuming that your two years' experience abroad and your husband's native speaker status are enough to produce a text that can stand on its own two legs, you are beaming out an "anybody can do this" message. Which immediately places you in a seriously unattractive segment of the market, one rife with semi-qualified competitors accompanied by their own helpful spouses, boyfriends, girlfriends, in-laws and more.

We are not denying that this market section of the market exists. We're just pointing out that it is not where a professional translator wants to be.

Although we are certain your husband is a nice guy and genuinely wants to help, there are also several other issues to consider, starting with the confidentiality you owe your clients. Not to mention the psychological flip-flopping that occurs in pricing when you are aware, deep down inside, that you can't really guarantee what you are delivering.

With that in mind, here's our advice: do the professional thing—get out and network. Locate a real live experienced translator working from English to Spanish and pass the jobs onto him or her. Who knows, you may get some in your language combination back in return.

FA & WB

SIGNING YOUR WORK

Q *I'm a translator living in Tarragona, Spain. You've suggested that translators include a clause in their Terms & Conditions specifying that they must do a final review of typeset documents before the text goes to press.*

This sounds like a good way to avoid over-confident non-native clients inserting errors in my translations—and me getting blamed.

Can you suggest wording for this clause?

Safety Net

A Dear Net,
Try a variation on "Our service includes compulsory review of final

copy by the translator before printing, failing which a 50% [or 100% or 200% or 500%] surcharge will apply as the translator's name appears in credits."

First-time clients always react—sometimes in a panic—to ask what this threat of extra fee is all about. Which is exactly what you want, since it gives you a chance to explain that you don't want to apply/collect the surcharge and won't have to if they respect their end of the deal. Better yet, you can explain why it is in both parties' interest to incorporate this final review phase: since your name appears on the document (normally right next to photo and layout credits), you are protecting your own "brand" even as you protect their image for foreign readers. Win/win.

This is also a good time to remind customers that the point is not to refuse their feedback and changes, but rather to ensure that these have been checked by a professional translator—you—before being set in stone or printed 200,000 times in full color.

An analogy to bring this home: if an audit company's client steps in and changes the numbers in financial statements after content has been finalized and signed, the auditors, too, will remove their name; it's a professional risk they cannot assume.

Note that if the customer cannot or will not comply with your conditions, there's no problem—but they must then remove your name (and pay your bill, of course).

Clients with experience of quality assurance generally have no problem with the concept or practice. Instead it is nervous translation suppliers who seem anxious to conceal their text paternity/maternity. Now why would that be? We're sure one of our readers will enlighten us, and in the meantime maintain that financial penalties are an excellent way to focus the mind and keep everyone on the straight and narrow.

FA & WB

Q *I thought you'd be interested in some feedback that I just received from a client:*

"FA & WB are right to focus on raising prices, but they don't say enough about the importance of quality. As a result, intermediaries like us find ourselves with translators who demand far too much money for the quality of the work they provide."

Just Passing It On

A Dear Passing,
Feedback always welcome!

We're certain you've already have pointed out to your client just how often we address quality in this column, but in case some joker has been quoting us selectively, let's take this opportunity to get everyone back onto the straight and narrow.

Quality is every translation provider's Holy Grail—on paper. And we certainly see very few suppliers (freelance or agencies) who claim to provide anything but the Best. Some of these people are absolutely, breath-takingly outstanding translators, too. Yet the proof of the pudding is in the eating, and the market opaque enough to hide lots of ropey practices. High prices don't necessarily mean impeccable quality, but low prices are a strong indicator of sub-par quality.

Moving right along, may we suggest once again that every client announce—indeed, insist—that its translation supplier's name will appear in credits on published texts, including commercial and technical documents.

This is easy to do and has benefits all around:

• Clients get proof, right up front, that a supplier is proud enough of its text-offspring to assume maternity/paternity in front of the whole world.

• Good translators (and intermediaries) get their name out and about, attached to the work they produce and sell. This is as it should be.

• Poor translators (and intermediaries) also get their name out and about, attached to the work they produce and sell. This is also as it should be.

• Translators are reminded that their name and brand are on the line with every job they do, thus have an incentive to avoid over-extending themselves in expertise or capacity.

• Last but not least, this easy step costs nothing. Zero.

Why, we wonder, do not more translators make this approach theirs? Why do translation agencies not embrace it? We are confident that readers will enlighten us.

In the meantime, intermediaries like your client should have the wherewithal to judge quality, and rap knuckles or simply turn to different suppliers if it is lacking. This is what justifies their slice of the action: project management including triage, testing, selection of the best translator for a given job, and revision.

Finally, while we're on quality, it's high time somebody laid it on the line for suppliers—big and small—who, when caught red-handed delivering a sloppy job, dismiss criticism with "at that price, what were they [the client] expecting?" To remind them, for example, that you get the clients you deserve.

Ah there, we've just done it.

FA & WB

TERMINOLOGY

Q *What is your favorite online dictionary? I would like to just type in a word and get an instant, full definition (maybe even a list of synonyms) rather than fumbling through the way-too-thin and heavily-mauled pages of my dictionary! Does a dictionary like that exist? Thank you.*

Fingers-to-the-Bone Fred

A Dear Fred,

Striking how print dictionaries have faded from the translation scene, isn't it? And your query explains why—the Internet opens new vistas for translators, making many of the assembled-on-the-cheap-despite-reputable-name-in-publishing offerings less attractive than ever.

We put your question to our favorite literary translator who answered as follows: "Most literary translators rely less and less on dictionaries. We use the web for research, first to find the word in as many source language contexts as possible and then to check out possible translations in the target language. We also have a raft of native speakers we call on to 'locate' problem words, plus target-language experts we can consult to check specific technical terminology. There are no shortcuts, quick fixes or one-stop online solutions."

She said it, not us.

For a few early interfaces designed specifically to help translators locate glossaries and parallel texts quickly, check out www.multilingual.ch. Another option: take a course to optimize your search skills.

FA & WB

Q *Our company is in a high-technology field and is an occasional translation buyer. We like to think that we are on a cutting edge.*

Because of the very technical nature of our work, we gave the translation agency handling a recent assignment both the documents to translate and an in-house glossary.

In exchange they signed a non-disclosure agreement.

Two weeks ago one of our researchers discovered whole paragraphs of our document in the "help" section of an online forum of translators. Several sections from our glossary were also posted there.

We have complained to the agency. They tell us that the irresponsible act was by one of their subcontractors, with whom they will not work again. That is of little help now; our confidential information was placed on the web for all to see, in breach of our written agreement. Who knows where else our document may be displayed?

Here is our question to translators: both the document and the glossary were marked "Confidential." Do translators not know how to read, or what that word means?

Unhappy Client

A Dear Client,
Curious, isn't it, that professional wordsmiths can be so clueless about notions as basic as "non-disclosure agreement" and "competitive environment."

But your query raises several issues, which you will want to keep in mind for any future purchases of translation:

• Clients are not always aware that agencies rarely employ translators in-house; more often than not, jobs get subcontracted out to one or more suppliers, perhaps even to another agency.

• A serious agency will have a structure in place up front to ensure that each and every one of these subcontractors respects the same degree of confidentiality you have insisted on from them. If they haven't, they are remiss and you have a definite claim against them.

• Employing only translators and translation agencies that are members of a professional association is one way to reduce risk, since all such associations include a confidentiality clause in their code of conduct.

Note to Unhappy Client: By all means seek damages from the agency. This is a healthy if painful wake-up call for the entire industry.

Note to agencies: Make sure you have professional indemnity insurance and a tight contract policy. Have all suppliers sign an NDA (non-disclosure agreement) up front, and enforce it through regular reminders and checks. Ensure, too, that they understand the full implications for their own work and research methods—or gird yourself for some first-hand experience in commercial litigation.

Note to translators: If you want to argue that using an egroup for assistance is "normal practice in the industry," fair enough (if your agency client agrees). But get real: it is both stupid and naive to do so in a way that discloses confidential information about a client and its documents. However warm and cozy your favorite egroup seems, anything you post can be cut and copied someplace else. If you have professional indemnity insurance, reread your contract now to get a better grasp of how insurers view "negligence." This will help you understand why you may not be covered if you do stupid and naive things.

With thanks to Unhappy Client for raising this important issue.

FA & WB

PROCESSES

Q *I am a student in the English Program at Brawijaya University, Indonesia and am now doing my report. Would you please tell me:*
- *what is editing in translation?*
- *how to do editing?*
- *what are important things in editing?*

Report Writer

A Dear Writer,
The first and most important editor is always you, the translator.

We all know how our translations benefit from letting them lie for a day, then reviewing them with fresh eyes. It is simply amazing how many things we catch that way: misunderstood passages in the source text, inconsistent translations of one and the same word, misspellings, bad grammar, infelicitous style.

The next editor is another translator or native speaker of the target language with subject matter expertise, hired and paid by you if you work directly for the customer, or by the translation bureau if you are working through an intermediary.

In practice, however, outside review does not always happen, for a variety of reasons.

In this case, make sure that the customer understands that there is still is going to be an editor, namely them! Quite apart from budget or time constraints, this kind of arrangement can work like a charm if the customer invests the time and effort required to do the job properly. After all, they usually know the target audience better than anyone. But even in this case, be sure to explain to them that you will be doing a final pass before the document goes to press.

Just make sure not to confuse the terms "proofreading" and "editing." The former simply means ensuring that a text conforms with rules of spelling and typesetting. It does not address accuracy, completeness or style. The latter means that you, the editor, actually climb under the hood of the car and get your hands dirty fixing, twiddling and adjusting.

It is difficult work and carries a big responsibility: make sure you do it well. And charge prices to match.

FA & WB

Q *I'm not a translator, just a monolingual editor. A client of mine (a government agency) has directed me to develop a Standard Operating Procedure for translating technical documents from English into Spanish. He doesn't have any examples, so I'm trawling the Internet. Are you aware of, or do you know where I could find, examples of SOPs for translators? Any advice you could give me would be greatly appreciated.*

Philosopher's Stone

A Dear Stone,
You are several steps ahead of the crowd, since your client appears willing to pay you to provide advice on this red-hot topic—which means they are probably going to read what you pull together, too.

Yet it's extremely hard to give an intelligent answer without information on document types, deadlines and volumes.

Example: assuming low volumes, reasonable deadlines, low repetition rates and the need for high quality, the best way forward could well be to interview experienced translators with a view to long-term investment by both parties in a long-term business relationship aiming for high, consistent quality, mutual confidence, continuous learning, etc.

But if any of the basic assumptions changes—high volumes? tight turnarounds? massive repetition? mediocre quality acceptable in some cases?— the best solution could be radically different.

As a general lite backgrounder we recommend *Translation, Getting it Right*, a brochure with which we are intimately associated. It can be downloaded for free in .pdf format in English, French, German, Dutch, Italian, Romanian and Czech from a number of translator association sites, starting with www. fit-europe.org.

For a more detailed approach, you will want to consult *Translation: Buying a Non-Commodity*, available in English, French and German (free)—and perhaps check out the various standards already developed by the translation industry (not free).

FA & WB

PAPERWORK

Q *Should I put my terms & conditions on my website or is it better to simply attach them to the estimates I send out?*

Lock'em In

A Dear Lock,
Do both. Getting things down in black and white is an essential first step in developing and maintaining a portfolio of happy, loyal clients. Which means adopting and publicizing ultra-clear terms of business is an excellent reflex.

Remember, too, that T&Cs are not only about payment: they describe how you work and explain what you deliver, while reminding your client of the input you'll need from them along the way.

It's that second chunk that you'll want to emphasize early on in negotiations, most effectively in a less legalistic format than your official T&C document, which comes in when you are actually closing the deal.

Onwards and upwards!

FA & WB

Q *I have a sensitive and urgent financial query related to a French agency for which I have recently done a first job (780 words for which I received just over £37 after bank conversion fee). The agency seems to be the subject of some kind of tax audit. They want me to send written confirmation that I pay into social security funds.*

There are three problems: first, in the UK, where I live, there is no requirement of this type (I really don't know which body could issue the "certificate" that they want).

Secondly, I obviously do not wish this to end up in the French courts—my spoken French is not as fluent as it should be and I know nothing at all about finance or law, plus I certainly do not have the money to pay a solicitor.

Thirdly, for a series of personal problems too complicated to go into here, all of my translation work is indeed undeclared. I know I should straighten this out, and intend to in the near future, but have not had time, energy or billable income to do so this far.

What should I do?

Urgent Query

A Dear Urgent,
To recap: you are working illegally and fear you've been caught and want advice from us because your French (and English) is not up to understanding the issues. Can we assume that the £37 was not for legal translation? Good.

It sounds like your French agency client's number has come up in an URSSAF review—not the tax authorities, rather one component of the (compulsory) social security system that applies to all independent contractors working in France. Such reviews are not uncommon. They are aimed at identifying people working off the books and forcing them to comply with the law.

If the offender is working in France, the person/company that paid him/her gets hit with a fine corresponding to the amount that should have been paid into the retirement/healthcare/family benefits fund (or as the employer's contribution for a salaried person), topped up by an additional penalty to discourage future negligence.

In your case, if the agency has to pay such a fine, they will not want to work with you again, for obvious reasons.

We think it unlikely that the French authorities will come traipsing over to Blighty to get you, although you should definitely phone your professional association's legal helpline for an opinion. It sounds like you might want to make this an anonymous call.

Perhaps a brief letter describing the British tax and social security system will suffice?

But consider this a wake-up call and—we bet you could see this coming—pull up your UK socks by this time next week. Don't procrastinate. When you work as a freelance provider of a business service like translation, breaking the law is not only a serious risk for you and your clients, it stamps a scarlet A on your forehead ("Amateur") and bars you from the lucrative end of the market.

FA & WB

Q *I saw your response to the Urgent Query.*
I have a similar, but perhaps much more serious problem: I'm currently living in Paris, and I've just gotten a letter saying that I've been rejected from the (compulsory) URSSAF social-security system, which means I don't have a numero de cotisation or anything, but in the time that I sent in my application I started working already, writing 'Siret en cours' on my invoices. What can I do? Why might I have been rejected by URSSAF? Can I re-apply and be instated retroactively? If you don't know the answers to these questions, could you suggest someone that I could contact who might?
Sincerely,

Freaking Out

A Dear Freaking Out,
Why not go to the horse's mouth: simply phone URSSAF and ask!

Normally you will have filed your application in person, at which point the pen-pusher manning the desk will have given you a stamped receipt. That is itself proof you were acting in good faith when you started issuing invoices.

Dealing with redtape-meisters is an integral part of working as a freelance provider of services in France, so consider this your first hurdle. If you were a member of SFT, the national association of professional translators (www.sft. fr), you might use their free legal helpline for assistance; then again, French residents applying for SFT membership must submit proof that they have fulfilled the legal requirements for working in France, so you, sir, are in chicken and egg territory.

With information from the source, we're betting you can supply the missing documents needed to straighten things out (Tax records starting in 1960? Certificate from your hometown justice of the peace certifying that you have no criminal record? Great-grandmother's birth certificate?) In the meantime, three cheers for you for taking the initiative and jumping through the hoops. At the risk of repeating ourselves, off-the-books translators don't get a crack at the lucrative end of the market.

FA & WB

4
Client/supplier relations

Translators create texts for clients at the other end of the phone, across town, or on the other side of the world. But they are not always good at communicating with these buyers and users—nor do customers necessarily explain what they want or need when ordering a translation (sometimes they themselves don't know).

CLIENT REVIEW

Q*I take your point about encouraging feedback from clients. But lately some comments have come too close for comfort. For three years I've been translating a corporate newsletter into English for employees of the US subsidiary of a Spanish engineering company. Last month a manager at the US company went through my text and changed a lot of it. This person is not a translator—he's not even a linguist— but about 75% of his suggestions were definite improvements on what I'd written. And since his comments reached me through my client, they've seen all his corrections: they know how dismal my effort was. How am I going to live this down?*

Heading for the Hills

ADear Heading,
An in-house target-language subject-matter expert prepared to take the time to review your work and make detailed suggestions is no reason to disconnect your phone and hide out in the basement, much less skip town. This guy is a find, a gem, a jewel.

Step back a minute and think. Your prime concern—your commitment to your client—is to turn out a top-quality newsletter in English. By taking the time to mark up your text, the US manager has already demonstrated that he can help you do just that. Which makes him a potential ally (unless he is angling for your job, in which case you *have* got a problem).

We suggest you accept his input as a wake-up call and view it as opportunity to kick your own operation into shape.

Don't dawdle. Phone your client and tell them how pleased you are to get the feedback. Mention that you won't be using every single suggestion (to save a little face, you might cite one of the guy's obvious mistakes in an offhand way), but confirm to them that this is precisely the type of exchange translators need to work well. (This happens to be true.) Ask if you can contact him through them. Put it this way even if you've already got the man's name and contact details, since it is good to keep their head office in the loop, at least for your initial exchanges.

When drafting your comments to him:

1. Ease in with sincere thanks and acknowledgment of a slip-up, but don't dwell on it.

Something along the lines of "Professional translators can get so caught up in their work that they lose sight of the forest for the trees, and I want to thank you for helping me get back on track" should do it.

2. Keep the flow going.

Ask for some assistance on a few more terms—confirmation of tricky technical vocabulary, for example, or his opinion of job-title translations. You do this because you actually need the information (or at least a confirmation), but also to remind him—and whoever may be skimming through the letter at head office—how complex your job is.

3. End with at least one big(ger) picture query.

Ask if the subsidiary he works for has a style book (references, please), or if he has any general comments on the journal that you might pass on to the Spanish editor. This information will be invaluable to you as you work on future editions, and is an excellent way to consolidate your position as the US subsidiary's interface with its Spanish parent.

In short, rather than view this out-of-the-blue editing as a catastrophe, learn from it, build on it, use it to expand your network of contacts in the company.

While your work is probably not as dismal as you say, may we also suggest that you arrange for regular, independent editing by this in-house expert or someone else. No secret here: when you produce work for publication, a second (or third) pair of critical eyes is essential.

Finally, a word of caution: the next time a client calls with a newsletter project, locate your in-house subject-matter native-language expert before the first issue goes to press.

FA & WB

Q *I had to smile at your advice to Heading for the Hills (page 59), whose work had been reviewed and improved on by an expert at the client end.*

Am I the only reader convinced that most client "adjustments" are anything but improvements?

I translate corporate documents from Italian to English. While I welcome exchanges with real experts, I have recently seen one of my texts massacred by none other than the Managing Director's wife, a native Dutch speaker who studied Italian in college years ago and has literary pretensions.

The job was a 16-page catalog for an exhibit featuring works from the corporate art collection. This woman fancies herself an artiste, so helpfully "corrected" my painstakingly researched and crafted text. If only!

Have you got some useful ripostes for situations like this?

Rewritten Seeks Revenge

A Dear Re,

Heading for the Hills' input came from a genuine subject-matter expert. What you've got here sounds like a dilettante with family connections, and there are several strategies for dealing with them.

For offenders under age 25, an appropriate response is a friendly chuckle and approving nod at Junior's effort, perhaps inquiring if s/he has plans to attend translation school after a few years abroad to get that basic fluency up to speed—this as you cheerfully uncap your red pen and get down to work. You can usually discard their input entirely after a half-page or so. Keep that regretful smile in place, of course.

A marital link is a little trickier, but can work to your advantage if you view it as an opportunity to raise her (and her husband's) awareness/appreciation of your skills.

You can be diplomatic or blunt. Diplomacy, a useful skill for any self-employed person, would involve customizing the tactics set out in points 1 to 4 below. If you don't think you can handle this, go straight to point 5.

In any case, act quickly. When the problem surfaces, establish contact immediately—in writing. If you limit your response to bitching to colleagues and friends or writing to FA & WB, you will miss the opportunity to recover control of the project.

1. Say something nice. We'll take your word for it that you can't realistically thank her for the quality of her input. But if she reworked 16 pages, hey, the lady did log some time, so acknowledge that, e.g., "Not many people outside the profession realize how time-consuming it is to produce high-quality

translation, and I want to thank you for the many hours you spent revising the catalog for the Arte Azzura retrospective."

2. Translation basics. Remind her that most professional translators work into their native tongue only; while her input was enlightening in some critical areas, you won't be able to use all of it. Make brief notes on her grammar, syntax, terminology and style problems, and tell her you would be delighted to discuss these points further at her convenience. It is always good to meet people face to face, especially well-connected ones.

3. Let the red ink flow. Three or four pages should be enough to bring your point home. While it sounds like you can safely axe 90% of her input outright, suggesting a third solution 5-10% of the time is tactful.

4. Insert a few subject-matter footnotes. Big fat ones. These show that you master your subject, and bring home the message that this is work, babes. In our experience, dilettantes have little stamina. If it looks like there's a sustained effort involved, they often back out of their own accord. (This is one reason why they tend to fiddle with art catalogs and not 320-page user manuals for clearing and settlement systems.)

What with the axing and revising and footnotes, you are now operating at a loss on this job. But don't despair—this person is in daily contact with the company's top dog. You have raised her consciousness, wowed her with your expertise, embarrassed her gently but thoroughly, and given her a graceful excuse to withdraw and stay withdrawn. (Or sign up for a translation course; why not?) This is long-term PR.

5. If she's a hardcore meddler, take a tougher line, up to and including informing the company courteously but firmly—in writing—that you will not allow your name to appear in the credits. Regardless of this client and this job, you have your professional reputation to protect.

See why it's a good idea to sign your work?

FA & WB

ASKING QUESTIONS

Q *Your response to Wearing Down Fast (page 67) sparked some serious debate in our in-house translation department. Like him, we serve authors who seem far happier when we deliver translations that are word-for-word transpositions of* *their original efforts. I'm the latest hire here, but I've heard some real horror stories. So far I've been flying the quality flag, but remind me again: why shouldn't we just give them what they want/deserve?*

Pass the Ammo

A Dear Defender of the Faith,
Negotiating with authors—asking questions to clarify source texts and explaining linguistic choices—is an integral part of the translator's job. And as part of an in-house team, you are in an ideal position to do this.

Regardless of the consensus around the translation department water cooler, we wonder if your colleagues are not simply ill at ease with the normal backing and forthing that goes on when authors review translations. To our knowledge, this is rarely mentioned, much less taught, in translation schools, which is a pity all around. Handling these exchanges requires not only language but people skills—skills that will serve you well whether you remain a staff translator or move into the freelance market. Once you've identified sections that need clarification, you must be able to ask questions efficiently and articulately, slipping in the odd technical reference to remind authors that you master the subject, and offering a choice of solutions. Rare is the source text that does not benefit from such discussions, which are also an opportunity to raise your own profile and that of the translation department.

Heading down the path of least resistance, even for in-house documents, carries at least one risk: seeing your own writing style corrupted. We urge you not to underestimate this danger, since it will ultimately disqualify you from the top end of the market—which is arguably the most lucrative (and certainly the most fun).

The bottom line: however willing your clients may seem, do not foist upon them anything that would embarrass you in front of native-language peers, especially if you can imagine life outside this particular company. Who knows where your career will take you? And in one way or another, shoddy work always comes back to haunt you.

FA & WB

Q *I was intrigued by your comments to Pass the Ammo (above). In translation school we were encouraged to resolve source-text ambiguities on our own, and at least one of my teachers suggested that authors would not take you seriously if you bothered them with questions. Now I hear I'm supposed to. I'm willing to try, but*

Chapter 4

I wish I'd known this sooner.

Better Late than Never

ADear Better,
Your comments are one reason we urge teachers (and translators) to commission translations of their own writings at regular intervals. Being on the receiving end is the best possible reminder of how frustrating it can be for authors when a well-meaning translator blasts through, "resolving" queries on her own.

We agree with your teachers that direct clients unfamiliar with translation will not always realize how valuable your input can be. Not immediately. You'll probably have to educate them. But rest assured, virtually all will appreciate your eagle eye and commitment to readability if you take the time to explain how you work and why.

Start with a reminder that we are not just lining up words here, folks (that service is available instantaneously online, and it is free, to boot). Nobody will ever read their work as carefully as you, the translator. Along the way, you will naturally encounter passages open to several interpretations, in which case questions/comments are absolutely normal—a page straight from the best practice manual. Questions are good news for text originators, since your comments will allow them to tighten up the original.

Ultimately, our own preference is for phone or in-person exchanges. Here practice in asking questions pleasantly, efficiently and diplomatically will serve you well. Keep in mind:
• Authors' time is money (so is yours), so no rambling.
• Slipping in a few technical or sector-specific asides early on is a good way to reassure and to establish your mastery of the subject. ("The reference here is to Alan Greenspan's comments at the World Economic Forum, right?") You master the subjects you translate (your teachers did insist on that, didn't they?) and you do your homework. That's good.
• Mention but do not dwell on obvious mistakes at their end ("...a typo, no doubt; I've fixed it for the English, OK?").
• Depending on your contacts' foreign-language skills, the number of queries you have, and the length of the text, it may be worth sending them a draft translation with questions clearly marked, proposing several options for each. This gives them a chance to tick their choice, or start mentally rephrasing what was unclear, prior to your call.

FA & WB

Q *I very occasionally pop into an online forum for translators (remind me what we are called—glunkers, glinchers, slinkers?) and its "help" section, where translators post questions about texts they are working on.*

I think the idea of mutual help is great, but I do occasionally wonder (a) why people take on texts in fields where they have absolutely no experience, which they obviously can't handle, and (b) if they ever pick up the phone and ask the customer what he/she meant before they post their questions on the forum.

I can only judge in the technical field, but some of the questions make me wonder what the final text looks like.

Speaking for myself, I virtually always phone the customer (or, at the very least, add a translator's note) to point out ambiguities, suggest modifications for an international readership, or admit I have no idea what they mean—even in industrial chemistry, where I have a PhD and 22 years' translation experience.

Usually my clients agree that the original text is not clear (or contained an error) and change it accordingly. In fact, I find the customer ALWAYS appreciates a frank discussion and exchange.

Without the right context, and without knowing the background, you cannot be expected to know what the customer means at all times, and trying to pretend you do just damages your credibility. And yet I sometimes subcontract out work to experienced translators, encourage them to ask questions, phone up to check again if they have any doubts about anything, then get back crap with no comments. Why?

Which brings me back to my original question—why do translators seem so reluctant to ask their customers questions, yet so willing to post a list of queries on translator forums? Is the big wide world so scary? Am I being too judgmental? Or should I stop being a glunker and get involved?

Science Translator

A Dear Scientist,
The link between (a) a readiness to translate anything that moves and (b) reluctance to interact directly with clients is not fortuitous.

In fact, it explains a lot of translator twitchiness—the defensiveness that comes from knowing, deep down inside, that one is on pretty shaky ground much of the time. Symptoms include alternating bouts of belligerence and forelock-tugging, with regular time-outs.

The only long-term treatment we know of involves taking a closer look at what clients really want and/or think they are getting, and acquiring the knowledge or skills to deliver just that.

Seen this way, a willingness to ask questions of one's peers is surely a step in the right direction. And for translators working in isolation, it can be immensely useful to run an idea past a group of fellow professionals. Questioners may be working on a text in their chosen field when a term (or paragraph, or page) from another domain pops up; help from a specialist colleague can be one way to move back onto familiar terrain. If initial searches on the web prove fruitless or confusing, why not seek confirmation in a supportive atmosphere before running options past the client?

But we suspect you are referring instead to the hapless souls who post a fresh round of questions every day, each time in a different technical field.

We know several specialized translators who supply non-judgmental responses to even the most hair-raisingly elementary questions on such forums. Reminding risk-takers just how complex the subject matter is can alert them to the danger of getting in over their head, says one. Some day the penny will drop. If you agree with this approach, you might consider leaving your lurking ways behind and joining in.

More generally, however, we have noticed a distinct difference in job satisfaction, self-esteem, and—wait for it—quality of output between translation suppliers who maintain the sort of easy back-and-forth with clients you describe, and those who clam up and/or limit their questions to exchanges with fellow translators.

When challenged, the latter often claim that customers would think less of them for "not knowing the answer." In a fit of orneriness, some will even argue that a translator should never consult a client on terminology and that to do otherwise betrays craven weakness. Sigh.

This group is at best misinformed, at worst trapped in the uncomfortable text in/text out/duck'n'cover/next job, please! segment of the market. (This applies to both translation companies/agencies and freelancers, incidentally).

Only when they jettison this mindset will they get a crack at the more attractive sections of the market—which, incidentally, pay at least three or four times more.

Ultimately, we see no better way for translators to win recognition for their expertise, and secure proper remuneration and working conditions than by reminding customers just how complex language issues are. Questions are an ideal way to do just that.

FA & WB

QUALITY

Q *I work as an in-house Houyhnhnm-Yahoo translator for a large Houyhnhnm company and have repeatedly observed a phenomenon which, to my knowledge, no one has openly discussed before: the more literal, i.e. the more "Houyhnhnmized" our translations, the happier the Houyhnhnm authors are with our work. If we put their texts in real Yahoo, the translation sounds too free to them and they often complain.*

Many of my colleagues have caved in completely and give them what they want. This way everybody is happy: the Houyhnhnms think they're getting a wonderful translation and the translators don't have to deal with constant questions. A lot of these texts are for internal use, so my colleagues feel that no harm has been done. Yet even when our work is sent to clients, they usually just respond without complaining about the quality of the Yahoo in the material they received, thus leaving the Houyhnhnms convinced that it was perfect.

How should I handle the situation? My colleagues tell me to get off my high horse and give our authors what they want and deserve: translations that look like Yahoo and read like Houyhnhnm. Although I can't get myself to do it, I must admit I do get tired of ramming my head against the wall day in day out. Any advice would be appreciated.

Wearing Down Fast

A Dear Wearing,
A treacherous sea to negotiate: too far starboard, and you crash head-on into the reef that awaits the reckless; too far port, and you get sucked under by the whirlpool of resignation.

There is, though, a way to steer clear of both dangers.

The key is to step into the shoes of your Houyhnhnm authors for a moment. After all, it is only natural that they instinctively shy away from what they understand but imperfectly. ("You there! What means 'but imperfectly'?" demands the Houyhnhnm peering over our shoulders as we write.)

However, there is no need to sacrifice your professionalism by giving them bastardized Yahoo. What they really want is clear and correct Yahoo but with vocabulary and grammar that does not overtax their limited command of what is for them a second language. Also, the presentation you translate may be one they have to give themselves, and so they feel extra-cautious about not being made to use words they understand but im- ouch! You get the point.

You can do it! Pretty soon Houyhnhnms will be trampling a path to your cubicle as your craven colleagues look on in envy. And with a little bit of luck, you can look forward to fame and fortune in a new career—as a political speechwriter.

FA & WB

Q *I head the translation department at a major bank in continental Europe. In addition to handling our company's more sensitive translations, my job involves coordinating workflows to subcontractors. We require half a dozen language combinations, but mainly French, German and English.*

Over the years our bank has been approached by any number of translation companies/agencies, big and small, each promising us high quality, specialized translators, fast turnarounds, etc. I know enough about translation, banking and management to sort out the sheep from the goats, and quickly send glib sales reps packing.

But here's the problem: even when the initial contact is good and we get excellent work and service at the outset, this never lasts. Within about a year (18 months at most) quality starts to slide and we are forced to look elsewhere.

We pay well and I go out of my way to provide healthy lead times, helpful feedback and so on. I have a feeling that the crux of the matter is these suppliers' fixation on growth at all costs; in expanding their operations, they somehow "forget" to serve the customers they've already signed up. How can I bring this message home?

Big Bank

A Dear Big Bank,
Why not grab the bull by the horns and ask the translation company representatives who come calling how they see their business developing? In this scenario, the guys who say "Well, we'd like to expand but it is extremely difficult; there are relatively few economies of scale in the segment that interests you and us because there are so few genuinely skilled translators, so we are growing only very slowly" go on your shortlist. The ones who announce exponential growth, upcoming flotations and offices opening in London, Paris, Milan and Zurich (not to mention major investments in the ultimate technology that will generate savings of 300%) get a cup of coffee and a don't-call-us-we'll-call-you. Past this initial filter, once you have selected a provider do be sure to set out your expectations in writing at the start, and hold the supplier to them—up to

and including charging a penalty for work that falls short of the mark.

You might also insist on knowing the names of the translators who do your work. Make it clear that you do not plan to circumvent the company, which will still be providing plenty of added value in project and glossary management, updating style sheets, etc. Maintain contacts with these people through the company by phone and email, and considering inviting them (the translators, not just the project managers) over for a meeting once every six months or so, to visit your in-house departments and see how their texts are being used.

Establishing and maintaining a personal link really does pay off. At the very least, you'll be able to see when the translation company starts replacing experienced translators with juniors.

FA & WB

Q *I recently had a translation flatly refused (the text was about property investment in a marketing context) on the grounds that it didn't flow in the same way as the English original.*

When I looked at the 'corrections' the German customer had made, they were (apart from one or two technical terms, which, in any case, I had raised in a question) things like:

- focus: he preferred 'Focus' instead of my choice of 'Marktschwerpunkt'

- real estate investments: 'Immobilieninvestments' instead of my choice: 'Immobilienanlagen'

    etc.

I pointed out that my translation flowed perfectly well, but was nevertheless keeping to a standard of the written word as reflected in such fundamental reference documents as the Duden, national daily papers, etc. However, if the client wished to represent a style as it is now often heard on television etc., he would have to do some copyediting of the text.

I have since discussed this with a few colleagues, here in the UK and in Germany, and am somewhat 'verunsichert': it seems that English words including 'peer group', 'case manager', 'hardliner', 'decisive moment', (not to mention many terms in the world of finance and banking) are in regular use now in German, even in some written documents.

My question is: what standard can we apply? I would have thought that the Internet with its many half-baked translations is hardly authoritative. Dare I mention the Duden? Even in its latest version it probably would be nicknamed 'dino from the last millennium'. So where are we to turn? Recent developments seem to be so rapid that there no longer is a clear guideline as to what is German and what is hype for marketing or some other purpose.

Stymied on Style

A Dear Stymied,
We are the first to recommend exchanges between authors and translators to fine-tune nuance and style. Indeed, for most texts that is part of the deal. So if you've made yourself available, tell the customer you expect your bill to be paid, and resend it to drive the point home. "Refusing" a translation for reasons of taste and individual preference is simply unacceptable.

Now for the next question: might you be growing out of touch with how the language is evolving back home?

The answer, of course, is yes.

How can you stay in touch with the latest buzzwords? Sure, you could jet back and forth between the UK and Germany every month. But this would likely be a waste of time and money, depending on how highly you value the opportunity to ask Lufthansa stewardesses for their telephone number.

The answer is twofold.

(1) Read. But not "half-baked translations on the Internet." Instead, make a point of regularly perusing the real-estate industry's trade news. This used to require expensive subscriptions, but we denizens of the 21st century are lucky since we can get content free—on the Internet!

No matter how cringe-inducing the indiscriminate adoption of English words is to you, suppress your reaction. The customer is paying the bill, and has a right—within reason—to impose vocabulary.

(2) Before you know it, another customer will throw your translation back into your face, citing your egregious lack of respect for the sanctity of German. To avoid this, make a point of noting in your correspondence and general conditions of business that clients MUST specify any special style preferences, as well as providing pertinent materials, such as press releases and URLs.

Good luck!

FA & WB

Q *I am a Latin American student majoring in English philology in Madrid. Our teacher commented that these days translation agencies in the US want their Spanish translations done by Spaniards rather than Latin Americans. He didn't explain why, but I guess he had in mind that it is a matter of language correctness. We didn't have the opportunity to comment on this in class, so I didn't say a word, but I can't get it out of my mind. Of course, I have my own opinion: the competence of a translator does not depend on his nationality but on his command of the languages he works in. Preferences are a different thing. What do you think?*

Hibernating Iberian

A Dear Hibernating,
Serious translation intermediaries with even a minimal understanding of the business try to match the translator to the target audience. Always. And since terms and expressions differ from one Spanish-speaking country to another, this means turning to a translator from Spain for a translation for a Spanish audience, a translator from Argentina for an Argentine audience, etc.

"Language correctness" has nothing to do with the country and everything to do with the educational level and writing style of the individual doing the work.

Perhaps your teacher was deliberately seeking to provoke your class (hmm, why didn't anybody speak up?). If he was extrapolating from a personal experience, he was making the same mistake that practicing translators do when they equate an incident with a clueless intermediary with the attitudes and priorities of premium clients (who are the ones you want).

So maybe your man is simply out of touch—in which case, listen carefully to what he has to say about the history of translation and translation theory, but take his marketing advice with a scoop of salt.

FA & WB

Q *I had been working with a translation company for almost two years when they stopped sending me work. I tried sending them e-mails and even designed a survey to get some feedback from them, but no luck. I finally called one of the people who used to send me work and she told me that they had another translator who didn't require extensive revisions on their part. Even though he was more expensive they didn't mind, she said. So I'm not sure if I should try to find out what happened or just forget about it.*

I admit I feel bad because I think that I'm not such a bad translator—it is just a matter of style. Maybe they give my translations to someone to review and this person makes comments which are probably not very positive.

What do you think?

Frustrated in Costa Rica

Dear Frustrated,

What we think? That you are history for this particular translation company.

But we sympathize with your efforts to find out precisely where the mismatch lay—that's essential to develop your own strategy for the future. A thought: maybe your feedback survey, while a good idea in theory, looked too time-consuming for your contact at the company.

What you need in any case is a close look at changes made to your input.

If none of the texts you worked on for this particular agency are available on the web or elsewhere in the public domain, get back to your company contact again. No bitterness, no weeping: simply explain that you are considering further training and want some concrete examples of what you need to focus on before signing up for a course.

To increase your chances of a response, make the translation company's job as easy as possible. Look through your own records and identify a few assignments where you feel you performed particularly well. Ask for their revisions of these, specifying file names, subject matter and date. `

With future clients, ask to see revisions as a matter of course and spend some serious time analyzing TC input (you might ask a trusted colleague for an opinion, too).

Finally, you note that the company's dissatisfaction may be "just a matter of style." That's not an argument to make to a premium client, where accuracy is the absolute minimum and style just about everything else. (Whether your ex-client enters that category is another matter—but do note that price is not their main objection here).

Keep in mind that translation is a writing skill, and that working on your writing style is one of the best investments you can make. An excellent book for translators working into English is William Zinsser's "On Writing Well" (First HarperResource Quill, ISBN 0-06-000664-1); we would welcome suggestions from Spanish-speaking readers for translators working into that language.

FA & WB

Q *My company recently commissioned the translation of a set of job descriptions from a group of UK translators that had been recommended to us. Our choice was based partly on the supplier's ability to work with translation memory tools, as we needed to remain consistent with an existing set of job titles and certain sections were quite repetitive.*

The results were disappointing. The entire text needed to be revised in-house: some of the French had been misunderstood, and the English structure sometimes matched the French so closely that clarity suffered.

Here is an example: "The purchaser then takes the lead as a summarizer, combining the contributions of his/her corporate internal and external partners in order to identify the optimum product-market combination, while helping the internal interested parties to identify and understand the risks associated with implementation of such suitability."

When challenged about the shortcomings, the translators responded: "We must stress that we have been commissioned to translate the text, not produce an English text which expresses what we might consider to have been the author's intended meaning."

Is this a widespread attitude in the translation community? I thought expressing the author's intended meaning was exactly what translation was about.

The choice of translation memory tools for our project may have been misguided. We gained in consistency and terminology management, but we were confronted with human translators who, in their quest for greater productivity, lost sight of the need to communicate clearly with human readers.

How can I avoid this happening again, but still benefit from the greater speed and consistency these tools offer?

Hobgoblin in Hoboken

A Dear Hobgoblin,
Start by striking these guys from your supplier list.

Translation memory systems are not a substitute for human thought and language sensitivity, and their comments reflect either total cluelessness or far too many late nights—neither of which you need. They have effectively disqualified themselves as serious contenders outside the gisting market (a pity for them, given the price differential).

We assume you gave the UK suppliers detailed project specifications, but did you ask to see samples of their work in advance? In translation there is never an absolute guarantee of quality, but a supplier with a portfolio of successful work is a better bet than an unknown quantity, even with a recommendation. For future projects, you might also ask to review the project together earlier on, i.e., not wait until final delivery to discover how much revision would be necessary.

In answer to your first question, the attitude you decry is—sadly—all too common, although few people articulate it as baldly as your erstwhile suppliers. In fact, one of our contacts claims this is the number one problem facing the industry today, citing translations that give you the impression the translator thought his role was to "describe" the document rather than make it understandable. Slavishly following the punctuation of the original is one flashing red light (e.g., French to English translators who mechanically put three dots instead of "etc."); syntax structured along that of the source text another.

Like raw machine translation, translation memory software is only as good as the people who use it. As the man said, translation is not about words, it is about the ideas behind the words. Exit machine, enter expert human translator (and beef up that budget while you're at it).

FA & WB

Q *I am a translation company owner and recently signed up with ProZ.com to get a feel for this market place.*

The jobs section is astonishing. How a serious agency (and all the jobs being offered there are by agencies) could put its business in the hands of almost complete strangers is beyond me. Talk about price pressure—"no more than EUR 0.08/word" is a common way of offering a job! Yet the bids come flooding in. Another thing that amazes me is how many freelancers offer translation in both directions, multiple language combinations and all subject areas.

But the most incredible thing must be their "KudoZ" system. Someone posts a question, you answer the question and if you convince the asker you're right, they give you a KudoZ point. The more KudoZ points you've got, the higher up the list you go when bidding for jobs. So, it's a meritocratic system—but bizarrely it's the least experienced translators who decide who's good and who's bad. And if you've got a bit of a name in translation circles, you go around bullying inexperienced translators into handing over KudoZ points. Some complaints indicate that people have even been putting up questions under invented profiles, then answering themselves and awarding themselves the KudoZ points!

The whole system seems designed to propagate bad translations: inexperienced translators asking questions which are answered by not very good translators (not very good because if they were they would be doing well-paid translations rather wasting their time answering silly questions). Would you care to comment?

Laugh or Cry?

A Dear Laugh,
ProZ.com's model is hair-raising, to be sure, but hey, take a look at the traffic. Sites like this flourish because there is demand—a reminder that there is not one translation market, rather a multitude of segments, including those driven by rock-bottom rates and/or lightning turnarounds, with quality a distant third.

Where you place your company on the quality/service spectrum is a personal and professional decision. We are convinced that skilled translators generally rethink their positioning as they gain experience, and shift their focus accordingly. That they enjoy, en route, the camaraderie of exchanges with fellow translators—both no-hopers and experts—is understandable.

So—is ProZ.com a flawed model? Sure, for those focusing on the high-priced, high-quality, direct-client end of the market. Populated by many inexperienced and/or clueless service providers? Absolutely.

But transparent, too, which is all for the better.

Consider: a few serious agencies that do dip in from time to time have been known to blackball translators on the basis of either their questions or—more often—their answers. Seen from this angle, ProZ.com's very transparency is fighting the quality fight, albeit in a bizarre, backhanded way.

FA & WB

PS: ProZ's job system has changed slightly since this Q&A first ran, but prices observed on the site are now even lower (gulp). We stand by our initial analysis.

Q *I'm currently reviewing the most incredible heap of crap I've ever come across in my translating career. It's a 10,000 word translation (Eng>Fr, from an English original translated from Japanese). The English translation is actually quite good, but the French is garbage, translated by a fellow with an impressive CV, who claims to be an MBA and a teacher of accounting in some private university in Switzerland. But he really made a dog's dinner of it.*

Two questions:

1. It's very clear that my revision is saving the ass of the translation agency that commissioned the original translation. How can I capitalize on that?

2. I'm irritated that a fellow "translator" did such a poor job, while claiming such lofty credentials. I've got his address. What's a good way to bring him down a notch?

Fire-fighter

A Dear Sarge,
1. Charge accordingly. You might also have a little chat with the project manager. But situate yourself above the fray—rather than get all steamed up about the incompetent job they bought in (they're probably pretty steamed themselves at this point), use more neutral quality-assurance language: do their terms of business forbid subcontracting, for example? They might want to think about that, as it could be where this assignment went wrong (other possibilities: over-reliance on translation memory or simply brain-dead human translation).

2. OK, you're looking for a "you scoundrel, casting discredit on the profession!" letter that is at once classy, witty and effective.

The most damning tactic we can think of is to address this guy as an equal while confirming that you are on to his tricks. Something along the lines "Cher collègue, this project slipped off track, no doubt due to misuse of MT or one of your students not living up to the trust you placed in them; as a fellow professional, I sympathize with these problems, and am happy to return my comments to you."

You thus remind him that he behaved unprofessionally (and possibly unethically) towards the client, while keeping to the high road yourself.

Venting can be exhilarating, but focusing on point (1) will do more for your business.

FA & WB

Q *A friend of mine made a mistake in a translation (one mistake in a two-page text) and the agency that commissioned the work didn't notice it either. This agency is ISO-certified and is supposed to have an in-house reviser.*

The end client, which is one of the agency's biggest customers (they say) got really upset and the agency waived its fee. It then asked my friend not to invoice the text either, since the original error was hers.

This agency represents a huge chunk of my friend's business, so she accepted just to keep on good terms with it. The bill was for €30.

My question: wouldn't it have been better to bill just half? After all, they were supposed to be revising.

Negotiator

A Dear Negotiator,
It would have been better to have billed €30—but with amounts this small, we think it is simply more professional to let the whole thing go,

especially if her relationship with the agency has been good so far.

But this is also a reminder that you really don't want to have all your eggs in one basket. Any time a single client accounts for more than 25% of your business, it's time to look for more. And an agency that puts pressure on you (er, your friend) for an error they should have caught may not be the ideal client anyway.

FA & WB

Q *An agency asked me to translate a 6000-word Ge>Fr document in my specialty area in a rather short time span. I declined, mainly because I considered the deadline way too short.*

This agency is usually serious about quality so when they later asked me to edit the translation I agreed.

Unfortunately, the translation delivered to them was substandard and, in my opinion, beyond repair. The only solution was retranslation, which was impossible in the editing window I'd been given (one evening).

I told them so at the start of business the next day, and backed up my comments with an analysis of a half-dozen serious mistakes (from the first page).

Now the client blames me for refusing to deliver a partially edited text. Who's right here?

Thwarted Ed(itor)

A Dear Thwarted,
Unhappy client, unhappy agency, unhappy translator: the blame game is one reason why written procedures are so important.

Mitigating circumstances in your favor were your familiarity with the agency and belief that they wouldn't stick you with a dead one. Well they did, didn't they? A pity, since they could and should have said no when a deadline-driven client showed up and they had no confirmed talent available. We're in this for the long term, or should be.

But you were cutting it fine, too. Editing is tricky; best not to get involved if there is absolutely no margin for error.

Here are some tips to avoid such situations in the future:
• Listen to your Inner Worrier. Your first reflex was right: just how likely was it that the agency would locate a qualified translator at such short notice?
• If you accept mission-critical jobs for which texts won't arrive until after normal office hours, demand a contact number with a human being on the other end up through 10:00 pm or even midnight. This is not only possible,

but best practice for genuinely quality-oriented businesses. The understanding must be that you will only phone in an emergency—which was clearly the case here. Use your time wisely and let your contact know immediately if there was a weak link in the chain.

• Never ever quote for an editing job without having seen the text first; if your intermediary can't guarantee that the work will be done by a known entity, just say no.

• Always charge a stiff premium for after-hours input, and quote an hourly fee for editing (as opposed to a lump sum). Explain why: it's an incentive! If project managers and translators invest sufficient time and effort upstream, your total fee may well be lower because you'll have less to do. It is simply not reasonable that a translation job be placed, by default, with an untested, unspecialized and presumably inexpensive junior translator, with you left to pick up the pieces.

But the best way to avoid situations like this is rigorous enforcement of the "just say no" principle as soon as your bad-vibes antennae start twitching.

In the case you report here, the time you spent analyzing bare-bones basic mistakes made by the initial translator and writing these up for your agency client represent added value sufficient to justify full payment in our opinion.

FA & WB

CERTIFICATION

Q *I am a professional translator from Angola.*
I have been working in a translation office for over 10 years, but I don't have any university degree in translation.
Do you think that I can have accreditation without a formal degree?
Would you please give me practical steps for being accredited.

Office Worker

A Dear Worker,
You don't say why you are interested in accreditation—do your clients know or care what an outside seal of approval might mean for the quality of your work? Will your employer recognize a qualification through higher pay or status in the office? Or do you simply want to test your skills against a benchmark?

We ask because it is worth thinking carefully about what you expect to gain before embarking on what is likely to be a time-consuming and expensive endeavor.

Ultimately professional translators are judged on the quality of the work they produce and deliver day in, day out. So while certification may help a beginner get a foot on the bottom rung, your 10 years' experience underpinned by a strong portfolio may count for more in many markets.

Those general comments aside, you don't say which accreditation interests you, nor are we sure whether you live in Angola or are simply originally from that country.

If you are thinking of the American Translators Association, note that ATA voted in November 2003 to rename their accreditation program "certification." For more information, contact ATA directly (www.atanet.org).

In general, overseas candidates must take the exam at one of the scheduled group sittings (none of which are in Africa), or take an individual sitting proctored by a current certified ATA member (none in Angola at present). All candidates must also meet specific eligibility/experience requirements to sit an ATA exam, but there is a provision for candidates without a degree to take the test if they can provide proof of five years of full-time experience— that's your cue if ATA certification is what you're after.

If you do live in Angola now, success would give you a monopoly over the in-country Angolan market for ATA-certified translators. Hmm, that's a thought (although Fire Ant & Worker Bee have no information on how big that market might be).

Depending on your language pair(s) and location, other options worth considering are exams given by the Institute of Translation & Interpreting and the Institute of Linguists in the UK. For more information, visit their websites at www.iti.org.uk and www.iol.org.uk.

FA & WB

CLUTTER

Q *I am a freelance translator with an office in my home and a reasonably successful business serving clients in the UK and the Netherlands. The other day I was caught off guard when a client phoned me out of the blue and insisted on dropping in to review a text in person (he happened to be in the neighbourhood, and the text was urgent).*

It was a chastening experience—not for the text itself and our discussion, which went very well, but because my office is a shambles, with papers papers papers and files files files as far as the eye can see. I will spare you the details, but from the look on this man's face as he crossed the threshold, I don't think my frantic hoovering accomplished much.

I've lectured myself and pulled up my socks (sort of) but am realistic, too: I am not a tidy person, and there is no way my working environment is going to become a slick, clean operation with a place for everything and everything in its place.

I know that visits from my clients are likely to remain rare, but never want to go through that stress and embarrassment again. Have you got any strategies for dealing with clients who pop in unannounced?

Litter Bug

A Dear Bug,
If your untidiness is grease and cockroaches, we can't help. But we can identify with paper clutter build-up, along with that sinking feeling as the doorbell rings.

Successful techniques we have observed firsthand depend on the size of your office, the size of the cluttered patch, and advance notice.

If you can, intercept the visitor at the doorstep, pretexting a prior visitor (e.g., your tax inspector has just shown up for a spot-check of your books, you'd like to leave him/her to work in peace, shall we retire to the café down the road?).

If this is impossible, your aim must be to lead the visitor quickly past the clutter to a clear desktop or other surface at which you will be working, then focus attention on the job at hand. To do this, we have five suggestions (note that for options 3 to 5, you will have to buy in supplies in advance):

1. Square Up the Corners: somehow piles of papers that are carefully stacked look infinitely neater than those in haystack format.
2. Strategic Lighting: carefully targeted, this can be a big help, depending on the time of day.
3. The Green Plant/Colorful Bouquet: a strategically placed decorative element may divert the visitor's eye temporarily.
4. Archives In Transit: a store of packing cases folded behind a bookcase will serve you in good stead. Should a client-intruder's call alert you to an impending visit, whip these out and place all extraneous documents/papers inside. Tape shut and stack neatly as per Square Up the Corners (above).

Explain briefly to your visitor that your archives have just been transferred in from storage or are on their way out.

5. Crime Scene: in extreme cases—and depending on the layout of your office—you might consider taping off the cluttered area with that striped fluorescent tape they use to mark out danger areas on construction sites or at crime scenes. Explain briefly to your visitor that there was a burglary the previous night and the police have instructed you to leave everything as is until they can get over for fingerprinting. (Let us know how this one works, OK?). The tape can be found in most hardware stores.

FA & WB

Q *I am a freelance translator suffering from office clutter not unlike that of your correspondent in a recent issue of Translation Journal.*

My solution is simply to lead the (rare) visitor to the living room coffee table with the (true) pretext that I have only one chair in the office. It works and nobody has ever raised an eyebrow.

Yours,

Lonely Rider

A Dear Lonely,
Even readers who have already invested in the packing cases and fluorescent tape will want to consider your excellent suggestion.

Thanks!

FA & WB

GIFTS

Q *My wife and I work together as freelance translators (G/E, E/G), supplying work to direct clients and agencies (about 50/50).*

Last December/January, as most years, we received a number of Christmas gifts from our clients—primarily office supplies w/corporate logos but also other assorted gadgets. A few good bottles of wine. A nice coffee-table book. And a bunch of calendars and diaries, most of which will go straight in the can.

My wife says that we should consider sending gifts to our clients in return but I am not comfortable with this. It seems to me that we are small fry compared to the companies that employ us, and anything we might be able to afford will look tacky (like a lot of those calendars and agendas, to tell the truth). I guess cards are an option. What do you think?

The Grinch

A Dear Grinch,
Celebrating the year end by expressing thanks and best wishes to those who helped make it a success is an appealing ritual, but you're right about the tacky trinkets. Ditto tacky messages, e.g., "Peace on earth—and you can call us any time for your German/English language needs." There's a fine line between sincere greetings and yet another marketing ploy. Do not cross over.

While cultural conventions and expectations definitely play a role in holiday offerings, we see no reason for you to splurge on costly corporate objects in response to your clients' largesse. A card, perhaps—why not. But even then, don't go into it half-heartedly: find or create witty cards, or at the very least buy them from a charity you support and add on a personal greeting.

If you do opt to go the gift route, find something memorable, personalized and easy to mail/deliver (light-weight, non-perishable). Why not put off the decision for now; keep the option in the back of your mind until November 30. If nothing suitable surfaces by then, forget it, or go for a card. Or nothing.

Other suggestions gleaned from our contacts here in Europe include:

• Spread the cheer: rather than a bottle of booze for the boss, a box of fine chocolates for the whole office, or case of premium lager for the next office party. Input from cheerful, organized secretarial staff often goes unrecognized; these people are your allies (or should be) and deserve a tip of the hat.

• Incorporate wit and wordplay: as translators, you and your wife are professional writers, poised at the interface of two cultures and languages. Even if you stick with cards alone, use your writing skills to create a short best-wishes message that sparkles and reminds them of your cross-cultural expertise.

• If you do opt for an office consumable, make sure it is well-designed and genuinely useful—e.g., a striking calendar with lots of space for notes, or a sleek desk version—or linked to your specialization, e.g., a space pen (writes upside down) for a translator working in aerospace.

If Fire Ant & Worker Bee operated out of Latin America, we might send our favorite customers gift-wrapped boxes of fried *hormigas culonas* from the Colombian province of Santander. Cross-cultural, unusual, clear link to name/image, easy to mail. And unforgettable. Unfortunately, we are assured that these crunchy insects are at their best in May. But you get the idea.

FA & WB

GLOSSARIES

Q *I've been keeping glossaries for clients and updating them on a regular basis. Now one of my direct clients has asked me for a copy of my glossary. Should I give it to them at all, and if yes, should I charge for it?*

Methodical in Miami

A Dear Methodical,
Your business relationship with a direct client will benefit enormously from agreeing on a common base of terminology, so look at this as a collaborative project, not a threat. And don't lose sight of the big picture: while terminology is important, your added value as a translator goes well beyond knowing the correct words (or should do).

Now, you know and we know that translation has nothing to do with word-for-word substitution. Many end-users pay lip service to this idea, but it's easy for them to forget just how complex the service you are providing is.

So to raise awareness all around and consolidate your ties, keep your eye out for terminology items of interest to them. Clip relevant articles, highlight terms and send them on to your in-company contacts with a short cover note. Send the same contacts client-specific glossaries regularly and ask them to send these back with corrections and additions. As a glossary grows and improves, your translations will improve and customer satisfaction will rise. We repeat: this is a high-profile way to present the behind-the-scenes work you put in year-round on behalf of your clients. And the message it conveys to clients is a good one: "I track your market; my skills go beyond terminology, but we've got to get this part straight first so that you can benefit from everything else I've got to offer."

FA & WB

CANCELLATIONS

Q *About a year ago a law firm contacted my small (2-person) translation company about a litigation involving foreign parties and documents. My partner and I had never done business with them before, but they're apparently a respectable outfit. When we realized that their immediate need was for an interpreter, we referred them to an excellent interpreter and translator who's worked with us in the past, and asked them to remember us if they had any translation work.*

Her experience with them was very unpleasant: they hemmed and hawed, refused to sign a contract, and repeatedly canceled previously scheduled bookings. Finally, after setting up an assignment in Paris (complete with demands to fly economy class and then work as soon as she hit the ground to save on hotel bills) they canceled only a few days in advance. Big mess, lots of arrangements to undo, and potential opportunity cost. The interpreter's reading is that their behavior is cost-driven.

A cancellation fee would have been an obvious choice, but with no contract, she didn't feel she could make it stick. In her defense, I should add that we've found law firms to be unusually resistant to signing contracts. This should feel like a paradox but somehow it isn't.

The immediate lessons are 1) to look for clients who are focused on value and expertise rather then nickels and dimes, and 2) to refuse to commit to anything until the client does (i.e. ALWAYS get a signed contract). The bigger question is how to negotiate effectively to get the signed contract—assuming that there are any strategies beyond Just Say No. Any advice?

Vexed in Virginia

A Dear Vexed,
A lawyer of our acquaintance suggests presenting the lawyers with the very thing they use themselves—an "engagement letter." Be sure to list the terms you expect, including the cancellation fee.

One way or another, all service providers benefit from having a written set of terms and conditions to send out before negotiations get under way. Putting essentials down in writing really does make a difference, forcing the drafter to consider what her minimum acceptable conditions are and why.

Content can be expanded to include, e.g., a brief explanation of why it doesn't make sense to hire a professional interpreter for a critical meeting and then send her into the arena in a sleep-deprived state. This is in the client's interest; it's all about spending money wisely. Just be sure to keep the tone firm and informative—not lecturing, not strident.

It will be scant comfort now, but you might tell your interpreter friend that with experience it becomes easier to identify clients with bad-risk potential.

Hemming and hawing is a red flag, or should be. And even with a signed contract, suing a law firm is to be avoided.

FA & WB

HARD TIMES

Q *I can see a recession is coming on; what should I do to protect my translation business from it?*

Bear

A Dear Bear,
We've got bad news for you: depending on where you live, the recession is already here. Yet it seems many translation providers are not yet feeling any pain—perhaps because client industries are still trying to figure out exactly how they themselves are going to cope, thus need a steady flow of information from abroad.

But if you are a regular reader, you'll have the bulwarks in place, right?
• Even in good times, the basic rule of thumb is "Make yourself indispensable." As the economy slows, get out of your office into client territory, go that extra mile, specialize.
• If there are more competitors chasing a decreasing volume of work, be sure to give your favorite clients ammunition to use with their hierarchy to justify your prices and services. This is not all that difficult, but it does mean spending more time explaining, holding hands, providing cheerful extras, and the like.
• Watch out for start-ups staffed by newly unemployed language-proficient folk, a trend observed in past slumps. They generally have little staying power, but are efficient marketers as long as they last.
• Stay focused. Keep an eye on new ideas and markets, but remember that it is easier to keep a good client than to win a new one.
• Read up on what other industry observers are saying—it's a popular topic. Here's one we like: thoughtsontranslation.com/2008/10/02/how-not-to-panic-about-the-economy/.

FA & WB

Q *My workload started plummeting a few months ago, which did not bother me at first as the weather was nice and I had a deck and pergola to build.*

The deck and pergola turned out very well, but my income is suffering! There are no background issues of poor quality or high rates that I am aware of. Indeed, my customers have recently expressed satisfaction with my work and I don't charge high rates anyway. Could you clarify things for me a bit? Having not yet gone through a recession as a freelance translator, I have no experience to draw upon. I remember telling people quite recently that what I did was recession proof, but I guess I was wrong.

Handyman

Dear Handyman,
Economic turmoil has put many business projects on hold, with obvious repercussions for translators. Many interpreters have been even harder hit with international conferences postponed or cancelled.

Yet even without such events, translation is a business and as such naturally subject to economic cycles. As a freelance professional, you must build this into your business plan, taking measures to ensure that even extended lulls at your clients' end do not bring your office crashing down, pergola and all.

You should have several months' income set aside before getting into the business in the first place. This nest egg will give you the breathing room you need to fine-tune your strategy to match your language combination, skills and field(s) of specialization. It will also help keep you from crumbling under price pressures; once clients have identified your pain threshold, it can be devilishly hard to negotiate them back up.

With a buffer, you can put slack periods to good use—for example, to buy and break in new hardware and software (impossible to do when the pressure is on). Or to read up on a new or related subject, and let clients know you are doing this (could kick-start some business). Or to catch up on glossary work, so that you can hit the ground running when your favorite client comes knocking with a 160-page training manual. And to get all of your paperwork up to date.

Above all, never ever express serious concern—much less panic—to your clients about the bottom falling out of the market. When you call them to investigate why business has suddenly dried up, phrase it "anything coming up? I'm reviewing my schedule for the next two weeks, want to be sure I can fit you in," rather than "good lord, I haven't had a call in weeks." Focus throughout on how to position yourself to take best advantage of the upturn when it comes. And don't worry—it will!

FA & WB

DEALING WITH CRITICISM

Q *One of our best external translators cannot take criticism—something my colleagues in the in-house translation department used to laugh about, but which is getting to be a serious problem.*

We always provide guidelines and background documentation up front, and make an effort to frame our feedback in a positive way, so I feel we are doing our part. We also pay well and promptly.

But he insists on arguing every (and I mean every) point, which means an author's request to change a single sentence or term takes on ridiculous proportions. What is the best way to deal with such an obviously skilled yet persistently contentious supplier?

Translation Department

A Dear Department,
Funny, isn't it, how in some cases the translator's laudable attention to detail can morph into the conviction that his solution is the only one that flies.

Part of this may stem from the good translator's appropriation of the source text: he lives it, breathes it, gives it a voice in the target language. It's his baby, an extension of himself. So a simple query becomes What, you don't like my offspring? You don't like me?! Who do you think you are?! And before you know it, the guy blows a radiator.

In this particular case, we have two suggestions:
- If you envisage a long-term future for him with your company, you must somehow get him to view your comments as feedback, not criticism. Why not invite him in and introduce him around, so he can see for himself that the authors are neither monsters nor idiots? Take advantage of his visit to reiterate that it is your company policy to keep authors in the loop. You might pull out some metrics: show him, using statistics, how your workflow operates, how you allocate time to this or that activity. Remind him that he is a valued partner—and confirm that he will be more valued still if he can help you respect your deadlines.
- If this doesn't work, cut your losses: find new talent and stop sending him work. No need to explain or discuss, especially if you find his current

contentiousness time-consuming. To quote an industry observer, he's been voted off the island.

Your letter is a reminder to all translators that being a provider of choice doesn't stop with the ability to craft an outstanding text. It entails a willingness and ability to interact with clients in a professional and service-oriented way. An author who questions a translation is not an enemy but an ally-in-waiting; the translator's job is to explain an initial choice and work towards an alternative, if necessary.

FA & WB

Q *I have just learned that my main in-house contact at a client company is blaming me, the external translator, for his own errors and delays. He's a nice person but sloppy. I don't want to look bad, because I am interested in developing my business with this particular client (other departments, etc.).*

Should I confront him? And if so, how?

Bristling

A Dear Bristling,
Confront him, eh? What exactly did you have in mind: a dressing down in the lobby? A head butt at the water-cooler? A set-to outside the accountant's office?

Not good. In fact, "confrontation" is, in general, an approach to be avoided, since it could well blow up in your face. As an outside supplier, there is no way you can be present at all the meetings where he might bad-mouth you.

What you must do is broaden your network in the client company. You mention that this fellow is your "main in-house contact." Make a point of networking with other employees (to obtain background documents for a job, or for billing information, or for scheduling issues) and get into the habit of copying them into your correspondence starting now—to get more people into the loop. At the very least this will establish the fact that you meet deadlines.

Just as we see no point in a "confrontation," it's a bad idea to criticize your main contact to his colleagues. After all, what do you know about internal dynamics?

But in similar situations we've had good results with the sandwich method. At the very least this allows you to identify potential allies.

Here's how it works: start with an admiring comment to his colleagues about how "incredibly dynamic Mr. Jones is" (you can even put this in writing; if he sees it, he'll be flattered).

But you move on immediately to a statement that is open to several interpretations: "What a guy! He's moving at about 200 miles an hour, but—and it must be me—I'm not always sure in what direction." This is the cue for the rest of his team to pile in with their impressions, at which point you may well learn what they really think of him. You keep the tone friendly and earnest, of course. End with another slice of white bread—an admiring statement about their entire company.

What is the point of all this?

It will give you a better idea of where the real power lies, and help identify people worth cultivating. Don't be surprised to discover that he also blames his co-workers for his slip-ups; character will out. But whatever you do, steer clear of internal conflicts. Your priority is to network and in so doing ensure that a reasonable number of people in the company understand your sincere commitment to them and your contribution to their success in the form of timely delivery of high-quality translations.

FA & WB

5
Pricing and value

Pricing strategies abound. Yet far too many translators price their work by default or through ignorance or over-reliance on success-averse gasbags—all potentially fatal mistakes. Negotiating good terms creates the space you need to deliver a top-notch job and earn a good living.

NEGOTIATING

Q *I've come to believe that commercial translation defies any rational explanation. What can one say about a market in which prices range from 2 cents to 100 cents a word?*

Baffled

A Dear Baffled,
That's easy. If you are a supplier, aim high. If you are a buyer, keep the peanuts & monkeys adage in mind as you shop around. If the translations you buy are cheap and good, they probably won't remain cheap forever; even translators who are clueless on pricing when they enter the market eventually wake up. Not that expensive work is necessarily good, of course. Commission independent reviews at regular intervals to keep your suppliers on their toes. If a translation is poorly done, it is too expensive at any price; if well done, it is usually worth every single cent.

FA & WB

Q *I head an in-house translation department in Belgium. While I agree with most of what you say about translation quality and pay, my company's accountants don't. To put it bluntly, they complain about per-word discrepancies from one outside supplier to the next, and keep insisting that we use the cheaper ones. Is there any way we can secure the services of top-flight translators even if we can't pay top prices?*

Tight Budget

A Dear Tight,
If your prices are rock bottom, forget it. If they are somewhere in the middle range, try a three-pronged attack.

1. Take the accountants' comments on board by drawing up, with them, a grid for the different types of texts your company requires. Even non-linguists will understand why you want a larger budget for the CEO's speech, televised nationwide, than for an equal number of words on scheduling a delivery of office supplies.

2. Use non-monetary initiatives to strengthen your ties to premium suppliers. For this top tier, client feedback, personal contacts and all-around job satisfaction generally weigh heavily in the balance. By treating them as the rare commodities they are, you may be able to get onto their client rosters despite your budget limitations. Concretely:

• Be a premium customer. Book important jobs well in advance and keep translators in the picture if timing is changed, even by an hour. Provide background documents, direct phone numbers for in-house contacts, and detailed feedback—including compliments—on all jobs.

• Pay promptly (by return mail if possible; talk to your accountants about this).

• Where appropriate, include translators' names in printing credits.

• Express thanks.

• Once or twice a year, invite translators to presentations on your company's strategy or new products, followed by lunch in the executive dining room or other well-appointed eatery (as your accountants will tell you, this is usually booked as an entertainment expense, so may not even come into your translation budget).

3. As head of your company's translation department, you are in the front line for client education. Budget limits will be adjusted if you manage to convince senior executives that outstanding translation is a priority. Circulate information about language snafus and successes, and use every opportunity to raise management awareness of what is at stake. Preparing a few sample translations into their own language at different levels of quality (fair, good, excellent) will help draw their attention to the differences.

FA & WB

Q *Where do you find your clients, FA & WB? My customers are in North America and there is no way they are going to pay a premium for quality. It's easy to say "time to raise prices!" but that is simply not possible here. They go for the cheapest supplier every time.*

It Won't Work Here

A Dear Won't,
We have a suspicion that translators who keep saying "Yes, but...," "You are dreaming when you talk about charging such prices," and "Clients are not interested in paying a premium for quality" belong to one of two groups:
1. Amateurs and semi-amateurs.

These include housewives/househusbands earning pin money, retirees collecting healthy pensions, university teachers and students moonlighting as translators, and heirs supplementing their trust-fund income. Sometimes they leave this group to join the ranks of group 2 below.
2. Professionals who do not make enough money sustain their practice.

They are scared that they might lose their present clients if they raise their prices, yet these clients do not pay enough for them to stay in business. Such translators have three options:
• Their slide into genteel poverty accelerates, they get evicted from their apartments, they discover there is no safety net for them, they become bums and then die from exposure on a park bench one November morning.
• They get a salaried job, move into a different profession or marry someone with money, so becoming a member of group 1.
• They decide to bite the bullet and raise prices high enough to earn a decent living. They specialize. They invest in marketing and advertising, and they accept that they are full-time entrepreneurs with all the risks and benefits that entails. There are no guarantees, no magic formulas. Failure is always possible. But there is no alternative. If you want to stay in business, do your math, figure out the prices you need to charge, and then do what it takes to find and keep clients willing to pay those prices.

FA & WB

Q *Last year I attended a translator meeting where an ex-senior civil servant regaled us with tales of her foreign postings and (current) translation assignments for which she charges 0.05/word. People in the room asked why she was charging such low prices. She replied that she "didn't really need" the money, and that she thought it was "unfair" to charge more when she was retired and had a good pension already.*

I thought of this when reading a recent discussion in an online forum. In it a semi-retired Translation Elder comments on rising inflation and falling prices, rails against the powerlessness of translators to negotiate good rates, predicts dire things to come. Later in the discussion you learn that both he and another elder are not making a living translating at all. Instead they are using occasional assignments to top up income from other sources.

You also learn that both of these gentlemen work at low (even very low) rates. So despite being articulate and experienced, they are the ones doing pin-money translation at pin-money rates—even as they condescend to "young people" like me. I realize there are other factors in play, but this general cluelessness about pricing and ethics is disappointing.

Globalization opens the world up to cutthroat competition say some, but I'm wondering now if our most insidious enemies are not translation elders and their mindless, cynical ways.

Ageist Reader

A Dear Youngster,
The enemy is not the elders, but the "mindless ways."

Here's an example: "Lookit lookit lookit the disgracefully low offer I received this morning! It's outrageous/depressing/deserving of a lawsuit, the market is going to hell in a hand basket!" Whenever a message like this goes up on a forum, a given percentage of the young, middle-aged, graying at the temples and decrepit all pile in for a moanfest on Chicken Little's heels.

Before you know it, it's self-fulfilling prophecy time all over again, as less vocal forum members take this nonsense seriously and ratchet down their prices.

Our opinion? If you are in the market for real, you charge for real—and make a point of raising your prices every time you realize you are in demand. That's every time you find yourself working more hours than you want. You cull low payers from your client list as you gain experience, you regularly take professional development courses in your existing and potential specialties to keep on top of things, and you just as regularly identify attractive new markets and clients—and lift your eyes off the screen and fingers up off the keyboard to go out and win their business.

All that is Economics 101, which your elders may have forgotten or skipped, just as they appear to have missed the class on "dumping" and its consequences.

Other advice:

• Take online discussions with a grain of salt. Some of these guys are teasing, playing devil's advocate. Others are whiling away a lazy summer's afternoon on the wifi-enabled air-conditioned porch before pottering off to the golf course. Still others are bullshitting from their abandoned trolley car under a bridge.

• The fact that so many translators tippytoe around rates leaves the gate wide open for these entertaining gasbags to monopolize the conversation. Speak up!

• Cynicism is more fashionable with elders than with younger people (thank goodness). The afflicted suck the oxygen and energy out of the room—who wants to work with them? So perhaps your know-it-all elders have scared all the potential clients away.

• Finally, older translators can be genuinely out of touch with changes for the better in markets, and perhaps too stuck in their ways to deal with demanding clients. Data in the latest SFT rates survey (www.sft.fr) indicates that price-per-word rises gradually as translators gain in experience and age, but falls off after age 60.

The bottom line? Everyone—every single reader—should be following our advice in paragraph three. We'll stop there so as not to get caught ourselves in another aphorism: Old translators never die, they just rant away.

FA & WB

Q *I get the impression that every time you do a translation, you negotiate a price with the customer. Since I am not very experienced at negotiating, I generally just use fixed-rate pricing. Any hints?*

Puzzled by Pricing

A Dear Puzzled,

We agree that it is useful to have a basic rate scale, if only to be able to quote an approximate figure when potential clients phone. But if you are supplying a premium product, you should look for opportunities to turn your relative rarity to your financial advantage. The same applies if you are prepared to accept particularly difficult working conditions.

Don't get us wrong: we will all walk that extra mile for customers. But since translation often comes near the end of the document production chain, you are certain to run into cases where someone else's poor planning affects your quality of life. In such instances, special compensation is in order.

In practical terms, you can charge by the word, page, hour or any unit that suits you and your clients.

But make it clear to those clients that you have a life beyond the work you do for them, including other customers, family obligations and the leisure activities you need to keep a smile on your face and your blood pressure down. Inroads on that time are available at your discretion and at a price. If your work is good, they will respect you all the more.

Do charge a premium for rush jobs, night jobs and weekend work. Announce this up front, and don't make any exceptions; rest assured that the lawyers and accountants who work for them charge overtime, too.

If you are swamped in work, your base rates are too low and you should start testing the upper limits by quoting a higher fee when new customers call.

What you must avoid is anything that smacks of arbitrary pricing—announcing higher prices for weekend work, then not applying them, or caving in immediately if challenged. This sends out a very unflattering message: "Just testing the waters here, this guy looks gullible, let's give it a try!"

In the end, transparency is your best ally. You value your good clients, but you also know your value to them, which is your ability to get their message across to target readers. And you are willing to pull out all the stops to make their projects a success—for a price.

FA & WB

Q *OK, translators are often poorly paid. But what you advocate is what I call gouging—taking unfair advantage of clients who are up against a deadline, or in a bind. Aren't you worried that this is going to backfire?*

Fair Play Please

A Dear Fair Play,
Ah, the G word plus the U word! Sounds like you've been working too many late nights.

Charging as much as the market will bear makes sense for many reasons. To name just a few:

• We assume most people would rather earn more than less for a professional assignment. We certainly would.

• Your price must factor in not only your hours at the keyboard, but the time and money you invest to keep up to date on developments in clients' markets. You cut corners on the latter at your own peril.

• Demanding a high fee is more likely to secure the conditions you need to produce a good job. A translator paid peanuts is usually viewed as an expendable member of the team—if she is a member of the team at all. In contrast, if you are paid a lot, clients are more likely to ask your opinion and follow your advice (advance notice of work, background documentation, that all-important "respect" thing).

• Even more important, the texts you translate are more likely to have been fine-tuned before they hit your desk. And as most translators will confirm, many of the real problems in moving from one language to another come from poor source-text writing.

• "Gouging" does not come into the picture if you are up front about what you are charging and why. What you do not want to do is play the prima donna—combining your expertise and awareness of your scarcity with arrogance. Nobody wants to hear "I've got you over a barrel, buddy, and I'm going to take you to the cleaners."

So we'll stick to our guns, Fair: many translators charge far too little, and their very humbleness helps maintain the poor working conditions they complain about so bitterly. Worse, it saps the quality of their output, disserving their clients and trapping both in a downward spiral of high volumes/so-so quality/poor pay/lower quality/rock-bottom pay/garbage.

FA & WB

Q *In your answer to Yankee Doodle (page 160) you stated "as for cutting prices to appeal to bottom-feeders—well, it's an unusual business strategy, but we can't get our heads around it as this column goes to press. Perhaps someone could explain?"*

I am convinced that what we translators do is extremely important, and that we must unite and create a common front when it comes to professional fees or rates. Cutting prices, I believe, is always a horrible proposition with terrible consequences for the translator and the industry alike.

Your recommendations to Yankee Doodle on planning ahead are right on target to endure the slow times. We all go through long cycles of abundance and drought. But with careful planning we can overcome the worst times and use the slow pockets to actually do something productive and proactively sell our service... getting our thankful clients to write testimonials, to recommend our services to their clients, and to keep us in mind. They say "out of sight out of mind" and I believe there is a fine thin line between slow-work and no-more-work. A client-targeted newsletter with accurate and relevant industry info collected from the Internet, for example, is a great way to keep them receiving our info.

There are many strategies and I am only an entrepreneur with little to teach and much yet to learn. But one thing I have learned the hard way is that my service is well worth my professional fee and I prefer to eat rice for months to come, rather than lower my professional fee for anyone. I extend freebies such as complimentary short phone/email consultations, or quick single (or two) paragraph proofs, anything that will not take more than 5 minutes of my precious time. *Added value stuff that everyone loves to receive and makes people feel special.*

Ed the Entrepreneur

A Dear Ed,
You said it. Periodic client outreach through the products and services you mention is an excellent reflex. Ultimately, high-profile pro bono projects make far more sense than cut-rate work.

FA & WB

Q *I occasionally do sight-translation work for a longtime client with branches in several locations.*

Last spring I took a short assignment in an office where I had never worked before: the work was interesting, and it was a good opportunity to meet a new set of people within the company. At the special request of the lady who contacted me, I agreed to lower my rate from the usual $125/hour to $80 for that job only. Disappointing, but probably worth it for a small project: once they work with me, clients often want to use me again, and my rate is less of an issue. Also, making a good impression on new people often results in referrals.

When the job ran longer than expected, I negotiated with the client to finish it out at my usual rate. I gave examples of the value I had brought to the project and showed how I had saved them time and money. They agreed and seemed satisfied with the job I did.

That was six months ago. I haven't heard from them since, and now I'm wondering whether I priced myself so high that they won't call me back. However, it's also possible that they haven't been in touch because they haven't had any need for sight-translation or interpreting. That wouldn't be unusual with them.

I've seen price pressure before, and in this economy I'll surely see it again. Do you have any advice on how to handle this kind of situation in the future? And do you have ideas on ways to re-establish contact with the original client and/or to emphasize the value I've given them?

Worried

A Dear Worried,
First you need some concrete information on why they haven't been in touch. Clients think about translation services when they need them, which is hardly surprising—the same applies to the legal, accounting, tax advisory, packaging and cleaning services they buy in.

So freelance service providers often worry needlessly when, as you speculate, the client is simply focused on something else.

What you want is a way to remind them that you are available and interested without being a bother, or, even worse, sounding desperate.

Here are two options:

• Phone your contact to say that you are conducting a year-end (or new year's, or quarterly, or half-yearly) review of your client base.

Mention how much you enjoyed working with them on [project, date]. Tell them your business was volatile in 2010 (not bad, just volatile) and given a few fire-fighting jobs, you're trying to improve your own forward planning. Don't put unreasonable pressure on them, and don't mention prices. You realize that translation needs can wax and wane unexpectedly, but do they have any projects in the pipeline that you should be blocking out time for?

This tactic may not generate any useful planning information, but it does give you a credible reason to call. And from your contact's answer, you'll get a better idea of the lay of the land.

• You say you saved the client time and money. It's always good to remind them of points like this!

Why not write an article on this very subject for your professional association's magazine or, better yet, for a publication in the client's own sector—an ideal way to highlight their expertise and yours.

Once again, start with a phone call to your contact.

Mention how much you enjoyed working with them on [project, date]. One of your aims for 2011 is to promote awareness of best practice among users of translation, a priority for your national professional association [this happens to be true for every professional association we know of].

So you're writing a piece on how smart businesses in [the company's field] make effective use of translation services, and you'd like to interview them, or at least refer to the project you did for them. You won't reveal any confidential information, and if they do not want their name mentioned, no problem, you can anonymize it.

Whether or not they choose to participate—or the article ever gets written—you've reestablished contact, which is what you want.

It's surprising how non-threatening, positive outreach to past and existing clients can generate business, sometimes immediately. Maybe it boils down to reminding them that you're around, that you're very good at what you do, and that you're pleasant to work with.

FA & WB

COUNTING

Q *I don't know if this is appropriate question, but I thought I would ask anyway.
What is the standard payment for freelance translators? How is it calculated
(keystroke, word, line, or page)? Does it vary with the type of document (pure text, fiction,
illustrative, legal, user's manual and so forth)? Does it vary with the language?*

*And finally (and perhaps more appropriately...), do you know of any web links
where one could find this kind of information?*

Thank you very much,

Beginner

A Dear Beginner,
Intriguing, isn't it, how many translators get the vapors when money
comes up—perhaps they all have trust fund incomes (money is so tacky, don't
you agree?). Which makes it all the braver of you to wade right in and ask.

Here's the scoop: translation is billed differently in different countries, for
both historical and language-specific reasons. Thus translators in Germany,
home of the *Donaudampfschiffahrtsgesellschaftskapitän* and the *Krankenhaus-
tagegeldversicherungen* are not too keen on per-word pricing and have opted
instead for characters per line.

Of the options you cite, per-word appears to be on the upswing, while
only per-page is on its way out—hardly surprising, given the variety of fonts
available at the click of a key. (One A4 page of 16-point Times has little in
common with a 21 inch x 29.7-inch swathe of 8-point Arial narrow). We're
sure one of our readers will write in to set us straight on languages using non-
roman alphabets. You must also be sure to specify whether your unit-count
is based on the source text or the target; most clients will be happier with the
former, as it can be relayed in your estimate (i.e., before you take on the job).

But whichever unit you use, the figure *you* must track is earnings per hour—
net of social security and tax. How many words can you reliably translate
per hour in field X, Y or Z, and what will your net (not gross) be for every
thousand dollars or euros invoiced?

We strongly advise you to calculate this regularly for each of your clients,
since it will identify areas where you are earning most. Those are the fields you
will want to develop. At the very least it will remind you how expensive your
addictions are (to notoriously poorly-paid literary translation, for example).

Following a number of legal challenges from anti-monopoly authorities, national translators' associations tend to be very skittish about quoting actual figures, but you'll find some interesting stats chez ADÜ (Northern Germany) at www.adue-nord.de, and the Swiss translators' association ASTTI also gives some specific figures at www.astti.ch.

Finally, the French national translators' association SFT conducts a rates survey that is downloadable from the public section of its website at www.sft.fr.

Note that in many cases figures provided are arithmetic means. Real live translators may charge less... but can also charge far more. The challenge is to identify what clients are prepared to pay, which, for a quality product, is far higher than what some people claim is "the going rate."

Let us just repeat that: there is no "standard payment" that we know of, and the translation providers (freelancers and agencies) that refer to one are often quoting well below what clients are willing to pay for top-tier work.

FA & WB

Q *I've been translating for about a year.*
I'm currently dealing with a first-time translation client who is complaining about the rate I charged her (8 cents a word). A grad student working on a film about a French sculptor, she had me translate some correspondence and psychiatric reports from the asylum the artist was confined in. We agreed on 8 cents a word, but after the project was completed she informed me that she had found other "professional translators" who "seem to require significantly lower rates" than myself.

She also complained about being charged for the repeated words in the text. There are a lot of repetitions, but it was a difficult job because the original was almost illegible (handwritten doctors' reports), so I figure it evened out in the end.

Do you know of any document that explains why most translators charge per word, even when there are repetitions within a single document? I was thinking of explaining something along the lines of how the word count represents the length and approximate amount of time needed to translate the text, and that we are not actually charging for the difficulty of translating each particular word.

Asylum Seeker

A Dear Asylum,
Have you got a written agreement with this person? Her comments are a reminder that you really should have one, especially with notoriously impecunious folk like grad students.

Beyond a certain point, don't worry about being polite. She's just doing a variation on the "Is that the best you can do?" routine (an old friend of ours tries this, at times successfully, at hotels of all types, from 4-star Marriotts through to B&Bs).

In any case, humor is the best riposte, although it may be too late for this particular transaction.

Concretely, when a client even starts to suggest that a reduction is due since "there are repeated words in there," you must laugh not in derision but in genuine good spirits. Chortle, chortle, what a fine sense of humor you've got, madame! Then read out (from a prepared text) a sample sentence or two from page 4 of a 5-page text eliminating all repeats. This will of course be incomprehensible. You might even read her an excerpt from which you've eliminated all redundant punctuation marks or spaces (hahaha, isn't this jolly).

The "others out there are less expensive" routine is also a non-starter, of course. But you have to be earnest—even blunt—in response here, volunteering that your client can get low-end machine translation for free if that's what she wants. She can also buy translations at 0.02-0.03/word in certain foreign markets and those translations might even be good... but then again might be (really) bad. If that's the kind of risk she is prepared to take, she should have taken it, by all means (—-> note verb tense, it's too late now). You have already gone below a reasonable US rate to help her out, so sorry, a deal is a deal.

Bon courage.

FA & WB

Q *I've been browsing some back issues of your column and came across this piece of advice from the two of you in April 2006: "Time-wise, calculate at least two full hours per 250-word page."*

This was for annual reports, which as you say are at a premium. But even taking that into account, this is the first time I have seen anyone quote a word/hour rate that seems anything like sensible to me.

I like to take the time to find the word or expression that's absolutely right, rather than just good enough—and then double-check it all—so I am uncomfortable with being asked to do more than 1,500 words a day. Yet in discussions about how long it was taking me to achieve the required word count before I could apply to take the ITI exam, "standard" figures of 2,500 to 3,000 words a day came up repeatedly. Reading your advice has reassured me that my working speed is professional rather than inadequate, and I just wanted to say thanks for the moral support!

Word Counter

A Dear Word Counter,
Thanks for your thanks. We see a growing trend towards charging per hour rather than per word, which makes awareness of these ratios—indeed, of the very wide range of word-per-hour counts, depending on market segment—all the more important.

FA & WB

Q *I am a graduate student in California and have supported myself for some time through teaching and occasional small translation jobs. I have just been offered my first large (400 page) book to translate and I need to know how much to charge. Do you have any suggestions as to where I can get that information?*

Opportunity Knocks

A Dear Opportunity,
Your first book—congratulations! But don't forget that money is only part of the deal. If your offer is accepted, make sure that your contract covers copyright, mention of translator's name, subsidiary rights, etc.

You'll find "A Translator's Model Contract" for literary translation at the PEN American Center web site. [www.pen.org/page.php/prmID/322]

For European readers, a model contract is also available from the Translators' Association of the UK's Society of Authors, which has the status of a trade union and advises members on contracts. You can download this at www.ceatl.org/docs/EnglishMC.pdf.

The current minimum rate observed by the TA is £85/1000 words.

Word has it that US publishers generally pay less. The American Literary Translators Association [www.utdallas.edu/alta/] is not allowed to suggest prices, but do check their web site and links; networking with published translators is the best way to collect figures for your market.

FA & WB

Q *I am constantly amazed at how clueless translators can be when it comes to the business side of things. In a listing on www.proz.com [www.proz.com/ profile/562593] there is one whose tagline advertises her as "fast, professional and cute"—maybe she's got the wrong profession?*

Wake Up

A Dear Wake,
By the time we reached this young colleague's page someone had clued

her in and, as readers will see, the "cute" bit had evaporated... replaced, alas, by worse: "fast, professional and *cheaper*" (our emphasis). Good grief.

May we take this opportunity to remind all readers that the arguments you use when pitching your services help define which clients end up on your doorstep?

Anyone, young or old, who announces on a website or in other promotional materials that they charge "low rates" or even "reasonable rates" or, as this young woman does, "rates that are always lower than average" is warbling through a bull-horn "low-ballers, come to mama!"

This is important, so we'll say it again: do not advertise low prices unless you are fishing for bottom feeders.

Our advice? Keep the photo—it's good to put a face on people—but let visitors decide for themselves whether or not they think you are cute. Above all, leave prices out of it and sell your expertise, your writing skills, your passion, your added value.

Unless you are looking for clients who want to pay very little, of course.

FA & WB

Q *I translate from English into Dutch and vice versa and from French into English and Dutch, and have been working as a freelancer for well over eight years now. At first, I belonged to your first category of translators, dabbling a bit while I was studying, but after I graduated I moved into full-time translation.*

I have a number of customers who ask me more and more often to write press releases and newsletters for them. One of them even referred a sister company to me, which suggests that they are happy with the copywriting jobs I do for them.

Now, my problem is that when they first asked me to do some copywriting, I had NO idea whatsoever of the rates that are usually charged for this type of work. So I upped my translation rate a little, and told them USD 0.25 per word. I am charging their sister company USD 87 per hour, after calling around a bit to find out what prices copywriters usually charge.

However, I am far from sure that these are reasonable rates (from my point of view, that is), and would like to ask you whether you can give me an indication of the rates that are usually charged for this type of job.

Also, if I am now below current rates, I would naturally like to discuss higher prices with them, but I am not completely sure how to do that without losing my customers. I would be very grateful if you could help me out on this.

Copy Cat

ADear Cat,
We are not experts on copywriting per se, although one of us does it from time to time. One thing that struck us is that you seem to be employing two different pricing schemes for copywriting—one, a per-word rate somewhat higher than your translation rate, and the other a straight hourly rate. This could lead to problems down the line because the two companies are related and might compare prices.

Secondly, it generally takes longer to produce a certain quantity of text when writing for hire than when translating an existing text. The reason is simple: in addition to research, client communications, terminology work, office management and the many other activities besides actual production that translators perform, a copywriter spends more time in briefings, progress meetings and on-site visits. Not to mention round upon round of revision hell. It is not uncommon to be asked to write a slender eight-page brochure by distilling reams and reams of raw client material: office e-mails, faxes, prior publications, business spreadsheets, news clippings, etc.

So while 87 dollars an hour appears acceptable, 25 cents a word appears low.

Keep in mind, too, that in general copywriters lose money at first with new clients, even when on an hourly rate. The reason is simple: you won't dare to bill all the time you put in at the start. After a couple of years, you start to break even, and after that you reap the rewards of your early investment as the learning curve (on both sides) favors your economics.

In our experience it is all but impossible to introduce a sharp rise in price for existing customers. But as word spreads of your prowess, demand will rise, and every potential new client then becomes an opportunity to lift your pricing structure a notch or two. It's one of the perks that freelancers enjoy.

An employee who asks the boss for a raise is practically taking his life into his own hands: if your boss says no, you must decide whether to quit or instead gnash your teeth and slink back to your desk, your motivation and self-respect in tatters.

You, on the other hand, can experiment, one prospect at a time. If you get several rejections in a row, it doesn't matter. A new buyer will come calling tomorrow and you can try a fresh approach then.

FA & WB

Q*I have just returned to my native Germany after four years in the United States, where I worked as a sales rep for pharmaceutical equipment & supplies.*

That assignment followed a twenty-year stint doing the same in Germany. I now plan to work at least part-time as a translator in this field; I'm putting together my business plan and have already been approached by several direct clients.

When I contacted the BDÜ (German translators' association) I was told that they are not allowed to give me any information on prices charged for translations since it would violate anti-trust laws.

I would really appreciate it if you could give me at least a rough guideline as to what average prices are commonly charged. Many thanks.

Calculator in Hand

A Dear Calculator,

How much do translators charge? How long is a piece of string?

The answer, of course, is that it all depends—on who your customers are, how long you've been in business, how you position yourself, what kind of material you translate, how short your deadlines are, and much more. Most translators in Germany charge by the line (50 to 55 keystrokes) of target text, yet some charge by the hour, others charge a project fee and still others by the number of words.

We've seen mass-mailed letters from German translation agencies offering work at €0.45 per line. It's hard to see how anyone can make a living that way, but hey, that's their choice. The top per-line price we've seen is €6.50, with most about a third that much or less, albeit with wide variations. With your experience and language skills, you will of course want to aim for the top quartile.

Our suggestion: as you move into the market, try offering project prices. This is a good way for you to learn how to calculate your income as a function of time and money. Concretely, figure out what gross revenue you need, divide by the number of hours a week you want to work, and you've got your hourly rate. Divide that by two because you're a beginner and will need longer at the start—even if your hands-on experience in sales gives you a leg up on many of your competitors. Be sure to allow for taxes and social security contributions.

If you do quote per word or line, you might explain to clients that this is temporary: let them know from the start that you will be reviewing your position in six months.

FA & WB

Q *I have recently retired from a US Federal Government position, where one of my functions was that of an official Polish translator and interpreter.*

I continue to perform the same duties for my former employer, as an independent contractor. We have a standard fee agreement.

I would now like to expand my translator activities. For that purpose I am joining an association. I have one problem (at least one that I'm aware of). While I feel some confidence in my translator skill, I'm a complete novice to the "business."

Proving that point beyond reasonable doubt, I asked the association for prevalent standards in the charging of fees. I was told about antitrust laws that would make an answer to my question illegal. I also noted that in your questions and answers this vital issue is discussed only in terms of "too much" and "too little." "Just right," is when you can feed your family, without killing yourself. Now, this is something that could be written into the plot of Alice in Wonderland.

Is there some source that you can suggest, from which I can, even obliquely, derive my personal fee standard? Luckily, I will not be relying on translating to make a living, but I would like to get started on the right track.

Straight Talking Please

A **Fire Ant rasps:** Dear Straight,

You write "Luckily, I will not be relying on translating to make a living."

Call us grumpy and cranky, but why are you asking us then?

As we see it, the only way to charge prices for translation that are at the upper end of the market is to be a full-time professional. This does two things:

• It means you put in the hours necessary to become good at your craft, i.e., staying current on your specializations; being a good writer; mastering the mental mechanics of turning words in one language into words in another. The muscles inside your brain that you need to do the heavy lifting of translation will atrophy unless exercised for hours every day.

• As Ambrose Bierce wrote, nothing concentrates the mind so well as the prospect of hanging from a tree the next morning. In translation, the barriers to market entry are so low as to be non-existent. Every single day new people are coming in hoping to undercut you and take away your business. Every single day one of your customers may go bankrupt, or your contact may be fired, or a bean counter may decide you are too expensive, or you may get into an argument with a customer and get dropped, just like that.

Unless you have the very real prospect of the bill collectors pounding on your door, how are you going to muster the guile, the cunning, the crazed single-minded determination to maximize your earnings that are your only safeguards against your bed being carried out from under your ass by the repossession man? How are you going to develop a "sixth sense"—an almost physical sensation of just how much you can ask for and be right more often than wrong?

Concretely, what is to stop you from defining what you want out of translation and then doing it? E.g., "I want to have $5,000 in supplementary annual income from translation."

Okay, then buy office equipment, write to agencies, and hope that work starts coming in the door. It pays better than solving the NYT crossword puzzle! But nine times out of ten you end up either churning out work of less than sterling quality, or working for too little money as you turn out high-quality work that takes you far too long to produce because... (see above).

Something tells us you know this already, and that you are turning to us because you think we have a magic bullet to offer. Sadly we don't.

Worker Bee buzzes: Dear Straight,

Ponder Fire Ant's advice—and see, too, our response to Beached in Bordeaux below.

See also the ATA's 2007 Translation and Interpreting Compensation Survey (atanet.org).

Q *Are my rates unrealistic?*
I live in Bordeaux, and recently sent a copy of my brochure (copy attached) to a colleague in the UK who said she might have some medical texts for me in the near future. I added that I was prepared to discuss rates.

Her response was that she was "flabbergasted" (at €158/1000 words, i.e. GBP 112...) and she added: "In England, you can charge half that, i.e. GBP 65. No wonder the French agencies come to England and offer even less."

The problem is, these days I am finding work very thin on the ground and wonder if I have indeed priced myself off the market. And yet (a) I don't always charge these rates, and (b) I haven't raised them much over the years. This year was the first time for quite a while. When I do charge them, the clients (all direct) don't quibble. They are very happy with the work done and pay more or less by return. I have been working for some of them for years.

However, it is becoming harder and harder to find work. I am not alone in that; my colleagues here too, in all languages, say the same thing. The French economy not being very buoyant (Bordeaux even worse), the unsettled international situation, financial scandals, etc., all don't help.

Any ideas for kick-starting my flagging business?

Beached in Bordeaux

A Dear Beached,
Your question highlights an intriguing side of the translation market.

In any business, it's essential to have a grasp of what you might be charging. But we are convinced that many if not most translators are flying blind.

Why?

Perhaps it's the much decried "poverty cult"—linguists feeling uneasy talking about money; "uggh, tacky," even when negotiating skills in this area could result in a direct improvement in their quality of life.

Skittishness may also result from run-ins with national anti-trust authorities. We know of two major translator associations that have incurred hefty legal fees after (awkwardly) wading into the fray and issuing what said authorities construed as attempts at price-fixing.

Or maybe it's simply a natural preference for discretion as regards one's own earnings.

Whatever the case, many agencies and freelancers appear to base prices on what their competitors are charging (or, even worse, what they *think* their competitors are charging).

This when they should be interacting with clients to determine what those clients are prepared to pay for a red-hot product—which is often a lot more.

Which brings us back to client education.

Clients not aware of what translation can do for them will tend to base purchasing decisions on price, full stop.

It does no good to complain about how foolish this is. What you must do is get out there and explain, in words your audience understands. Not rant, not whine, not wave a diploma, not insist that translators "deserve respect," etc.—those are all huge turn-offs—but explain to them how your expertise is going to give them a competitive advantage.

Concretely, you have to get out from behind the keyboard and schmooze. Tacky? Of course not. A little scary to start, perhaps, but also both exciting and stimulating, and the only way we know to get a handle on where your clients' heads and budgets are. Not to mention the invaluable insights you will gain on what the texts you produce are supposed to achieve, which is an excellent way to improve quality.

It sounds like you've already built up a good practice, and we suspect you've simply let things slide on the commercial side. Maybe your in-company contacts have moved on to other positions. Maybe your competitors—larger outfits with schmooze budgets to spare, or young & dynamic (or old &

dynamic) rivals your size—are out there pitching harder than you.

There's only one solution: get out to those chamber of commerce meetings, attend the wine-tastings with expert foreign journalists (hey, sign up for a refresher course yourself). Rebuild your contacts to the decision makers. Be pleasant, self-confident and above all interested in clients' markets and products.

There is no question of lowering your prices unless you get independent confirmation from far more sources that this might be in order—and even then there are ways of appearing to lower your prices without actually doing so.

As straight talkers, let us add that your prices are absolutely in the ballpark. Your UK contact is working in a segment of the market where clients have long been left up to their own devices. She is paying the price, and ultimately so are they. After all, the bottom end of the market is €0/1000; as we all know, volunteers abound and some computer translation is free. But remember, too, that the sky is the limit at the top. You get a crack at those markets by reaching out to clients at every opportunity. Good luck!

FA & WB

Q *To establish the size of a project, I tend to look at the text and number of pages. I normally count the words of the target text to assess volume after I've translated the text. In my current project, we agreed on 300 pages based on a word per page figure, and additional payment according to this formula for "some" additional text.*

But it turns out there is so much small print that the volume is nearly double of what was agreed. I will be paid for it, that's not the issue. The problem is to demonstrate to my client that the volume is so much more than agreed and expected.

My client, which in this case is a "coordinator" I work with, thinks I can simply count the words in the source text to get a good idea of volume. To my mind, this is totally beside the point. I only know what I've done once I have counted the words in the target text and have operated this way for 20 years. I am not even sure it would be even an approximate indication of volume in the target text. Am I correct?

Wordcount Worker

A Dear Wordcount,
No, we think you've got the wrong end of the stick, although your letter is a reminder of how useful it can be to compare perceived "standard practice"

with what other people actually do.

Note that source text wordcounts are common, the advantage being that they give your client (and you) a clearer idea of what you are getting into before you start—before you sign on the dotted line. Which is as it should be.

But not to worry, you seem to have a good relationship with your coordinator, and this ain't rocket science anyway. To calculate a reliable ratio between target word-count and source word-count, simply select segments of a few texts you've translated in the past and use the "statistics" function in Word to count the corresponding words in both source and target versions. Calculate the difference, and note the average as a percentage. Bingo!

If your coordinator needs a visual "demonstration," you can always convert five pages of Exhibit A (your original-format source text—the one with all the fine print) into Exhibit B, the same document in 12-point Times Roman. The increase in length will be obvious. For fun, offer an Exhibit C, too: the same text in 2-point Times. Hey, this might even fit on one page—would you still charge the same as what you do for one regular page? Exhibits A, B, C = case closed.

But remember, however you decide to bill translation work, it ultimately comes down to how much you earn per hour, net of social charges and tax.

FA & WB

Q *The attached correspondence is about a book translation for a publisher I'll call FILUP ("Famous Ivy League University Publisher") and I'm being asked to quote a price.*

I want my usual rate which is $15,000 for 100,000 words. Should I ask for more and let them beat me down? My advantage is that the author is very keen on having me because we tend to live in each other's shoes when doing a job together, and she likes that. But I know that FILUP have their own preferences and I don't want them to look elsewhere.

You will notice that the author has "forsaken" royalties on the English edition. Also note the publisher's noises about not wanting to spend too much money on the translation.

I am counting on (a) your experience and knowledge of these matters (b) your experience and knowledge of Americans.

Mother Goose

A **Fire Ant says:** As you are surely aware, FILUP is rolling in dough. Of course, that is no guarantee that they will take you on and accept your quote, sight unseen. Even at the most profitable corporations, people are under increasing pressure to justify each and every outlay, and FILUP is no exception.

What is more, very likely they already have a small cadre of translators (more often than not, academics on the faculty of FILU) whom they know and value from prior book translations. So on the face of it, your chances of getting the job—never mind the money—are slim to none, and Slim just skipped town.

Your one trump card would appear to be your excellent working relationship with the author, and it is a strong card indeed. Play it for all it is worth. If you and the author plot your strategy right, suddenly the odds are very much in your favor.

She will need to make it clear to FILUP—pleasantly but very firmly— that getting the book translated by you is very important to her. Eventually, after some back and forth, and after duly rolling out your credentials and explaining how your involvement will save the editor lots and lots of time because the two of you can handle all the tedious and tricky cultural and linguistic issues by yourselves, FILUP will relent.

The second part of the decision phase is money. They may try the standard ploys of "Just think of the prestige you gain by getting your name on one of our publications," and similar gambits to "beat you down," as you put it. That is all poppycock.

Once FILUP decides they want to publish a foreign book, cost becomes secondary. (We told you, they're rolling in money.) Browse a few of their titles, and you'll notice that in many cases, on the Acknowledgements Page, the publisher thanks ABC Fund or the XYZ Foundation for their generous contribution towards enabling the English-language publication of the book. (And, we might add, some of FILUP's translations are indeed very well done; you can tell that the extra money paid to the translator paid dividends in the form of especially thorough research and beautifully polished style with no hint of "translationese.")

Once FILUP have their minds made up that they want to do this, they will find the money, even (or rather, especially!) if it does not come out of their own pockets. All that you and the author need is patience and steadfastness while the decision-making process plays itself out.

Good luck, and we hope to receive a signed copy in about a year and a half!
Worker Bee opines: Not to discourage you, Goose, but we're told the cards are stacked against translators in this particular area.

Given immense pressure on academics to publish, university presses are among the most exploitative publishers around, with the result that many academic authors get paid virtually nothing—some publishers even reckon the authors should pay them. Nor is forgoing royalties a big deal: since most academic books are expensive and bought only by libraries, sales of 1,000 count as a roaring success, so nobody gets any royalties to start.

In this distinctly less rosy scenario, publishers could care less about the author's preferences unless they are dealing with, say, Umberto Eco. They may even go out of their way to avoid a translator imposed by the author, worried about being stuck with an author's friend's friend who is not a very good translator.

What to do? "State your price, blow your trumpet about previously published work, offer to do a sample, and sit tight. But don't hold your breath," says our local expert.

Sorry for the downbeat take. If it's any comfort, once you've moved on into the "how much" phase, Fire Ant is right on the money.

Q *There are several translation rates surveys circulating but I've never seen any guidelines on rates for proofreading. What rates do people charge, and how do you charge—per hour or per thousand words?*

Down to Detail

A Dear Down,
We trust you already know how much you earn per hour on average (gross and net), if only to help identify text types that you, personally, should steer clear of.

Whether translating or proofreading, keep that figure in mind.

For editing, revising or "simply" proofreading, our contacts advise strict compliance with Rule No. 1: Never issue a fixed quote, much less accept a job, without seeing the text or a sizeable sample first. (How do you say "lost my shirt" in Tagalog?)

Rule 2: When your client sends the text, be sure to scan not just page one but also a few passages in the middle and towards the end. That's where the going will get seriously rough if a mad dash to the finish line preceded your arrival.

Rule 3: Be absolutely clear with your client about expectations on both sides. Proofreading is not revising, but many buyers confuse the two. In our experience, you will almost certainly be fixing errors and omissions, not just flagging them. And if the fixing is the equivalent of a rewrite, you'd better quote high.

Rule 3: Keep your eye on the clock and on the ball. Log time meticulously. Let the client know if things are getting out of control, and try to renegotiate.

As always, the hours you spend on the job are not just those hours on that day. They reflect the thousands of hours of experience you bring to this particular task. Remind your client of this if necessary.

Remind yourself, too—and be sure to factor them in.

FA & WB

Q *Yesterday a major French carmaker asked us to revise a text they'd had translated by an agency in Slovakia. My Slovakian being as rusty as my Slovenian, I turned down the offer.*

"But the translation was from French into English, and it's terrible," they replied.

Here's the good part: "Please bill the Slovakians. After all, it's their fault. Oh, and don't bill them too much because they have extremely competitive rates."

Ergo:

i. It's cheap but bad.

ii. The poor quality is the fault of the agency working, at the client's request, with two "foreign languages."

iii. Do it properly, bill the Slovakians (whom we chose), but don't charge too much in order to remain competitive.

We discussed it in-house, and our reply was:

i. We won't revise it. We'll re-translate it or nothing.

ii. We'll bill you, not the agency.

iii. We'll charge you 25% extra for the rush.

iv. We'll charge you 75% extra for being so stupid.

Were we overly aggressive?

Sandwich Bar 2

A Dear Sandwich,
An exquisite exchange, thanks for sharing.

As a colleague points out, these people are perfect candidates for the Clients To Fire list.

Doing business on their terms hurts not just you, the translation supplier, but the whole profession. If you accept, you become an enabler, which makes you just as guilty as they are—only more so, since you ought to know better. Subsidizing shoddy suppliers in Slovakia (or anywhere) with a cheap rewrite guarantees that these same suppliers will continue to undercut your prices.

Bringing that message home to your clients firmly and professionally (we're assuming you added "for being so stupid" for our benefit) is the way to go.

Your letter is a useful reminder that it is not just clients who need educating, but also translation providers.

FA & WB

Q *I am a freelance translator based in Germany, working from German to French. I was recently asked to quote for a job, but my offer was judged too expensive. That said, the prices cited by the "Vendor Coordinator" who refused my bid were, for me, astounding. He/she/it states outright that "prices in France" are 0.08 for non-technical documents, 0.09 for technical documents, 0.04 for 75-84% matches, 0.03 for 85-99% matches and 0.02 for full matches. Revision is paid 0.025/word for "non-technical documents" and 0.03 for "technical documents", or €30 an hour.*

"N'hésitez pas à revenir vers moi si ces tarifs vous conviennent," says Mr. Vendor Coordinator—"Get back to me if you are willing to work at these rates." The agency is SDL.

My question: can people survive at those prices?

I Want More

A Dear More,
Translators who choose to work for this particular agency obviously can. In its defense, the company claims that it invests heavily up front to "prepare" texts for translators, providing translation memory modules that speed up the job.

Maybe, maybe not.

Keep in mind that your eye should be on per-hour net earnings, not per-word gross.

But let's step back here: what tells you that this particular buyer is a reliable source of "prices in France"?

What they are referring to are *their* prices in France—prices which are perhaps an indication of their positioning out in the market. And hey, if their business is booming, ticking over or even limping, there must be buyers out there for whatever they're selling.

But this in no way means that there are not other, better-heeled customers on the market with different priorities. If those are the ones you want, give SDL a miss and devise a marketing strategy to hook up with more attractive direct clients or more specialized agencies.

Your example is a reminder of just how vulnerable individual translators with little training in business practices are. All it takes is one buyer (who by definition will have a vested interest in lowering prices as far as they will go) announcing that X is "the price", sometimes with great assurance, even huffing and puffing. The rumor catches hold, as one horrified translator after another passes this tidbit on. If all are equally naive, everyone tugs their forelock and ratchets down their price: a self-fulfilling prophecy that needn't be but is.

While pondering that, you might want to consult the annual rates survey published by France's national professional association, which shows figures well above SDL's.

Our advice? Time to cut loose from the low-end agency scene and focus on specialized agencies or direct clients.

Onwards and upwards,

FA & WB

Q *Some of my agency clients pay me 8.5 cents a word for all types of translation, including legal texts. I've told them that others pay more, but they're not having any of it. To be sure, a direct client will pay more (I know that), but how high do you think I can go with a small agency?*

Pushing Hard

A Dear Not Hard Enough,
See our reply to I Want More above.

The key is not to simply "refer to" others who pay more, but to actually locate those others, lock them in as clients, and then cull customers whose rates are no longer in your ballpark.

In any case, equating "small" with low prices is a mistake. Some of the best-paying intermediaries we know are small, specialized outfits that have understood the importance of focusing on what you do best and selling on quality, not price.

FA & WB

UPWARD PRESSURE

Q *I need advice on raising my prices. I'm thinking of one client in particular, for whom I've worked at the same per-word price for far too long. They really resisted the last time I brought this up (several years ago now).*

What's the best way to raise the subject? Do I use the phone or email or a letter? What percentage rise should I go for?

Counting

A Dear Counting,
Phoning will give you a better idea of their state of mind, but involves more ebb and flow. If you're nervous, a carefully crafted email might be better.

The main thing is not to get defensive or aggressive—easy to say, but not so easy to do, since money matters do make lots of folks nervous.

You've made a decision and are imparting information. You fully expect your clients to stay on board.

Once again, the sandwich method has definite appeal.

Here's a possible scenario:

1. Let the client know how much you enjoy working with them [because their texts are so interesting, they themselves are so pleasant, their sector so dynamic]. And you really do know their operations and requirements intimately at this point.

2. But your accountant has reminded you several times now, most recently at the end of [previous month] that the special rate you're working at with them is well below the one you apply to all your other clients. You haven't fussed to date because their texts are so interesting, they themselves are so pleasant, their sector so dynamic. But your accountant is adamant—and he's right. (Standard good cop/bad cop here).

3. So you are raising your special rate, although you still plan to keep it at the low end of your pricing scale because their texts are so interesting, they are so pleasant, their sector so dynamic. (You say this even if their texts are boring, they are hopelessly disorganized, and their sector is in the doldrums.)

This new rate will apply from [date of your choice] and you sincerely hope that your relationship will continue.

Should this client dig in their heels, you might agree to postpone the increase to, say, July 1. You might also reduce it a tiny bit. This is called negotiating. But in this case be sure to start by announcing an increase that is higher than what you will ultimately settle for. You should also be prepared to address other factors affecting your net take-away, including surcharges, payment within ten days, etc.

A good rule of thumb is never to fold on price without winning a concession in another area.

FA & WB

Q *The other day I was clearing out some old papers and found some of my very first translations. I think the quality of my work has improved 500% since then. Yet my prices have hardly risen at all. I would like to earn more for what I think is a very good product. How can I raise my prices?*

Gearing Up for Action

A Dear Gearing,
By doing it—by announcing to your clients that effective January 1 (or June 1 or whenever) your prices will be 10% or 15% or 20% higher.

If you feel an explanation is necessary, point out that your prices have been steady for X years or that you are raising your rates to cover rising costs all around. It's important that you be neither apologetic nor defensive (nor arrogant, for that matter): you have become aware that you are underselling your services and your current adjustment is aimed at rectifying the situation. And be wary of those who claim that "the going rate" is X, Y or Z. Translation buyers base their choice of supplier on many factors, among them subject-matter expertise, writing style, availability, language combination, speed and price. (Note that price is ranked last—at least for the quality-driven type of client you want).

That said, it's probably a good idea to check two things before you make a move.

• Is your output really as good as you say? Not to knock your +500% improvement, but you may have been a dismally poor translator when you began. To confirm that your work does make the grade, submit texts to peers and subject-matter specialists for review. Explain that you are considering a price rise, and ask them for an honest assessment.

• Is the demand there in your market segment? If you are constantly swamped with work, it is time to raise prices in any case (Economics 101). But some price-driven work will probably evaporate as you move up the ladder, so you will have to replace those clients with new customers willing to pay more. You may even have to redirect your efforts towards a different market segment altogether. Rest assured, quality-driven clients exist. But you will have to track them down. The place to link up with them is on their home turf—trade shows, industry events, etc.

In concrete terms, we suggest you continue to serve your existing client base at current rates and apply your higher rates to new clients only. Once you are sure the pool of new clients is there, announce to your old clients that you are adjusting your price scale upward in response to market conditions, and see if they are interested in continuing your relationship on that basis.

And remember: just as there is no minimum price for translation (after all, Google Translate supplies it free on line), neither is there a maximum. If you are targeting the quality-driven end of the market, be sure to quote high enough to start.

FA & WB

Q *I graduated six years ago and after two years working in an agency set up a freelance business with my partner. We specialize in energy and want to build a direct clientele. Right now we are at 50% agency and 50% direct clients. Our minimum per-word price is 0.20 for direct clients. My partner thinks we are spending too much time actually winning the clients, and I am starting to agree. It usually takes one industry event plus two follow-up meetings with the departments involved for the first job to arrive; during that time we have transport expenses plus hotels plus living expenses and no money is coming in.*

Do you have any advice for speeding up the process without looking too pushy?
Tracking Expense

A Dear Track,
Rather than look for shortcuts to winning clients, we suggest you raise your prices. As you point out, there is an acquisition cost involved (something agencies know all about) and the more specialized you are, the lower 0.20 a word looks. Track your per-hour net income, not per-word gross. And next time pitch for 0.30.

FA & WB

Q *I am baffled! A year ago, I met a fellow translator working in the same language combination and specializations as I do. He is a very good translator and a pleasant guy who began translating a couple of years ago after a 20-year career in the industry for which both of us translate most of the time.*

I have been translating for 15 years and I was very happy to share information about resources, training, software, marketing and other tips, since I generally view good translators as colleagues rather than as competitors. I have also frequently referred my own clients to him since I have more work than I can handle and I knew they would be happy with the quality of his work.

I thought that all this information, as well as my complete transparency about the rates I charge, would gently entice him to raise his own rates which are abysmally low.

Once I realized that "gently" was not working, I clearly and repeatedly explained to him that the quality of his work justified an increase in his rates.

Well, it has now been almost a year and the only projects for which he charges rates similar to mine are the ones which we share, and for which I am the client contact person. I don't think that he deliberately wants to undercut me, but he is lacking in self-confidence and tells me that he has to "pay his dues." He is also afraid that raising his rates would diminish the flow of work that he receives.

I have explained the very simple marketing tools I use which enable me to work as much as he does, albeit at higher rates. However, this otherwise intelligent person is always "too busy" (with lower paid projects, evidently) to follow through.

He has already attended four different conferences/translator gatherings, where he has met plenty of other successful translators, so he is not operating in a vacuum.

How can I convince him to stop acting like a scared nitwit? I am contemplating cutting off all ties with him, but it would be a shame because he is a very good translator.

Tired of Mentoring in Vain

A Dear Tired,
Your account speaks volumes, and you appear to have tried just about everything.

If it's any comfort, we know people like this. And if you consult back issues of this column, you will see that some of our correspondents tell similar tales, in each case emphasizing the "little ol' me" angle, worrying about getting too big for their britches and swearing they are going to start putting their practice on a more professional footing—tomorrow.

Suggestion: recommend that your skilled but clueless buddy read the next issue of Translation Journal (or buy him a copy of this book!) and check after a week or two to see if the penny has dropped.

So much for him. But your letter raises other questions, especially when you write "I have more work than I can handle." May we suggest that your own prices are too low? A mid-summer boost might be just the ticket.

FA & WB

DOWNWARD PRESSURE

Q *It's all very well to talk about raising prices and targeting premium segments, but that is light-years from the daily experience of the vast majority of translators. I should know: I have the knowledge, the diplomas (PhD), the experience (18 years). I log long hours and always deliver excellent work on time. But I haven't been able to raise my prices for eight years, and am losing work to cheaper suppliers abroad all the time. The reason is simple: the agencies I work for refuse to negotiate, and they are the ones who call the shots. I am one person; you have only to look at their advertising budgets and influence.*

I have studied for years to get where I am, but sometimes I wonder why I've bothered (except that I love languages). I sincerely believe that I deserve better, as do the many translators like me who are struggling in good faith but not able to make ends meet.

Failing a guaranteed minimum price, with sanctions for agencies that go below this, I see no solution. Our national translators' association should get out of bed with the agencies that are responsible for this state of affairs. It should be working to establish this minimum price, rather than organizing conferences that are far too expensive for most members to attend.

Unfair

A Fire Ant rasps: Forgive us if we've misunderstood, but your letter is not about associations (or even agencies) at all.

What you seem to want is a fairy godmother to wave her wand and bring you high-paying work without you having to do a thing. And maybe give you a little kiss to make it all better in passing.

Here's the bottom line: it takes two to tango. The only way for an agency to get away with paying low rates is to find poor helpless little people who will accept low rates. If you are still laboring in agency hell after 18 years, it's clear that you have made a few bad choices over the years. You are living with the results now.

Worker Bee buzzes: Over the years we have offered many practical solutions to translators in your situation. We urge you to consult the TJ archives (or this book).

For the record, we've never said that creating a successful translation practice is easy. It takes language skills, business savvy, hard work and a willingness to strike out in new directions.

But the first step is to accept that change is inevitable where the market is concerned, and not only possible but positive where you and your own practice are concerned.

When you read a tip that worked for a fellow translator, your first thought should not be a gloomy "Well sure, she managed to make that work, but I don't have her language combination/specialization/social contacts/wardrobe/

[fill in blank]" but rather "Hmm, maybe that could work for me, too."

FA & WB

Q *This week I received an offer of work from a translation agency here in the US—the first time they've contacted me. The job is in a field I know and I am interested. The company says it can give me "as many words as you want throughout July if this goes through" and promises more (maybe) as the year progresses.*

But then this: "We need to bid very competitively as we are up against a translation company that uses cheap translators in Africa and Europe. What would be your rate per target word (files are pdf, translation to be done in Word) and the volume you can handle (days available and words per day)?"

Sounds like a challenge, but I'm game. Should I cut my rates to lock this deal in? If so, by how much?

Big Break

A Dear Big,
Have you heard of the Stockholm Syndrome? Coined in 1973, the term describes an emotional attachment or bond of interdependence between captive and captor. It's based on gratitude (of a sort) and develops "when someone threatens your life, deliberates, and doesn't kill you." (Symonds 1980)

The Stockholm Syndrome is the only explanation we can see for this phenomenon of experienced translators caving in at the mere sight of a loaded gun. The gun in this case is the mythical "cheap translators in Africa and Europe" whom you must now underbid—or so they say.

Get real: Europeans' cost of living is generally not lower than in the US. And even in Africa, cities with educational facilities able to produce skilled translators are not that cheap. However, some translators will always lay down their head under the guillotine. Some even helpfully draw a CUT HERE line on their neck.

Susceptibility to the Stockholm Syndrome is just another occupational hazard.

Note that working with suppliers like this has three serious drawbacks: (1) you won't earn much money, (2) you are unlikely to learn anything from the process and will certainly get no credit or feedback, and (3) you have every chance of getting unceremoniously dropped at some point along the way (hardly surprising: there is always somebody prepared to charge one unit less).

If you think this is a sweet deal, think again.

FA & WB

Q *I've recently received a spate of emails from price-sensitive translation agencies. Example: "We want to know the languages you translate and how much you would charge us; please let us know the lowest possible price as we are looking for certain translators to regularly perform translations as our business grows and are obviously looking for an arrangement which would be profitable for you as well as for our company."*

Is it ever worth answering these?

Starting Out

A Dear Starting,

You might consider responding if you are, say, researching an article on bottom feeders for your local translator association magazine. Yet with one or two exceptions, such publications do not pay their authors, which puts you in double-penalty territory.

The very positive thing about pitches like the one you quote is that you know from the start what you are, or might be, heading into. The "you're getting in on the ground floor here" argument? Why not (and we have a terrific deal on this bridge, contact us privately).

If you are capable of producing smooth, accurate translations, price-driven buyers should not be your priority. If you are not sure that you can produce smooth, accurate translations, you might nibble—then again, don't count on these companies to give you much feedback, which is what you'll need to break into the lucrative end of the market.

FA & WB

Q *Our highly specialized translation agency is having a problem with a corporate client busy tightening the screws.*

Following the arrival of a new bottom-line-obsessed CEO, all of their suppliers have to commit to publishing a "productivity index" annually, meaning a percentage reduction in prices from one year to the next (or "N / N-1")

I've told the new translation department boss that we try to keep a lid on costs by efficient use of translation memories and by checking for previously translated material (even though the client department doesn't tell us when they've recycled some of the text).

This, I was informed, was "synergy," not "productivity." What a fool am I!

"Consider machines: once they are up and running, they work more and more efficiently, which means they produce goods at a lower cost," he said in his charming accent.

I pointed out politely that our "machines" were people and that if we lowered prices every year, they'd soon be working for nothing. He admitted that this could be a problem but opined that maybe we could do a mixture of "synergy" and "productivity," with reductions "for fuzzy matches, etc." in year N-2 vs N-1.

Should I close down the agency and open a sandwich bar next week?

Manager

A Dear Manager,
Ah, the temptation to cut costs in translation services!

Situations like the one you describe are legion, with saber-swinging chief executives installing new translation bosses who draw on years of experience as bulk buyers of paper clips, machine tools or laundry services.

Since your own operation is already client-oriented and specialized, and unless you really do want to shift over to commodity translation, your best bet is simply to remind the company where your strengths lie. Remind them, too, that your services are available in case of emergency, without being smug about it. Then sit back and wait. Recovering singed and reeling customers 12 to 18 months down the road is immensely satisfying. By that time, the cost-cutting CEO may well have moved on to another position, too.

But your example underscores why it is important not to have all your eggs in one basket. If this company accounts for a significant share of your business, you may feel obliged to accept its conditions, which is the first step on a very slippery slope.

FA & WB

Q *Why do clients always always always spring for the cheapest supplier? And then they regret it and people like me have to pick up the pieces.*

Angry

A Dear Angry,
Perhaps because you aren't charging these particular clients enough for your text-repair services?

At the risk of repeating ourselves, a translator who agrees to "fix" poorly translated texts at cut rates is part of the problem. So if your clients come to you regularly for this service ("always always always"), you may well be an enabler.

Perhaps, also, because you are Angry? Don't forget that clients, too, can get frustrated if everything they buy in is garbage. By the time they reach you, they may be intent only on finding a short-term solution.

If they haven't figured out where the problem lies (pay peanuts, get monkeys), set up a meeting and walk them through the figures. Be patient and pleasant—and be sure to put a price on the frustration at their end and yours.

Good luck!

FA & WB

Q *I know that you're often asked to give advice to eager translators. As one of your eager readers, I'd like to provide some unsolicited advice myself.*

One of my agency clients recently sent out a letter to all their vendors informing them that they'd received some glossy business award in their country, which was great considering they were experiencing such tremendous growth, etc., etc.

This was all fine and good, until I discovered that in the same breath they'd decided "to communicate a necessary change in the payment terms set by [the company] with its translation service providers:

Your (MY!!) standard rate will be reduced by 6%."

As you may expect, I was not a happy bunny to read that.

Then I wondered: do I need this specific client that badly?

Answer: No.

Question no. 2: Do they need me?

Answer: Well, let's find out.

So I replied, no doubt rather tersely, "Please be informed that I have just decided to increase the rates I apply to you by 20%."

And pronto, two days later, came the answer: "Whilst it seems you are unwilling to reduce your rates at all I would like to ask that in view of the above you can maintain your current rates as they stand. These are challenging times for many businesses and if we are to prosper in the current economic climate, we all need to play a part."

So what do I infer from this anecdote?

1. Business is business. Agencies are brokers. If their margins are squeezed, they need to cut costs. That's OK with me, as long as they don't play with MY income.

2. No matter how hard they try to convince translators of the opposite, agencies are nowhere without top-quality vendors. So don't let them bully you: finding good translators is a hard job. If you're good (or at least if you think you're good) RESIST!

3. If they want me so badly that they not only instantly forget their "decision" to reduce my rate by 6% and instead beg me for a status quo, I would be stupid not to push my luck a little, don't you think?

Standing Tall

A Dear Tall,
You've hit the nail on the head, while omitting a key factor that we'll add in for the benefit of Passing's client: you can stand tall because you have something to sell—a specialization and writing style that this translation agency needs, and knows it needs.

You've also made the right decision in viewing this entire exchange as a business issue from start to finish.

All too often translators take announcements like the letter you mention as a personal insult and let their indignation rip—which is probably the least productive option.

FA & WB

Q *Only a week ago, I attended a business workshop on getting through the economic downturn. One of the things that they stressed above all was that businesses should AVOID RUSHING TO CUT PRICES, especially if there was no reduction in value. The woman who presented the workshop has a business making beautifully embroidered handbags that usually sell in the $90-$150 range: when she saw the downturn coming, she developed a new product. It's a much smaller handbag for about $35. The craftsmanship is exactly the same—there's simply less of it.*

The question I've been mulling over since then is this: where's the $35 handbag for the translation industry? How do we apply the same principle to our product?

Strategist

A **Fire Ant asks:** Are those $35 bags selling?
Worker Bee muses and enthuses: An intriguing idea. Let's do a little lateral thinking.

Text-wise, you'd want a short document that displays your outstanding translation/writing skills.

A text with enormous personal appeal for a discerning clientele would be nice, especially if recognition and appreciation of your outstanding job might lead to future assignments.

Here's one: bioblurbs for famous speakers at international conferences.

A lot of the examples we see are clunky, even laughable, no doubt produced at the last minute by a gofer or stressed-out coordinator. Or perhaps a student intern.

To be sure, these little blocks of text are labor-intensive to translate (think exquisite embroidery).

But they are also the type of text that international VIPs—especially those

125

who speak several languages—would rather not be embarrassed about once the issue has been brought to their attention. "Sure this is short, but it's important to get it right" is an argument that will resonate with them. And every prominent political or business leader on the world stage needs one or more, depending on the language environments they speak in.

It might be a good idea to drop the $35 price tag entirely for your first round of candidates: make your "free trial offer" elegantly crafted revisions of flabby or clunky or inarticulate bioblurbs. Send these directly to the CEO or billionaire philanthropist or Prime Minister or Head of Worldwide Sales: existing (bad), new (good) + cover letter (it will have to be a very good cover letter).

Word of mouth should do the rest, and you can slap on a $35 (or $350 charge) when a new contact mentions that George Soros, Michel Rocard, Sergio Chiamparino or Pierre Dartout sent him.

What a hook for subsequent top-level work! Talk about getting in on the top floor!

FA & WB

6
Marketing and finding clients

Producing outstanding translations won't get you far if buyers don't know you exist or how to find you. To move beyond dabbling and pin money, translators must invest time and effort to link up with clients.

NO MAGIC WAND

Q *Getting jobs from reputable agencies is incredibly hard. I've been tested by several, only to wait for months on end with no actual assignment. Their explanation is that project managers act independently from the HR department; they encourage me to keep waiting.*

But waiting is the one thing you cannot do when you are starting, so instead you (at least me) end up working for less reputable agencies at their own (rock bottom) rates, meeting impossible deadlines. I may be marketing myself terribly wrong, or translation in the new era may have became a terribly competitive business, or both. Ideas, please, for us beginners.

Drumming My Fingers

A Dear Drummer,
What you are looking for is a means of hastening your Big Break. You don't mention how long you have been hammering at the door, but unless you are extraordinarily lucky, amazingly skilled and/or possess a rare language combination, you are probably going to have to log some more time at the less glamorous rungs of the ladder.

In practical terms, count at least two years to accumulate the strict minimum experience/feedback you need to gain a foothold in the market. If by the end of this period you are not getting repeat business and attracting a better-quality clientele there are two possibilities.

- The first is that your skills are not yet up to scratch. To judge this, you'll need feedback, and unfortunately the less reputable agencies rarely provide it. So even if you do of necessity start working through low-end outfits, use every single opportunity that comes up to solicit comments on your work. Commission a critique from an established translator or editor. If your work is found lacking, you may want to think about a translation course, or better yet an internship in a translation department or company.
- The second possibility is that your marketing is skewed. Agencies are loath to assign a job to an unknown quantity, so the challenge is to make your strengths better known. You can do this by highlighting specialist skills in your résumé or by establishing personal contact with agency staff and owners.

The good news is that this is easier than you'd think.

If you are keen on working for agencies, attend language-industry events, where translation companies and agencies are traditionally well-represented. Since you are not applying for a job but offering a service, don't distribute a CV. Instead, list your specializations together with relevant work history, recent seminars and workshops attended, resources including dictionaries and software, membership in a professional body, any published work, and references. If you feel tongue-tied or worried that you have no published work to show (yes, we realize you are a novice), try another tactic: ask translation company reps present to critique your skills sheet for you. And use the one-on-one exchange to impress them with your enthusiasm and knowledge.

Finally, as one contact reminds us, while part of marketing is what you write, the other part is where you send it. From your letter, it sounds as if you are tackling some mighty big agencies ("HR departments"?).

Don't confuse big with good; clients do this all the time, and many get seriously burned as a result. In our experience some of the best translation companies around, offering good pay and interesting projects, are the smaller, specialized ones.

FA & WB

Q *In your April column, you said you were "amazed at the number of skilled translators who assume there is no alternative to working through an intermediary" (page 211). My reaction: is there one?*

I have been a freelancer for five years now, exclusively for translation agencies, and I just can't understand what clients want from a translator.

Over the past few months, I have tried very hard to find direct clients (in telecommunications and shipping/maritime transport mostly), but have had very little success. My offer included competitive rates, fast turnaround, specialist knowledge, etc. I have used all the Internet resources I could find to customize my offer to potential clients, and I even did translation tests for a telecommunication company thinking of setting up in Asia, but nothing came of it.

So my question is, where is this "thriving market" you mention? Is it just a matter of being in the right place at the right time or is there something I've overlooked? I am starting to lose hope of ever working for direct clients, so all suggestions are welcome!

Desponding in Slough

A Dear Desponding,
Tip of the month: don't start your pitch with "competitive prices." What good clients are crying out for is subject-matter expertise, backed by effective writing. There is plenty of time to discuss prices once they understand the added value you offer.

As you note, it is important to identify what clients want from a translator. We are convinced that the only way to find out is to get out and mingle with them.

One of the first things you may discover is that many don't really know themselves.

Others may be skeptical about your input, especially if they have been burned by sub-standard work from other suppliers in the past. For these buyers, translation is not a solution, but an unknown—and as such a source of worry and trouble.

This being the case, one of the best ways to establish and consolidate ties with both groups is to shift your focus from language to specialist knowledge of their industry. Train yourself to speak their (subject-matter) language—literally.

At the risk of repeating ourselves, you must read what your clients read. Trade journals, but also a daily business paper such as the Financial Times or Wall Street Journal, or your source/target-language equivalent (the business pages of your local daily will not do the trick). And don't kid yourself, this will take time.

Next step: hang around client watering holes—trade fairs, chamber of commerce events, etc.—to sharpen your feel for their concerns and markets. If you are not at ease in business circles, this may seem daunting to start, although by now you'll have been tracking their industry closely for long enough to be genuinely curious about some of the projects they are up to.

Opening gambits at a trade fair can be as simple as a request for multilingual documentation, or asking reps to explain how their product X compares with competitors' Y.

At an industry conference, ask delegates next to you which trade events they would recommend. At this stage, you are not a seller (yet), just an interested observer seeking input from them, the specialists. All of this is to ready yourself for face-to-face contact, for you will at some point have to meet clients in the flesh—this time as a genuine supplier!

Mastering your subject is the best way we know to gain the confidence—and credibility—you need to demonstrate how your skills can serve them. Good luck!

FA & WB

Q *I worked in-house at an agency for four years but only went freelance (F>E) last spring.*

The transition has been difficult. My former employer and I are on excellent terms, but they don't do much into-English. I met some great translators through them and have kept in touch, but these people work in other directions and I've had no referrals. I've done mailing to agencies and have received many Translator Information Sheets to fill in, but not a lot of actual jobs.

In short, I am beginning to wonder how a fledgling freelancer can get her foot in the door! I know that I am an excellent translator (from glowing colleague/ proofreader/agency feedback), but finding clients is turning out to be much harder than I had imagined.

I should mention that my preferred subject matter is medical, and I have also done quite a bit of legal translation. Do you have any advice?

Awaiting Big Break

A Dear Awaiting,
First the good news: the positive feedback you have received puts you in a stronger position than many fledglings. Without this, we would have advised you to solicit or commission a detailed critique of a few pieces from an agency or fellow freelance (or subject-matter specialist).

More good news is that you've already got a preferred field: medical (+ legal?).

But even "medical" is vast. Try to identify some particularly attractive "translation products" (pharmaceutical inserts? research papers? medical reports for insurance companies?...). Build up a library of examples from different sources. Study them. Identify what makes them good, then locate companies likely to commission such work.

Networking with fellow translators is a good first step. But if you want to build up a clientele, you must target translation buyers, preferably direct clients.

Here are some suggestions.

1. Set aside 4 or 5 hours a week to find out who/where your customers are and what products they are buying.

2. Take out a 3 or 6-month subscription to a business daily—even if you are not targeting the business market, your potential clients are. The business pages of your local paper will not do the trick; if you work into English, it's got to be the Wall Street Journal or the Financial Times. Remember; your market is international. Ideally, you will be working for companies outside the US, trying to sell their products and services to English-speaking buyers.

3. Every day—every single day—skim through the paper for 30-45 minutes. Note developments in your target markets. Watch for big-picture news—an EU decision; release of an industry report, etc. But don't neglect the details: Company A moving into market B, Institute C teaming up with Association D, launch of a new drug for treating malaria, breakthroughs in HIV research, etc. etc.

Notice names—of companies, people, products.

Clip relevant articles and set them aside.

After a few weeks, you will start to recognize names and issues that are hot.

(Note: 1 to 3 can be done on the Web, as one of our correspondents reminds us. Your costs will be lower. But a newspaper will bring in a more varied haul and let you do your reading away from the screen).

4. Short-list the companies that seem to be most active or aggressive in tackling markets where your language combination is needed.

5. Use the Net to obtain information on them: order annual reports and/or brochures in your language combinations. Study this material. If the bilingual documents are well translated, you're in luck: use them to build up subject-specific glossaries. If they are poorly done, you are also in luck: these people need your services.

6. Establish contact, preferably not as a workseeker, but as a language expert seeking background information from them, the subject-matter specialists. The work arrives automatically when they see how informed and enthusiastic you are.

Three options for establishing contact come to mind:

• The glossary: contact your target companies. Explain that you are a translator, currently specializing in their field. Mention in passing some international project that they've got on the boil (shows you've done your homework). You are working on a glossary. You have questions on two or three terms. Could one of their engineers/researchers help?

You can do this by email, but phoning is more effective. Experts love to explain things; chances are, they will be flattered by your request and genuinely helpful.

But do not wear out your welcome. Ask about two or three terms—no more. Offer to send your contacts a copy of your glossary as thanks for their assistance. If the opportunity comes up, visit their lab/plant/office.

• Attend a trade fair or two in your specialism, and hit the booths with your glossary project or simply to collect bilingual documentation. Any of these contacts may develop into work; even if they don't, you will learn a lot.

• The free trial offer: locate a poorly-translated document in your field and retranslate a chunk of it. Poor foreign-language websites are obvious candidates.

Send your translation + photocopy of original text + photocopy of first translation to the company.

Your cover letter should be short but pleasant—a sentence or two indicating that you know their industry, that you appreciate the outstanding quality of their products/services, that you think the text they've got does not do justice to these products/services, that you think your text is more suitable. Do not harangue them about their original bad text.

Suggest that they show both versions to a language-sensitive mother-tongue partner for an opinion. And end with a sentence like "I will take the liberty of phoning you next week to discuss this further."

Send your letter to the chairman of the company (w/copy to head of communications). If you target the head of communications alone, it may well go in the bin (who commissioned that poor translation, anyway?). And—this is important—actually phone them.

Good luck!

FA & WB

Q *I am 28 years old, and for circumstances too complicated to explain here, I put my medical studies on hold in 2002 and moved from my native Venezuela to Denmark. Looking for ways to earn a living in a new country and support a 9-year-old child without having completed an education has proven to be depressing, hard and just plain nerve wrecking.*

But first some background: My father, an English-Spanish translator, had his office at home, which means I grew up being a receptionist, then also a Spanish proofreader, and finally in 1994 I did my first English to Spanish translations.

I have been translating ever since. During some periods it has been my full-time occupation and in others an occasional occupation (my medical studies required a lot of time) and a way of earning some extra money in the comfort of my own home.

My father always encouraged me to follow his profession, but at this point, I felt that without his protective wing, I did not stand a chance, and without any degrees in translation or languages, it would be disrespectful to compete with others who had gone through an education.

The turning point was that I actually fell ill due to my workload and—after lots of encouragement from my boyfriend and my parents—I decided to start marketing myself and register my own translation company.

I realize now that there are a lot of people out there with no degrees who are excellent translators. That said, I have the advantage of a background in medicine and 10 years of experience (where does time go?).

But now to get to my question: how to succeed in a situation like mine?

I worked 7 years with my dad, the last 3 I have been freelancing, but only for one agency. New agencies ask for references, in the translation field I can only cite my dad and this agency (I have many references from my teachers at medical school, though), how would an agency see this? Especially how valuable is it to cite your dad as a reference? I mean, he is my dad, he cannot really be objective.

I have successfully passed the two translation tests I have taken so far, I have registered at a ton of sites and applied to many agencies. Only 3 have added me to their databases, but I have not gotten any work from them yet.

There was one which especially detailed the tests results and made wonderful praises about my translation, giving me the highest grading in technical content, grammar and syntax and style. That boosted my self-confidence a lot.

I know I am good, I learned from my father the importance of meeting deadlines, inspecting your work carefully, not being shy to ask for assistance and taking overall responsibility.

But how can I make myself attractive to potential clients without having to offer unfair rates, or seem desperate? Which I am. My only income comes from one agency and even though I have a solid relationship with them, sometimes I feel I cannot put my feet down on some issues for fear of loosing the contact altogether. I have almost no savings, so I cannot really wait for months and months until my business picks up, I am actually depending solely on this agency to survive, which is very precarious.

I am sorry this has turned to be a bit short of "War and Peace", but I hope you can give me some pointers and advice!
Sincerely and desperately,

Natasha

A Dear Nat,
To summarize, you've got a raft of skills—you've been a receptionist, a proofreader and a translator; you have both freelance and agency experience, you've got a specialty, you've done some medical school and you have lab experience.

But you've also got a dilemma—how to pitch these strengths successfully to clients.

First question: do you know who and where your potential clients are? We may be missing something here, but were surprised to read that you set up a translation company (presumably in your own name) only to market your skills to... translation agencies. With your skills and experience, why operate through an intermediary?

It's high time you did some online research to identify direct clients in need of your services, then developed strategies for linking up with them.

True, the English to Spanish market for medical translation in Denmark may not be enormous, but there are fewer competitors, too. And how many words a month can you handle, anyway? Keep in mind that once your initial contact is made—in person, if possible—you will be working over the internet, making location less important.

Trade fairs are an attractive option in medical equipment and pharmaceuticals, and here Copenhagen's central location should serve you well. Test the waters with a few visits to pick up documentation, then consider a variation on the glossary ploy, in which you ask a potential client for help on a glossary to get a conversation going.

Second question: how many references are required, anyway? Direct clients will be more interested in the actual work you produce, so it is worth putting together a portfolio with some of your strongest recent pieces. Be sure to respect confidentiality agreements with your present agency, of course. If you have no outstanding examples, produce some now, perhaps by correcting poor texts published by a potential client (see Awaiting Big Break, page 130).

But if you do need references, use current ones. Teachers in medical school are not a good idea—that was another life.

Which brings us to our final point: for your translation practice to take off, you must above all commit to translating as a profession, not just a fill-in-the-gap activity to pay the rent and put rød grøt med fløte on the table. Which means developing greater focus and—above all—believing in yourself (as we've seen, there are plenty of reasons to do so).

In discussions of your career and study decisions, present these as a progression, not a series of upsets and choices made by default. Each development has given you strengths and resources that make you a uniquely qualified supplier of a sorely needed service. Once you are convinced of that it will be easier to convince potential customers. And hard as it may seem at present, make sure your rates reflect your experience—not your desperation.

FA & WB

Q *I finished my translation degree over a year ago and took a seminar on how to set up in business that advised me to do all the things you recommend: attend trade shows, rewrite poor translations ("free trial offers"), mingle with businesspeople at chamber of commerce events, etc.*

But this does not seem to be paying off. I have had no responses to my offer of services, except last week when an agency offered me a job at about 2/3 the price I want to charge.

At a business event last week, the head of the chamber of commerce came over to me and asked how I was doing (she recognized me from the seminar, which was held at the chamber earlier this year). I said fine. I could have said something about getting discouraged (even desperate), looking hard for clients and did she know anybody who needed a translator, but I felt uncomfortable exploiting our acquaintance that way.

My point is, I want to succeed, but I want it to be on the basis of my work, not the people I know. Do you have any suggestions?

Beginner

A Dear Beginner,
Yes: change tactics immediately.

You sound very conscientious and your pride in your work is great, but if you are setting up as a freelance, you are also a business person and it is in your direct interest to view people you know as the invaluable resources they are. Forget Frank Sinatra, and use every single contact you have—ex-colleagues, your brother-in-law, parents in your kids' school, neighbors—to get your name out and about.

Concretely? Call the head of the chamber of commerce today!

FA & WB

CLIENT OUTREACH

Q *I've identified a company that needs my services. We would be a perfect match, in fact. But they are not answering my emails (four to date). I phoned and spoke with their communications department person; she didn't seem wildly enthusiastic. In fact she didn't offer me any work. But she didn't say no either. I don't want to give up yet.*

Do you have any suggestions ?

Match Made in Heaven

A Dear Match,

You don't say exactly how you phrased your pitch in the emails, but it sounds to us like your offer may well be filed in the "pest" folder.

Suggestion: ease off for a bit, and swing back around again after a six to 12-month break. Alternatively, identify some professional events where this prospective client will be on hand and try to meet up with a representative in person. Face time is always good; you can't shake hands by email or phone.

Should you meet a representative:

• use a question or two to get him talking, then step back and do some intensive listening.

• don't overstay your welcome: unless you really hit it off, exchange an insightful comment or two and business cards, then move on.

• above all, do not remind him of how many times you've tried to link up unsuccessfully. He may wonder if his colleagues at head office know something he doesn't. It comes across as whining; it's the equivalent of trailing a hot-air balloon marked "loser" behind you. Your emails were then, this is now.

Good luck!

FA & WB

Q *I am a freelance translator and I need your help. I would like to get some advice on how to get in contact with direct clients. Perhaps I should subscribe to certain translators' magazines?*

Bulgarian Reader

A Dear Reader,

Subscribing to translators' magazines, on its own, is not a terrific idea if your prime aim is to link up with direct clients.

For that, you should instead subscribe to magazines that your target clientele tracks to keep up with developments in their industry. Reading these will help you identify both clients and issues of interest to them, along with venues where you are likely to meet them in the flesh (see our answer to "Bouncing Back" below).

Other suggestions: join a translators' association, since a lot of contacts are made through word of mouth. Participating on translator elists is a good move, too—you'll pick up a lot of useful information and, provided you become an active and expert contributor in your fields of expertise/language combination, you may well find list members passing your details on to clients. For this to work, be sure to indicate your contact details in your signature.

Above all, you must market-oriented, i.e., specialize in areas where the strongest growth is, whether telecommunications, banking, environmental services or transportation.

How do you find out which areas are showing the strongest growth? Well, one way is to read the business section of at least one major business newspaper every day (this is good as a general principle, too).

However, business news often reports on developments or events that have already happened, which is not necessarily a good predictor of the future. So depending on your market, a better leading indicator might be the "Job Openings" section of the top business newspaper in your country/region.

Say you are in Bulgaria and see that company XYZ has placed ten 1/4-page ads advertising for product managers and other senior management positions. That's a substantial outlay, and they would not be doing it without robust expectations for the future. Two or three months later, once they have their team in place, they may also start looking for freelance translators. You do not have to wait this long: contact them now, with carefully crafted letters detailing your specialist knowledge of their industry, and follow up with phone calls. This is one way to get in on the ground floor—before your competitors.

FA & WB

Q *Early this year I began a new career in freelance translation. I've now had sufficient experience with translation agencies and direct clients to know that I really want to focus on working for the latter.*

Armed with a long list of prospects and some referrals from generous and well-established translators, I'm ready to introduce myself and my services. I've begun sending well-crafted e-mails or nicely-printed snailmails.

Results have varied, naturally; I can't say for sure whether distinctive paper letters prompt more responses than e-mail (and don't really expect you to be able to tell me that, either).

But what I would like to hear are some ideas on how to effectively follow up with prospects who don't respond, without coming off like a stalker: a second note? Another e-mail? Or maybe—gulp—a cold call?

Flummoxed

ADear Flummoxed,
Technology being as glitch-prone as it is, we think you can reasonably send the same message a second time with a neutral cover message, e.g., "I've had some email problems recently and wanted to make sure this reached you." But careful: no whining, and certainly no hint that your target is somehow out of line for not having answered first time around.

Note that you can improve your chances of a response by avoiding peak periods. These will depend on the sector you are targeting. Aerospace translators are up to their ears in the run-up to the Paris Air Show, subtitlers bleary-eyed in the countdown to the Cannes Film Festival, automotive translators frazzled as the Detroit Motor Show looms.

An auspicious time to write to your prospects is a week or ten days after such peaks, when these same top-tier translators and their clients are catching up on lack of sleep with still-vivid memories of just how hectic it was. This is when both will be particularly attracted by the idea of getting a better system in place for the next rush, and may well look more carefully at your offer.

Vacation periods can also be attractive, especially in countries where many people go on holiday at the same time. Make your first contacts a few months before the vacation begins, and position yourself to step in as back-up.

Finally, if you are feeling particularly energetic, you can always make your closing paragraph "I will take the liberty of phoning you next week to see if my services can be of use to you." Then phone.

Good luck!

FA & WB

QRegarding your advice to Flummoxed, I would like to sound the following note of warning.
Your correspondent is talking of e-mail, telephoning, and even cold-calling prospective direct clients, but he/she should be aware that such activities are now

strictly regulated in the UK.

As a self-employed translator, I myself was unaware of quite how difficult it now is to source direct clients until I attended a business development course run by my local Business Link agency. There is the TPS—Telephone Preference Service, MPS—Mail Preference Service, FPS—Fax Preference Service and even an e-mail preference list. If companies are subscribers and listed as not welcoming unsolicited approaches, transgressors may face prosecution and a £5000 fine. I do not know of any prosecutions, but unlucky the translator who becomes a test case!

The regulatory framework is now so tight it seems the only way to get direct clients is by recommendation, or by networking, the latter being an expensive and time-consuming process, as I am finding to my cost.

Business Grower

ADear Business,
Thanks for that update on the UK scene. Point taken: it would be suicidal to launch any type of outreach without checking first to ensure that your plans comply with local legislation.

And true, networking can be expensive and time-consuming. But is there any other serious option? All too often translators take a short-term view, rejecting out of hand investment that business people in other sectors would view as normal, even essential.

A self-employed translator is at once business development strategist, project manager, chief accountant, head of marketing, R&D expert and tea lady. Not to mention factory-floor operative, of course. Investing to hone your expertise, then making potential clients aware of those skills and your availability is part of the deal.

Example: One of us recently spent just under €600 in upfront expenses, plus billable hours lost, to attend a two-day conference for business leaders. Big bucks? Perhaps. But contacts made in the first two hours generated €1500 in business over the next month, with more to come.

The trick is to identify the most promising events by tracking what your client companies (and potential client companies) are up to, then studying attendance/exhibitor lists before shelling out. You might also simply ask existing clients which industry events they consider the best opportunities to learn more about their sector. This sends out the right message: you are developing your knowledge of the field to serve them better. That you coincidentally link up with new prospects is the icing on your cake.

FA & WB

139

Q*I have identified a business sector where I think there should be a substantial requirement for quality translation in the areas in which I specialize (commercial, advertising/marketing) and am planning to attend a trade event next week with my husband, who is involved in this sector.*

Can you give me any advice on how to introduce myself to potential customers? My previous experience has always been in dealing with customers who have already identified a need for translation. Moreover, I'm quite a shy person and not good at selling myself; I don't think just walking up to the people on a stand and saying "Do you need translations" is going to be very productive.

Off to the Front Line

A Dear Off,
You're doing at least two things right: planning ahead and linking up with an insider (your spouse).

As we have pointed out in previous columns, merely attending an industry event and doling out business cards is not a particularly fruitful exercise—unless a year's supply of logo-bearing freebies from machine-tool suppliers makes your day. Nor is trawling aisle after aisle at trade fairs asking outright for translation work; with clients of potential clients milling around, there is too much going on and your offer will often be dismissed as white noise.

A far better approach is to identify a promising business sector—as you have done—then select a key event and work through the following steps:

1. Secure a list of attendees and/or exhibitors. For trade fairs, this is often on the website or in the catalog (which you should buy for future reference).

2. Shortlist five to ten companies whose needs match your service offering: these are the guys you will want to speak to (to select likely candidates, draw on the same reading that helped you identify the appeal of this sector in the first place).

3. Draw up a one-paragraph profile of each target (key products, markets, executives (including names) and competitors); read through this before heading for the event, and again on site before approaching their stand. Remember, for the purposes of this trip, you are not selling to "the electronics/catering/food/advertising/[fill in blank] industry" but to this specific company, so it is in your interest to know all about them. Your spouse may be able to help by providing background on key issues facing the industry.

4. Use the glossary ploy (page 131) to collect examples, and your writing skills to get back in touch (page 132) with a free trial offer.

Your aim, this first time around, is not to trumpet your availability for translation (unless they ask), but rather to plant your name and face in the minds of promising targets as you seek examples of the translations that they are currently producing. You are a professional translator documenting herself on their dynamic sector so as to better serve them in the future.

To get the conversational ball rolling—and bring on-stand discussion over into matters translational in a relaxed but productive way—consider taking along A4 print-outs of strikingly silly translations *into* your target's language (signs and ad slogans are good examples).

These examples speak for themselves, bringing home to monolinguals just how bad flawed translation can make them look. You might also leave a copy of "Translation, getting it right", a client-education brochure available in a number of languages (new UK edition from ITI (www.iti.org.uk)), with your business card attached.

Beyond your own knowledge of and enthusiasm for these businesses' operations, your real pitch will be made from the comfort of your home, through your (written) revision of something they have already translated poorly—an approach where even the shy translator/word artist can shine.

FA & WB

Q *I am desperately nervous in the presence of clients. The other day I'd planned to go to an information day for professionals in my specialty area but didn't make it past the registration desk. It just seemed too daunting: once in the room, I would have had to dart around shaking hands and making small talk. I can appreciate (theoretically) why that might be a good move, but it's not me.*
Any advice?

Cave Dweller

A Dear Cave,
What's with the darting and small talk? First-time participants at such events learn a lot by simply watching and listening—if necessary, you can don a potted-palm suit and melt into the background or fiddle with your cellphone (an excellent "I'm-busy-doing-deals" prop).

You will quickly realize that attending client events serves three main purposes:

• you consolidate existing ties and drum up new business (at the very least, there are always a few speakers whose PowerPoints need your expert input)
• you pick up news of issues (and terminology) that are likely to surface in jobs over the weeks ahead

• most important of all, however, you experience how these people—the very ones who will be ordering, using and reading your translations—interact with each other; you observe how they chat and joke and make a case for their products and services over coffee. Which makes it easier for you to make a case for your own services when you pitch to them at some point in the future. Invaluable!

But to get that far, you'll want to take steps to avoid a meltdown in public, with or without the tree costume.

Tips for cave dwellers preparing for a client event:

1. Do your homework. Identify a half-dozen clients or potential clients likely to be there, and read up on what they and their companies do. This is not just to avoid asking stupid questions; it also reminds you how very interesting their business is.

2. Look the part. If you're selling professional services, threadbare sweats and a plastic-bag-cum-briefcase won't make the grade.

Some translators we know object to donning suit and tie. "I feel like I'm attending a costume party as a corporate banker," says one. But that's beside the point, which is to blend into your prey's environment before moving in for the kill. Trust us: knowing you are appropriately dressed will calm your nerves and allow you to focus on the important stuff like listening harder.

3. Take it in bite-size chunks. If you're feeling jittery, you needn't stay for the entire event.

Example: start with a meeting where you know existing clients will be on hand. Have their names handy and link up briefly for even a few minutes of face time. Extend hand and say "Hi, I'm [name]. I'm so pleased to meet you at last! / I thought you might be here and wanted to meet up in person to tell you how much I enjoyed the project we worked on in April." After a little back and forth about that job or a speaker at the current event, announce with a regretful smile that you're booked for a meeting at a venue across town and dash off—confirming the impression that you are much in demand.

4. Remember that your concern is to get them—the existing client or prey—talking about their operations, not to yap on about yourself. Have an elevator speech in hand and use it, but move the spotlight to them fairly quickly. As a seasoned networker has pointed out, often a simple "tell me about your business" will be enough to unleash the floodgates—their floodgates. Which is exactly what you want!

The bottom line? Meeting clients in the flesh is good for you, your translations and your business. It can even become addictive.

FA & WB

Q *I've been a full-time freelance translator for over a decade, and I've never been out of work for more than a few days. However, this year, July was flat—and I mean zero sales. Now, in July, I was fortunately busy on volunteer work during the first fortnight and on holidays during the second—so that was not too bad.*

However, after I came back from hols in August, things looked set to head in the same direction and I invoiced exactly zero again until August 18th. Fortunately, my billings for August 18 to August 31 came to approximately 25k€ on a few extremely urgent and technical documents, which has smoothed things out nicely.

My wife tells me that it's just a matter of clients being on vacation over the period, but I must confess that sitting in front of a silent phone was getting on my nerves.

Do you think I should review my marketing strategy?

Slight Panic

A Dear Panic,
Your letter is a reminder of just how important it is to have a cash buffer in the bank or under your mattress for those lean stretches. Small-business gurus in the US put this at about two years' worth of living expenses.

• Good for you for sitting tight and not lowering your prices (speaking of which, sounds like a nice end of August you had there!).

• Less impressive is the image of you sitting in front of a silent phone—unless that was just a turn of phrase.

Business slack? The lull is in itself a business opportunity. Use it to get out to client events—log some face time at business lunches, conferences, and trade fairs, where you can mingle and pick up strategic information about who's doing what and where you might fit in. Be seen, and be seen to be knowledgeable, professional and passionate about your customers' specialties.

While out and about, never ever mention that business is flat or (even worse) in a slump; they don't need to know: you're at the dairy-farmers' convention or insurance brokers' breakfast on tropical storm coverage because you are analyzing their industry in preparation for an upcoming job (which you can't discuss, it's confidential).

It's astounding how many translation jobs materialize in precisely these conditions, when your presence reminds demanding clients of a text they'd shelved, convinced they'd never find a knowledgeable, professional and passionate translator to take it on.

FA & WB

Q *It was heartening to see your column on the web, and without the need to pay out large sums of money, to be given some idea of what is out there.*

I worked for six years as a translator-interpreter in Italy and now find myself in a position to take up some work It>Eng, or Fr>Eng over the next few months.

Whom should I contact (if anybody)? Should I merely keep my eyes peeled for work on the newsgroup or are there agencies or organisations that I should contact?

Daisy (Fresh)

A Dear Daisy,
Start by mining your contacts from the past six years for job offers and assignments. Since they already know you, they will be the most likely source of referrals.

Are you still in Italy? Then join the local translator association, attend trade shows and workshops in your fields, and if you do not live in a major market such as Milan or Turin, visit at least once per year to build up business contacts.

Another source of jobs is colleagues: by participating actively on translator discussion lists and demonstrating your expertise and all-round pleasantness, you may well start receiving requests to join fellow list-members on large projects. Note that this cuts two ways: if your answers to questions are clueless, you will quickly be relegated to the clueless sub-list—which is only natural, of course.

FA & WB

Q *I am nearly 29 and live close to London. I started working as a freelance translator full time in June 2007.*

Strictly speaking, my mother tongue is English as both parents are English, however I lived in France from age 7 to 25 and went through the French education system, up to university (BA politics, economics and finance, MA international relations), thus making me completely and truly bilingual. I have been living in England since January 2004. I would say my level in both languages is roughly the same now, however as I am living in the UK, my English is likely to "overtake" my French at some stage.

Until now I have tried to market myself as being able to translate both ways (Fr>En and En>Fr), as I thought I would get more work than with only one pair, but several colleagues have questioned that strategy.

In the long run, I believe the logical thing would be to concentrate on Fr>En, however the demand for that pair would be in France whereas I am based in the UK, and my dip. trans. diploma is En>Fr.

Thank you for your advice.

Bilingual Briton

A Dear Bilingual,
There are so few people capable of translating both ways that you are indeed damaging your credibility by making that claim in, say, an online directory. A website is different, since it allows you to back up your bilingualism with information like that you've just sent us. As you are no doubt aware, oral fluency in both of your working languages is a plus when pitching to and working with direct clients (a point that native English-speakers often forget).

FA & WB

LOCATION

Q *You two are always boasting about charging customers an arm and a leg. Well I'm a damn good translator from German to English, yet I can't get anyone to send me prestigious, highly paid jobs. Maybe you should both just shut up and leave us working stiffs alone, instead of adding insult to injury.*

Injured in Indiana

A Dear Injured,
We hate to rub it in but there is a reason why you cannot get the high-priced work—you're out in the sticks! Even in today's globalized economy, physical proximity to your target market counts. Supposedly the Internet makes physical distance obsolete, but don't believe the hype. High-priced translation—the type that allows you to earn a middle-to-upper-class income—is never purchased anonymously.

In many other industries everyone agrees that you have to be where the action is. Could you be at the South Pole and sell a script to Hollywood for half a million bucks? In principle, yes, of course. In practice, fuhgeddaboudit.

Can you become pro wrestling champion of the world if you never set foot in the USA? Sure, in principle. In practice, geddouddahere.

If you never leave Hicksville, Indiana, you are doomed to stay in your rut—more likely than not churning out volume work for companies that will drop you without a second thought if you raise your prices by even a measly cent per word.

The terrible truth is that while the US leads the world in most industries, it is in many respects a backwater when it comes to premium translation. After all, who is going to pay top-of-the-line prices for translations? Not companies like Wal-Mart or Home Shopping Channel. They already have their supply contracts in place and know they will sell the entire batch of Taiwanese inflatable mattresses regardless of how well the instructions are translated.

For clients willing to pay top dollar, you must cast a wider net. First of all, look for documents that have been written to persuade, sell or impress—advertising, PR articles, glossy brochures and the like. This is what some people call "outbound" texts (as opposed to "inbound" ones, which are often far less demanding in terms of style).

In your case, the most lucrative work is likely to come from non-US companies anxious to break out of their home market. Such buyers are extremely self-conscious about presenting their best face to English speakers, whom they (rightly or wrongly) equate with the world. They're nervous and they've often been burned before, which makes it unlikely that they'll send their material thousands of miles away to be translated by an anonymous service provider.

So how does the image-conscious client find the translator who will lavish care and attention on their marketing materials (for a price)?

Well, this is where the proximity thing comes in. What most Internet gurus don't tell you is that despite the globalization trend, location is just as important as ever. No matter what the industry, if you look closely you will find that there are centers of excellence with clusters of specialized suppliers servicing their client businesses.

True, for the commodity end of translation it no longer makes a difference where the work is done. Anything that is routine or standardized can be done anywhere.

But if you are not doing routine work—if you have invested the time needed to acquire specialist knowledge and have honed your translation skills to near perfection ("damn good" is a good start)—then you need to link up with a small, discriminating clientele. And that means being where the clients are. It means linking up with the firms listed on the Neuer Markt who must publish in both German and English, it means selling directly to French companies and their advertising agencies, it means winning the business of high-tech manufacturers in Northern Italy. It means being part of an informal network of buyer-supplier relationships, where somebody picks up the phone to ask a trusted supplier for a recommendation and your own telephone rings five minutes later. In this respect, relationships with your peers can be as important as marketing and salesmanship to end clients.

If you cannot physically relocate to Germany, then research the market from Indiana and spend at least a week every year in Germany visiting potential clients. Emphasize your competitive advantages—you know how to weave in the latest cultural allusions so that texts have maximum impact on target readers, you can turn out work overnight because of the difference in time zones—and go get'em. Good luck!

FA & WB

Q *I am a graduate English and German translator from South America, got my BA degree one and a half years ago and have tried very hard to get a job as an in-house translator and find clients paying adequate prices. I haven't done badly so far, but I don't really see a promising future as a translator in my country. There is work for translators, but we are hardly paid "decent" prices, either as free-lancers or as in-house translators. That's why, although I really love languages, I'm losing hope of making it as a translator here.*

I currently see only two possible solutions:
1. going abroad (Europe or the USA; by the way, do you know in what country translators have the best possibilities?) In that case, do you have any advice for a foreigner translator who would like to make it there?
2. studying something else (probably computing), so that I have more job chances.

However, since I wouldn't like to abandon languages, do you think there's any way to combine both activities?

No Retreat, No Surrender

A Dear Soldier,
Extended stints abroad are an essential part of the translator's career path. How else are you going to consolidate language skills and acquire the insights you need to act as a bridge between cultures? For you, it sounds like one of the best times to do this might be now—with an initial experience of professional

life in your own country under your belt, and plenty of get-up-and-go. We nonetheless suggest you keep the following considerations in mind.

• Visas & such: get the red tape out of the way before you go anywhere.

• Experience does count, so wherever you end up try to be patient. It sounds like you are only 18 months out into the working world; how many business school graduates get senior positions that quickly? To make it into the top tier—where, rest assured, prices are more than "decent" in many, many language combinations—you must consolidate your book-learning by logging at least a million words. Look for opportunities to work with top-flight revisers, and be prepared to accept lower prices if that is part of the deal. This is an investment in your future.

• Further studies in another field are always a good idea; specialized translation—where a lot of the action is—is impossible unless you take the time to acquire in-depth subject-matter knowledge in promising areas.

• Where to go? Business logic says set up someplace where your language and subject-matter skills will make you a rare-ish commodity, or demand is strong. Network with colleagues abroad and read the business section of the paper to see where deals are being done and projects launched by client industries that involve your language combinations. Give yourself at least three months to carve out a niche, and spend the time attending professional events (for businesspeople as well as linguists) in your area of specialization. Thanks to modern technology, you can always build up a clientele abroad and retain good customers when you return home, with regular follow-up visits back to their market to touch base.

One terrific thing about language skills is that they can be combined in an almost infinite variety of permutations, opening doors into all sorts of exciting activities. We wish you the best of luck as you explore them.

FA & WB

Q *I was very interested in what you had to say recently to the person who translated in Indiana and who wasn't earning very much. I currently live on the U.S. west coast, but would not want to raise my family here and am considering a move to the Great Plains—my original home.*

I have a presence on the Web and have already worked for some clients in the U.S. and Germany, but have only been in the business for about a year.

Do you think that if I were to move north it would affect my business at this point? I would think that if a person marketed him or herself well, where one lives wouldn't be that much of a problem—especially since most of the work I do is via the Internet. I think that having a degree from a well-known school would also be helpful in building a client base, no matter where you are. What is your opinion?

Big Sky

A Dear Big Sky,
We're glad you've given us the opportunity to revisit our reply to Injured in Indiana (page 145). Others, too, have e-mailed us, asking whether our comments were meant as a secret dig at them personally (the answer, in each case, is no).

We understand that it may sound paradoxical to sing the praises of locality in this age of globalization and interconnectivity. But our position has support from no less a management guru than Michael E. Porter of Harvard University.

Prosperity depends on productivity and productivity growth, and these are highest where there is a cluster, not isolated firms or industries. As defined by Porter, a cluster is a critical mass of companies in a particular field in a particular location, whether that is a country, state, region, or even a city.

Let's examine how this concept of clustering relates to the translation market.

A vast portion of the market is probably location-insensitive. Dominated by translation companies who are themselves under severe cost pressures, this is a world populated by translators typically selling their work at rates that may look attractive to someone just starting out as a translator, but are not—in our opinion—sustainable beyond the age of thirty-five or thereabouts. Thus if the translator is the sole or primary breadwinner for the family, a fee of thirty dollars per hour (gross) will be woefully inadequate and doom her to laboring under a crushing workload, struggling to make ends meet.

As this column never tires of pointing out, there are smaller segments of the translation market that are far more lucrative. Example? Press releases that must impress the target audience with style as well as substance. When performed for quality-conscious direct clients, such work can fetch far more than bulk jobs. Contact the authors directly for specific figures.

But can you tap into the high-priced end of the translation market from anywhere?

One of us sat down and diagrammed how a half-dozen of his most lucrative clients came to him. In all but one of these cases, location played a critical role. Clients were acquired through (local) direct-mail advertising, referrals from (local) busy colleagues, word of mouth from (local) happy clients, or a combination of factors. In only one case was a client acquired through attendance at a professional seminar in another country.

Our conclusion? It is not enough to know one or two colleagues nearby who also target the high-price segment and can give you referrals and pointers about the market; it is not enough to have one or two clients nearby who are relatively price-insensitive and will gladly recommend you. For your weblet of contacts to grow and snowball into a strong network, there has to be a critical mass of both factors.

We believe it will be far more difficult to tap into a higher-end market if you are not physically present—if not all the time, at least at regular intervals—in such a cluster. Fortunately this is not all that difficult to organize!

FA & WB

FREE TRIAL OFFER

Q *I have ten years of experience in English/French to Spanish translation. A year ago I began reading two international magazines, both with an English (original) and a Spanish (translated) version. I have found and collected a lot of serious mistakes in the translated editions, which is surprising given these magazines' worldwide reputations.*

Question: should I contact the editors to demonstrate that I would be able to do a better translation/quality checking job? Is this an acceptable way of getting translation assignments? If so, who should I contact (I have thought of the International Editions Manager)?

Bad Tidings, Me?

A Dear Bad,
Taking the time to correct a published translation is an excellent way to make contact with a potential client. But only on five conditions:
1. Note your remarks simply yet stylishly in the potential client's language.

One of the reasons your target publications goofed in the first place is that editors were unable to judge what they were getting in Spanish. To bring your message home, you'll need flawless English, zero typos.
2. Assume from the start that the publishers really are committed to producing a top-quality magazine. Your letter should reflect this—no berating, no finger-wagging and stridency: you enjoy their magazine, and are confident they will seek a solution once you've let them know there is a problem.

3. Leave scope for face-saving.

The mistakes you've identified are almost certain to embarrass someone, somewhere, who may in return seek to discredit your remarks. That's life. One way to keep the temperature down and discussion constructive is to give this person some psychological room. Anybody can make a mistake.

Concretely, mention in your letter a few factors that may have contributed to the problems, e.g., "I realize publishers work to extremely tight deadlines, which may explain why 'scalpel' was rendered 'cell-phone' in your March issue." Suggest how you would deal with these. If you win the contract, you'll have to.

4. That said, slipshod suppliers are usually good at playing the "well, it's all so subjective" game, so be sure to include some specific examples they cannot wriggle out of. Your potential client needs this sort of ammunition.

5. If you decide to pitch your services straight away (rather than wait for the magazines to come back to you with an offer), explain how your expertise might fit in alongside that of the current supplier—as reviser or checker, for example.

There is plenty of time for you to move to the fore once the publishers have seen how efficient you are, and how pleasant you are to work with.

Who to contact? We'd advise starting fairly near the top, with the editor of the international edition. These people want their magazines to work (see 2), and will probably be grateful that you've taken the time to let them know something is amiss.

FA & WB

TESTIMONIALS

Q *Are anonymous testimonials worth using? And at what point in a business relationship can a translator ask a client for a testimonial?*

Man in Black

A Dear Man,
What a coincidence. Karen Klein wrote a column in BusinessWeek on this very subject ("Happy Clients Spread the Love" www.businessweek.com/smallbiz/content/oct2005/sb20051028_460132.htm).

We'd add simply that you should consult businesses in your country to get a feel for what will work. Certain practices that demonstrate energy and entrepreneurship in one place are perceived as pushy and overbearing in others.

We stand by our comments as quoted in Klein's column. There is so much churn in so many translation markets that even listing client companies can be laughable to those in the know.

It can also land you in hot water. We recently phoned a few businesses whose names appear on various translation agency sites in the "satisfied clients" list. None of the client companies had any recollection of ever having worked with these agencies, and all were seriously unhappy to find their names in print.

So whatever you do, remember to keep it transparent and focused.

If a named individual can't or won't testify on your behalf, consider writing up a short paragraph about a specific successful project you did, with enough detail to attract clients in your target audience even if you don't name names. Here's a good example: www.lingualegal.com/flexible.html.

FA & WB

SIGNED WORK & PRO BONO

Q *I'm with you on the signed work crusade (pages 49-50), and confident enough in my work to believe that a portfolio of signed pieces will help me win clients. But the agencies I work with don't like the idea. I understand their point of view. Have you got any arguments to bring them around?*

Dotted Line

A Dear Line,

There is no better promotional material than an outstanding piece of signed translation, so it is worth investing some time and energy to pull this together.

Despite some tentative interest a few years back, we know of no agencies that run a double by-line featuring translator names, so if you have no direct clients perhaps you'd be better off trying a different tack altogether.

One win/win option is to volunteer to translate a brochure or other document for a charity or cause you support. Start with some big players, but don't neglect the more obscure outfits—groups like Riders for Health [www.riders.org/us/about.aspx] and the Kakapo Recovery Programme have a lot going for them, and may be more receptive to your generous offer.

Meticulous planning is essential to keep your project on track:

- Contact the charity's head office to propose your services.
- If they decide to go ahead, get an agreement in writing: your services are free, but your name appears in the credits. To focus their attention (and yours), specify the print date or the date your text goes live on their web site. Note in writing—very important, this—that you have full control of text production, including revision and proofreading.
- Ride close herd on the project (excellent practice for assignments with your paying clients). Remember, the buck stops with you. This can be both exhilarating and a little scary for translators who have always had an agency interface.
- Have the charity acknowledge your role in a testimonial-style letter on their letterhead (e.g., "Jackson Throgmeyer's German brochure was sent to 15,000 potential supporters of our Sea Turtle Survival League, and the response has been overwhelming"). You draft the letter, especially if your contacts are not native speakers of your target language and have a limited translation budget; it goes in your portfolio opposite the brochure.
- If your translation appears in paper form, be sure to collect a few dozen copies of the original print run. You will want to be able to distribute these to prospects, and originals look better than photocopies.

Good luck, and report back!

FA & WB

Q *I'm in the process of getting back into the market after a parental leave. To build up a portfolio and get my name out and about, I followed your past advice by contacting a British charity for a pro bono project.*

They seemed very organized and told me they were used to working with volunteer translators, whom they "pay" with an acknowledgement in credits: "Many thanks to our translation volunteers (list of names)."

That is exactly what I wanted, so I translated a number of short texts for their website.

Imagine my surprise when I read the rest of their site in my language: a catastrophe! It is full of embarrassing errors that only a non-native speaker could make. And now my name is up there, but in the general acknowledgements, not on my own work.

I'm scared this might scare potential clients away. I realize it is my fault, as I should have checked the charity's existing text first. But what should I do now?

Do Gooder Done Wrong

Dear Do,

Good for you for getting the ball rolling so proactively, but—ah, hindsight!

Start by making screen captures of the pages you've translated, including the charity's logo and URL if possible. Keep these in an easy-to-send format for potential clients (with a header or written indication that you produced these translations "which are selected parts of XXX's website"). That way you've still got an addition to your portfolio—a sample demonstrating your translating and writing style—even as you distance yourself from the rest.

Next, explain to the charity why your name cannot be used as they propose. You can point out that it's not their fault (say this, even if it obviously is): note that one or more of their well-meaning multilingual fans tried his/her hardest, but the result is unprofessional and is not something that you can afford to have your name associated with. Depending on how they react, you might mention that the current texts reflect poorly on them, too.

Indicate that there are two options: either the charity moves your name up to the pages you've translated or they remove it entirely (no hard feelings).

Assuming the poorly-translated text does not run into thousands and thousands of words, you might offer to fix the rest, in which case your name would appear alone in the credits for your language version. In this case, they should delete your name from the credits for the time it takes to do this, of course.

If you (and they) are feeling magnanimous, the new credits might name the poor translators, too, but in parentheses "(with contributions from A, B and C)."

FA & WB

MOVING UP A GEAR

I'm a Bulgarian translator, now living in France, with three small children. So far, freelance work (F>B) has trickled in without me making too much effort. Nothing too well paid or interesting, but a steady stream nonetheless.

However starting in September all three of my kids will be in school, and I think the time has come to move up a gear. Basically, I want to leave the poorly paid, rush work to newcomers to the profession, and, building on my experience and skills, seek out and serve better-paying, higher quality clients—direct if possible. I'm sure they are out there. What I'm not sure of is where, or how to get them to take me seriously. Any marketing tips?

Diving Back In

A Dear Diving,
You've picked a good time—not just on the home front, with your kids in school, but also on international markets. Eastern Europe is clearly developing closer ties to the West, which is where you, the interface person, come in.

If past openings to the east are anything to go by, there will be plenty of competition among translation providers as barriers fall. You will not be able to compete on price with suppliers back in Sofia, so don't even try. Instead, position yourself in the quality segment of the market, using the suggestions below to help get your bearings:

1. Subscribe to at least two business magazines or newspapers: one Bulgarian, one French. General newsmagazines will not do the trick; you must be reading what your potential clients read in their offices every day. Elections in the offing? Track what the bankers and investment specialists say; how will this affect business? Who is hiring/expanding/divesting?

2. Identify promising sectors: spend 30-45 minutes a day scanning the wires and business press for mention of Bulgaria and neighboring markets. Nothing on Bulgaria today? Use the time to read up on French companies now operating in the country or planning to do so, and Bulgarian firms seeking contacts abroad. Study the industries and markets they deal in, and attend a few trade shows or chamber of commerce events (in France, for a start). Translators are still far far too thin on the ground at such events—and often ill at ease in simply talking with their fellow businesspeople. Practice makes perfect: attending such meetings, first as a spectator, and only later to market your skills, is an excellent way to acquire a feel for the business world. See our advice to Awaiting Big Break (page 130).

True, the French>Bulgarian market may seem small compared to, say, French>English. Yet a quick poll of expert contacts in Paris and London reveals that there are also very few names circulating—the case for many minority languages. These same colleagues indicate that they would welcome reliable names to pass on to their own customers should your language combination come up. Get out to translator events and link up with them!

No doubt about it: meeting people, meeting people and meeting people are the three top priorities when you don't have enough (lucrative) work. Over to you!

FA & WB

Q*I've always thought of myself as a fairly creative chap. However, in the not-unlikely event that I don't get a record deal in the near future, it looks like I'll have to continue making my living from translation.*

I've spent the last six years translating stockmarket-related texts, which has been fairly enjoyable, and also fairly lucrative.

The thing is, I'm now getting a little tired of writing "economic slowdown" twenty times a day, and would like to do something a bit more creatively challenging, and better paid, in corporate communications.

What should I do? Cold-call some communications departments of large companies, or some communications agencies, in the hope that they'll throw me the odd press release or brochure? Or is there a better way?

DJ Rumpus

ADear DJ,

Have you considered annual reports? You already have a leg up on the competition because of your experience in translating investment advice. Don't worry about cold calls; yours will be toasty—after all, you know your target companies inside out (or should do, at this point).

Before pitching your services, we suggest you build a few bridges: when you translate your next brokerage report, phone the company profiled for input on job titles, names of strategic programs and the like. Ask for corporate communications or investor relations teams—they are there to provide precisely this information. You will of course not be able to tell them who commissioned the report you are translating (highly confidential, etc.; don't worry, they know all about this), but if you play your cards right you will have ample opportunity to impress them with your linguistic expertise and knowledge of their business.

These are the same people who hire translators for press releases, the CEO's speech, pep talks to the masses and the like. Perhaps even advertising copy. Get the picture?

Are you an expatriate? If so, you might zero in on companies with headquarters in your geographical market (convenient for you to visit and make a sales pitch) but listed on a stock exchange in the country of your target language. For example, many French and German tech companies have opted for a NASDAQ listing in the hopes of attracting more US investors.

You mention another good idea, which is to critique (unsolicited and for free) existing communications such as Web sites or brochures. This can be a very effective way to win business. It doesn't have to be discreet, either: "Wordsleuth" Marc Alan Wilson, a copywriter in Utah, does this very cleverly on his website, replete with a "ransom request" typeface and fingerprints. www.wordsleuth.com/html/copywriting_crimes.html. (His testimonials are also top-notch.)

FA & WB

Q*Is it worthwhile to subscribe to expensive trade journals in one's industry as a way of being able to say "I saw in [name of magazine] that you were involved in such and such a deal" to personalize a mailing and show that one has done one's homework?*

Eye on Budget

ADear Eye,
Anything that generates personal hooks to get the flow flowing is worth it, but perhaps you could tell us first how expensive "expensive" is (€700? €1000? €2000? More?) and how you know your clients actually read the publication(s) in question.

Do you see copies lying around their offices? Are these well thumbed? Do clients themselves regularly refer to articles in these titles?

As an alternative, you might try to benefit from the free copies always available at top-level professional conferences—where the registration fee may exceed €700, but the face time with key senior players can generate higher returns.

FA & WB

HARD TIMES

Q*I'm a freelance French-English financial translator, and I'm worried about the future. I do a lot of work for brokerage firms, and have been feeling the pinch recently. I know volumes are bound to fall during this kind of bear market, given that analysts don't feel quite as clever as they did in the boom times. But what happens if most of the analysts get fired? Also, what happens if French banks merge, focus cost-cutting efforts on their brokerage units, and turf out even more analysts, along with significant numbers of in-house translators who then join the hunt for freelance work?*

I like to think that good translators will always find work, and that I'm one of them, but we all know what a slump in demand and a surge in supply means for prices. Maybe it's time to bail out altogether—I hear that there's a serious shortage of plumbers in the UK. Am I being over-pessimistic?

Buffeted

A Dear Buffeted,
Over-pessimistic? No, you are far too optimistic, sir! For if past patterns hold, many of those unemployed securities analysts will set up as translators themselves while waiting for markets to recover. And don't kid yourself: as experienced power lunchers, these guys will find it far easier to sign up new clients than your average people-shy translator. Unlike many money-shy linguists, they will also have used the last bull market to negotiate higher pay for their services and thus have a nest-egg to fall back on. If you do nothing else, keep this in mind next time the Dow Jones heads up, and raise your rates.

But not to worry, most of these out-of-work analysts lack the language skills, commitment and stamina needed to make a dent in the market beyond the very short term.

Ah, but your query concerns the short term, doesn't it?

Well, we assume you already track developments on financial markets in the daily business press. Now is the time to cash in on your hard work: even if investment reports have made up your bread and butter to date, step back and look at the big picture.

Draw up a list of issues set to pose particular challenges to the banks and brokerages in your client portfolio. Note publications that will soon be required of corporations discussed in the reports you now translate, paying special attention to international regulatory issues and reporting obligations, since these require client action regardless of the state of the market (e.g., IFRS, executive compensation, social responsibility reporting and corporate governance).

Identify the most promising, perhaps an area where you have good contacts—say, a particularly knowledgeable analyst whose work you've already translated (and who is unlikely to get laid off herself). Read the background materials and directives. Attend industry events to ask questions of the experts, subtly positioning yourself as that articulate well-dressed British translator who spoke so knowledgably about hedge funds over drinks at the Europlace luncheon. You get the picture.

Boom or bust, demand for financial translation is always there. The trick is to identify clients' needs before they do, invest the time to become a genuine expert, and let buyers know you are available. At a price.

FA & WB

Q *When I fled office politics to become a translator, I was happy to be working alone at last. I was fortunate that I did not have to work my way up through a patchwork of poorly paid jobs. Instead, I got a steady stream of assignments from a machine tool manufacturer.*

This worked well enough for eleven years. I've never earned great riches but have always been able to provide for myself and my family in our little neck of the woods. Recently, however, my primary client, who accounts for nearly all my income, has informed me they are going out of business. I am at a loss as to what to do. The idea of knocking on doors and asking for business hat in hand terrifies me. Do you have any suggestions?

In the Woodwork

A Dear Woody,
This may sound cruel but the hole you are in is one you dug for yourself. Here is what you did eleven years ago:

You escaped the sharks in the office pool, you got off the greasy pole and stepped out of the rat race. Fine. But at the same time, you placed most of your eggs in the basket of your no. 1 client, and now the chickens have come home to roost.

Do not *ever* become that dependent on a single client again. Giving more than twenty per cent of your time to any one buyer is risky, giving more than forty per cent to one is courting disaster.

Translators are seldom extroverted go-getters. However, in your present situation you don't have much choice: you have got to start marketing yourself actively. You can do this by networking with colleagues and attending industry events to find clients who will value your skills.

If all you need is a push, consider yourself pushed. And cheer up: you probably know an awful lot about machine tools by now, and we assume you already follow the specialist press in this field. Why not start by contacting advertisers and companies mentioned in articles who might need your language combination(s)? Be sure to emphasize your years of experience.

FA & WB

Q *I have noticed that little attention seems to be paid (including in professional publications) to the effects of the weakening US economy on the translation industry, and specifically on free-lance translators. I have observed a marked decline in free-lance work into US English, especially in the past several months. How should this be gauged, and what should a veteran freelancer be doing under such circumstances aside from the proverbial distribution of resumes, reminders, etc.??*

I would assume that notification of lowering of prices would be a rather delicate issue, especially if agencies have not proposed this in the past and are happy with the translator's work, since it would suggest that the translator is not very busy.

I should add that some agencies have told me that they too have noticed that things have been "quieter" lately, though this is little consolation to a freelancer who depends on them for ongoing work.

Yankee Doodle

P.S. My languages are Spanish, French, Italian, Russian and Hebrew. I translate contracts, academic texts, business correspondence, journalism, insurance and the like, not to mention the usual certificates, certificates and certificates (plus transcripts).

A Dear Doodle,
Let's take it from the bottom up, since in our opinion your P.S. holds one key to the slump in your business.

In translation, less is often more. Not quality, of course, but language combinations and fields of expertise. Economic turmoil notwithstanding, with five source languages and a half-dozen very broad subjects you seem to be stretching yourself pretty thin. How can anybody track issues and usage in all of these? Impossible, at least not to the depth that premium clients demand.

We suggest you trim your language list, boost your reading in the one or two languages you decide to focus on, identify subjects where demand is rising or set to rise, and start developing the in-depth knowledge you need to stake out your share of the market. See, too, our recommendations to the pergola man (page 85).

As for spontaneously offering to lower your prices to agency contacts—no, this is not a good idea. In fact, it's a terrible idea. Like premium direct clients, serious agencies base translator selection on candidates' expertise and writing skills. Assuming fire-sale rates will win business sends out the wrong message altogether.

As for cutting prices to appeal to bottom-feeders—well, it's an unusual business strategy, but we can't get our heads around it as this column goes to press. Perhaps someone could explain?

FA & WB

Q *I am a financial translator working from French to Spanish. You may not be aware of the state of the Spanish market these days, but my experience is that competition has driven most work into the arms of translators charging rock-bottom rates in Latin America and Spain, many of them working illegally. Things are so bad that I've almost decided to close down my business, because I refuse to work at such rates. I can't afford to.*

I've been sending CVs to stockbrokers, banks and financial institutions since last December, but they never seem to reach the right person. Have you got any tips or is my language combination doomed?

Last Act

A Dear Act,
If you are genuinely specialized, don't despair. There is a market for your services—but not one you can break into through mailings alone. To get a foot in the door, you need some face time or at the very least online interaction where you can display your knowledge and skills to potential clients (who may include fellow translators; ponder Unhappy Buyer's preference for referrals on pages 214-215).

• Step up your networking with colleagues, perhaps by joining a specialized elist (e.g., the financial translators' forum) where you can provide reliable answers to fellow translators' questions. Be sure to include your full contact details as a signature in each message. General "global translator marketplace" lists will not do the trick; despite the jolly atmosphere, they are populated by too many amateurs.

• Read the publications your potential clients read; there is no better way to stay on top of the issues that interest them and identify topics where they need, or will need, your expert input. Investing time here will equip you to leap into the breach if a make-or-break situation arises. Think Antonello Palombi, the stand-in tenor who swept to stardom at La Scala when the star stomped out in a huff.

• Attend industry events where you can put into practice the famous glossary ploy and free trial offer. If this means traveling to a large town or city, do it. You can cut costs by making day trips only or by staying with friends.

• Don't get obsessed with cheap providers abroad. The clients you want are not price-driven; they value expertise and the more sensitive their texts, the more hand-holding they will want, making proximity a definite plus. Let's repeat that: good clients do not buy translations from anonymous providers over the internet. But to link up with them, you yourself will have to have a business plan that goes well beyond sending out CVs.

FA & WB

161

Q *This is truly depressing. I had lined up a big job with a translation company two weeks ago. I gave them a discount because of its size (reluctantly). So Friday, after 12 days of waiting, they write to tell me that the client changed the deadline and it's shorter, so now I agree to take roughly half the job. Not ideal, but even half represents $5,000-6,000, so that's fine, since work is very slow. They ask me to wait until they send the job ticket in a day. I get a call the next morning from the translation company owner telling me that the client had gone ahead and used Google to translate the documents (over 200 pages of technical material).*

End result: I'm out desperately needed cash, the translation company is out their profit on the job, and the customer gets crap.

However, I cannot compete with free. This sucks.

The translation companies have pushed for automation for the past 15 years. This is the monster they have created by pushing automation. I wonder how many clients are going to simply use Google? Hey, it's free! It's instant! It's automatic!

Disgusted

A Dear Disgusted,
The medium-term solution we see for you is to take a marketing course—or two or three—and get yourself some direct clients.

If not, you've outsourced your marketing by default and must live with the consequences. The Supremes got this right: whenever an essential person, however sizzling, "just keeps [you] haaanging on", the only way to take control of your life is to get rid of them and move on.

It clashes with our generally upbeat approach, but here's another thought: what if the agency placed the job with somebody else and simply fobbed you off with the Google story?

The good news is that an unsatisfactory client base is something you can fix, with dedication and effort.

Look again at precisely what you are selling (or not yet selling) and identify what sets you apart from the competition. That's what you should be promoting. And if your perceived competition includes automated translation systems like Google, it's high time to reposition yourself.

Moving right along, should a choice between free computer-generated translation and your own expert services ever come up again (in your contacts with your future direct clients, for example), here are two useful arguments:
• Naïve consumers generally don't realize it, but both source texts and computer-generated translations produced by Google become part of the Google Translate database: that is one of the conditions for using the system.

This alone rules out the use of Google Translate by professionals and businesses with even remotely confidential documents.

• Running 200 pages through Google Translate is not free. It means cutting and pasting vast numbers of 500-word segments. Which costs somebody's time for—as you point out—unreliable output.

Automation the enemy? Well, there's automation and automation.

True, it is in bulk buyers' and sellers' interest to commoditize translation, and pretend that the humans involved are interchangeable. Some hint or state explicitly that automation allows them to do this. And for certain bulk products—where nuance and accuracy are not all that important, but speed is—they may even have a point.

But is this necessarily an agency vs. freelance issue?

After all, plenty of bulk freelancers have headed down the commoditization road as well. It starts as soon as you pitch on the basis of price rather than expertise.

Surely the challenge is to harness useful automation options to do the grunt work (think consistency, for example), and invest the time you save to hone other, exclusively human translation skills, of which there are many. That plus more marketing and time logged at the client-education front is the way to go.

FA & WB

DIFFERENT APPROACHES

Q*I worked as a professional translator (and enjoyed it very much) before moving into IT in a salaried position, but am now planning a return to translation and want to position myself properly.*

You've often emphasized the importance of networking. Since I am not that good at networking, I'm thinking of employing a person to help me. Is this a good idea? If so, what profile should I be looking for?

Back Again

A Dear Back,
We are in favor of translators focusing on what they do well, hiring other professionals as needed (e.g., a professional accountant, a professional IT technician, a designer for their business cards, etc.). And it's true that some of the best translators we know are more at ease with words on the page than

with the humans across the desk or on the other end of the phone. Which means employing someone to help market your services can be a good idea (1) if you find the right person and (2) if the numbers add up.

But before getting into buying marketing services, remember that enthusiastic word-of-mouth referrals by satisfied clients amount to the same thing—and they're free! By providing outstanding service to client A, you set the stage for them passing your name on to client B, then C, then D.

If you do decide to purchase marketing services, consider whether you are looking for an individual or an organization. Are there business networks or business service providers in your city or elsewhere that could usefully list your services in the palette they offer? Your local chamber of commerce might have some ideas and/or training courses that could help you to link up with likely candidates.

If you are thinking of an individual agent, will s/he be representing you alone or you and several competitors in the same market? This must be clear from the start. To give your rep a running chance of pitching your services successfully, you must have an offer that sets you well apart from the competition. We don't see this working if you are not targeting the top end of the market.

Money-wise, work out very clearly what the agent/PR person's remuneration will be (percentage of sales won is safer than a retainer) and decide how many hours a month s/he will be working for you. Again, for this set-up to work, you will probably have to be pitching to the upper end of the market—highly specialized content or very well-written work, which by definition is not fungible.

Note that in an ideal world, a savvy translation agency might also be your "agent"—a terrific idea in theory (see "translator more at ease with words on page" above). But this ain't gonna work with agencies that view translation as a commodity, and as long as translators themselves share this misconception. When was the last time you heard a specialized translator tell a potential client "fine, talk to my agent"?

FA & WB

Q *I have read your previously published comments about sharing glossaries with clients and would like to know your opinion about sharing glossaries with prospects (i.e., potential clients).*

After 17 years as a freelancer doing many different types of legal & business documents for (mostly) agencies, I have become specialised in translating certain very specific types of legal documents for a specific area within finance, an area in which France is the European leader. These documents require a very decent level in both legal and finance and a solid knowledge of this sub-specialty within finance.

Until now, I have only translated these documents for one large American law firm in Paris and they are very happy with my work.

I would now like to translate these same types of documents for other Paris law firms specialised in this field, but am not sure what approach would be most effective.

I have developed a highly specific glossary (including both legal & finance terms from this field) tailored to these law firms and am toying with the possibility of sending it to them, together with my business card.

I'd be grateful for your comments/suggestions.

Glossary Guy

A Dear Guy,
A regularly updated, highly technical glossary shows you know your stuff and are constantly honing your skills—a very good message for demanding clients.

In fact, at least part of its commercial value lies in using it as a pretext for contacting prospects to "help you complete entry A, B or C." (In exchange you can offer the prospect a copy, for example). So yes, go for it!

Another option: display entries for a few letters of the alphabet on your website, alongside your pitch in this particular field. Those in the know will appreciate your insights and feel all the more secure in turning to you for highly specialized (and highly paid) work.

A glossary is just the starting point for premium translation, but spadework at this level is a good sign of commitment to the field.

FA & WB

Q *I have French-English & German-English dictionaries for archaeologists on my web site. They are works in progress in that I'm still editing heavily, but they provide full context as well as definitions, and I think it's relatively clear where I'm headed. Eventually I'll use an automatic translation program that searches and replaces whole sentences rather than individual words.*

But before I pour more money into this endeavor and begin heavy marketing in my fields (Egyptology & archaeology), I'm having a difficult time getting any kind of feedback—even from those who constantly bemoan the fact that many important books aren't being translated into English.

I would appreciate it if you could give me a ballpark estimate of the time it takes to translate a book (let's say 300 pgs) and how much a translator is paid to translate a whole book in Egyptology, for example. I think with my automatic translator I'll be able to cut down the translating time by several hundred percent.

I also thought my existing dictionaries might be helpful to translators in general, since archaeology covers vocabulary from art & architecture to philosophy & religion. I would appreciate it if you would take a look at my site and give me any suggestions or criticism [www.archaeologicalresource.com].

A Crazy Dreamer?

Dear Dreamer,

Fire Ant & Worker Bee think crazy dreamers have a lot going for them, and feel your focus on specialization is right on target. We are also reassured to hear that you specialize in archaeology and not math, since a reduction of several hundred percent would get you into negative figures.

A quick review: for a project to be viable, there must be existing or potential demand. You are banking on the latter, assuming demand will materialize (presumably from the moaners) once the price comes down. You are also confident that some form of automated translation, integrating terminology from your glossaries, will allow you to produce smooth translations of specialized books in record time.

We see at least three flies in the ointment here.

First, there is no way machine translation or translation memory (your speed factor) will, on their own, produce a stylish, seamless translation of a book or academic paper. Automatic word/phrase substitution can be helpful in some cases if writers agree to use controlled language when writing. Authors of books and academic papers don't and won't, as far as we can see.

Second, whatever time you save by slotting in expressions is nothing compared to the hundreds (yes, hundreds) of hours you will need for actually translating, revising and editing.

Third, book translation already pays lamentably little. Academic work is not particularly lucrative either. If your plan calls for driving prices even lower, you are asking for trouble (see revision time above).

But what to do with all those glossaries of yours?

Well, first tighten them up a little. We skimmed through the letter A only, but did notice a number of terms that don't really belong in a specialized dictionary.

You can then use them as a marketing tool—a means of establishing and/or consolidating your reputation with buyers of premium translation in your fields. Observers tell us many buyers in specialized areas have withdrawn from the translation market altogether, burned once too often by generalist suppliers. If they discover that expert talent is available, they might re-emerge.

Consider making the glossaries available free on your site and soliciting feedback, or using them as a hook for contacting high-profile experts in your specialisms—the very people who might be in need of your skills.

In short, make yourself the translator discriminating buyers in your fields automatically contact when they want a top-quality job. And adjust your prices accordingly. Good luck!

FA & WB

Q *I enjoy your column and will launch a marketing campaign at some point. But that will cost money. And with the recession, my business is very slow so I prefer not to spend anything until I get some orders coming in. Do you have any advice for a translator with zero budget?*

Penniless

A Dear Hard Times,
Plant a Victory Garden to reduce your grocery bills? Although even there you'll need some seed money.

Letters like yours are surprising for at least two reasons.

First, you seem to have missed what this column is all about. A full 50% of our tips require no money, just time, energy and initiative. If you have time on your hands, we urge you to read and ponder other queries in this book, or consult them online (free!). Please note that even the tips are pointless if you lack the requisite skills in writing and translation.

Secondly, we are writing for people who see translation as a business, not a pastime. Business Admin 101 teaches us that when business is booming, you should be investing in it (and yourself) and building up a buffer. When times are difficult and work more sparse, you should put the lull to work: get out and network more aggressively with potential clients, take courses (there are lots of these to choose from) to hone your expertise, and upgrade your IT systems.

All of which costs time and money, you say? Of course. And we pointed out in one of our very first columns, you can't stick one toe in the water and expect the fish to bite. You've got to invest in bait and tackle. You, sir, appear to have retreated from the waterfront altogether. Perhaps that garden is your best option.

FA & WB

Q *Two years ago I used your techniques and caught my first direct client—a mid-size manufacturer in my region. Things were going great, but today I learned that my contact there is leaving at the end of the month. This is bad news, since (1) the company accounts for about 30% of my income and (2) he's a very pleasant person to work with. I'm concerned that the company will use his departure to switch to somebody cheaper. What can I do to remain in the loop?*

Baby Blue

A Dear Blue,

Don't despair: unless your man is heading into retirement or ill, chances are he's moving on to an even better position—which is your chance to expand your client portfolio. This is especially attractive in your case: when a single client accounts for more than 25% of your business, you're in risky territory.

But we suggest you start by consolidating your position at the first company.

• Phone the man set to move and refer (briefly) to a particularly successful project you worked on together. Tell him how much you enjoyed it; this sets the mood.

• Ask who your new contact in the company will be. Speak confidently and phrase it just like that. After all, you now know their products, organization and priorities, and things are going swimmingly—why ever should they change? (Why are translators so convinced that even good clients are driven solely by price?) Ask if you should contact this new person directly or if your soon-to-be ex-contact will be passing your details on.

• You might also ask if he can tell you where he's moving, keeping in mind that this may be confidential. If he does share the information, mention—with a smile—that you will start reading up on product X, Y and Z of theirs just in case. A handy reminder.

• Depending how the conversation goes, offer to translate his farewell message to former colleagues. Do this for free—he's a nice guy, sure, but is this above all an investment in his remembering you as he moves up the ladder Over There. And farewell messages are never very long.

• Call your new contact at the current client and say how much you are looking forward to working with him/her. Suggest a meeting—face time is always good.

An irresistible topic for most corporate contacts (and one far more effective than "I'd like to meet you face to face so you'll remember to throw work my way") is "I've got some ideas about how you might save money on your translation budget."

This does not mean that you are going to slash your prices or recommend cut-rate solutions. What you'll do is walk the new contact through some basic best practice points to ensure that you can continue to supply outstanding translations with no rush charges, no screw-ups as they move into print, no frazzled Friday freak-outs. Win/win!

FA & WB

Q *I have read your column and appreciated all your interesting answers.*
Here's my story: after streamlining and job-cutting at a company where I'd worked for thirty years, I decided to set up as a freelance marketing consultant. The job is interesting, and slowly but surely I began building up a clientele.

Through one of my international contacts I was asked to translate a trade magazine in the rubber and plastics sector from Italian into Spanish. (I'm a native Spanish speaker). I'd never given any thought to working as a translator before, but I find this job very rewarding. The magazine comes out twice a year. Now I'm looking for customers among Italian manufacturers of machinery for rubber and plastics with interests in Latin American or Spanish markets. I'm now prepared to invest some more time in the translation business, quietly, from home. It's a completely new world.

Bouncing Back

A Dear Bouncing,
Thanks for your comments—a reminder that practitioners entering the translation market later in life can grow their translation business organically out of a present/former career, building on specialist knowledge, writing skills, an existing network, and hard work.

FA & WB

7
Payment issues

Scoundrels and deadbeats aside, elusive quality issues are often the trigger for late, partial or no payment. The solution: transparency, forward planning and global vision, plus strict attention to detail.

SHORTCHANGED

Q *When is a translation agency legally entitled to refuse to pay for a job?*

Fight in Sight

A Dear Fight,

When the job delivered is not up to mutually agreed specifications—assessed, if necessary, by a neutral third party. Which is one reason why both you and your agency client have a vested interest in spelling out exactly what is expected at both ends before any assignment gets under way.

FA & WB

Q *I'm a freelance translator. Three months ago I accepted two jobs from an agency in France—the first time I'd worked with them.*

They seemed pleased with the work, but they have not yet paid my bill. Now the same agency has asked me to do some more work. I have completed the new texts but am loath to send them until I get confirmation that my earlier invoices have been paid. Would I be justified in withholding the work?

Getting Nervous

A Dear Nervous,

Is it any consolation to hear that many payment problems with agencies have far more to do with their home-grown mom & pop shop approach to doing business than evil intent? (Yes, we realize that that in itself is a depressing comment on the state of the translation industry.)

But we do sympathize. Better yet, we ran your query past an ex-numbers expert who once headed up an accounts payable department. Here is what he suggests:

1. Have a copy of your invoice handy, and give the agency a friendly phone call. Tell them you want to "check the status of my January invoice." That in itself should be enough to give them a gentle nudge.

2. You are more likely to avoid a round of buck-passing if you deal with a named contact. So ask the person on the phone: "Can I just make a note of who I'm speaking to in case I need to get back to you?"

3. If they stutter something about "not having received your invoice," respond pleasantly—even apologetically (practice beforehand if necessary)—"I wonder if I could seek your help in sorting this out? I'm currently working on another job for you, and I want get all the paperwork on this previous project sorted out so that I can be sure to get the present one back on time."

Keep in mind that you are more likely to get your money if you are friendly and courteous at all times. As our accountant friend says, people often mess up chasing debts because they get tense at the idea of money being overdue. So the bottom line here is definitely to keep cool.

That said, you are not a doormat.

If despite your good humor and constructive approach payment is not forthcoming, refuse further jobs from the agency and take a more aggressive tack. There is strength in numbers, and transparency is a useful weapon: consider posting a message on translator discussion lists to locate other translators who have had problems with this agency. And let translators' associations in the company's home country/region know.

Longer term, we think one of the most constructive initiatives that top-end translation companies/agencies might consider would be to draw up clear instructions on how to take deadbeat companies to court in different countries.* Compiling this information is beyond the means of many freelance translators. And surely it is in the interest of all quality suppliers to unmask operators with shady business practices.

FA & WB

*Years ago we also suggested as much to FIT, the International Federation of Translators. FIT-Europe has since followed up and the relevant information can be found at www.fit-europe.org under "Bad Payers project." Documents include the new EU Regulation establishing a European Small Claims Procedure, plus documents from Austria, Belgium, the Czech Republic, France, German, Israel, Italy, Poland, Spain, Switzerland, the UK and the US.

Q *Last summer I replied to an ad in a UK daily placed by a European translation company looking for freelancers specialized in finance. They emailed me a test piece and soon told me it was satisfactory and that I would be contacted. In September, there was a follow-up call from the European office to discuss terms, starting dates, ways of working, etc. I received a package of sample translations, documents, style sheets, etc. to study, along with a list of specialized dictionaries that were to be used impérativement—all quite hard to get hold of and very expensive, needless to say. I said I was ready to start on 1 October.*

Since I had heard nothing by the end of November I asked what was up and was told training new translators was taking a long time but work would come. In December, they said I would be contacted within the next few days, but now, well into the new year, the message is that I "may be contacted when the need arises."

Is this how things operate or am I just unlucky with this one? What if anything can I do? Apart from the totally unprofessional approach of the outfit concerned, it is no joke to invest money in this way.

Out on a Limb

A Dear Limb,
Yes, you were unlucky. The agency was unprofessional and you've been treated shabbily. It sounds to us as if they were bidding on a project that failed to materialize, and were trying to line up talent just in case.

The best thing to do is view this as a learning experience—a series of events that will help you develop the sixth sense you need to sort out the good guys from the fly-by-nights. You might also write them a letter stating your objections to their unethical ways, with a copy to your national translators' association.

That said, we advise you not dwell too much on this injustice. The good news is that you now have some excellent dictionaries to help develop your specialization in financial translation (a very lucrative niche, as you may know).

FA & WB

Q *Last spring I translated a 110-page insurance software manual from German into English for an agency in Austria and my bill was paid in full. But when I took on a separate job for the same agency over the summer, they paid late and I complained.*

Following my complaint, the agency announced they would be deducting about £60 from payment on the second job to offset errors in the previous (unrelated) assignment. They deducted the money but have not provided evidence of any errors.

They had no complaint about the second job.

I cannot help feeling that I am being "punished" for daring to complain about late payment, and that it is unjust to deduct payment from a previous job which had already been paid in full. I have requested payment but they refuse and I have had no further work from them. I plan to pursue this further with the [UK] Institute of Translation and Interpreting, of which I am a member. What do you say?

Shortchanged

A Dear Short,
The time to contest invoices is before payment, not after, so your client has clearly overstepped the line. But your investment in time, energy and money to recover the amount due is sure to run over £60, which may be what the agency is counting on (sly devils).

One option would be to chalk this up to experience, turn the page, and devote your time to more lucrative activities.

But we assume you are pursuing this for the principle, right? Good for you; read on.

There is strength in numbers, so your decision to contact your national translators' association is a wise first step. Fortunately, ITI offers members a legal help line. Call now. You will have to be able to document your claims with correspondence from the agency, etc., so start getting the paperwork in order.

Depending on the advice you get, ad hoc solutions include quietly severing your business relationship with the agency; volunteering your experience when other translators ask you about this outfit; or notifying the agency that, failing payment of the contested amount by date x, you will post details of the dispute on Internet translator forums.

FA & WB

Q *I recently did a financial translation for a new client (they found me on the ITI site and I was recommended by two colleagues). The document was highly specialised and was for a "prestigious" client. They had the job checked and told me that although they were happy with my financial terminology, they were not as happy with my French. They said that their checkers had spent three hours (!!) checking it (2500 words) and that they wanted me to reduce my invoice by 25%.*

I looked at the amendments, consulted two other French colleagues and we both came to the conclusion that most of the amendments were not justified (some were either wrong (!) or did not improve the text at all, some were just substituting one word for another which meant the same; apart from one sentence which was a bit awkward and which was possibly improved by the checkers, all the corrections were aimed at changing the style). So I explained this to them and told them that the reduction of 25% was not justified.

I have not received any reply yet.

However, this morning after a good night's sleep, I actually think that they are out of line. Depending on their reply I am thinking of reclaiming my work and preventing them from using my expertise. How do you think I could go about it? Is there any copyright rule that I could quote and would I need to ask them to sign an agreement not to use the translation?

Still Fuming

A Dear Fuming,
In the absence of payment of the agreed fee, the Institute of Translation & Interpreting's Standard Terms of Business, lodged with the UK Office of Fair Trading, make it clear who owns the translation—and that owner would appear to be you.

Yet in this case we would advise against "reclaiming" or litigation for the simple reason that it will cost you far too much in time, effort and money. There is a point at which a pursuit of justice may turn into a vendetta, and we're sure you do not want to be a latter-day Michael Kohlhaas. Instead keep your eye on the ball and seek a resolution through negotiation and compromise.

Concretely, this means that you retain the option of covering the client in customer service if it comes to that, i.e., accepting the 25% hit, however unfair it may seem. Depending on the agency's response, decide for yourself whether they are clueless low-bidders (in which case you won't want to work for them again and might have some interesting input should their name come up on translator forums) or trainable; in the latter case, view the complaint as a springboard for discussion leading to closer interaction, a means of "talking methods" with them and perhaps teaching them something in the process.

For the agency clearly does deserve a wake-up call. Three hours' revision for 2,500 words in a field as demanding as financial services is by no means excessive, especially for a "prestigious" client. Stylistic tweaking is notoriously time-consuming, (and of course a reviewer who introduces errors puts them on very shaky ground).

But keep in mind that for you, too, there is always a learning curve on first projects. Did the agency provide you with enough background information and examples of what they considered appropriate style? Next time be sure to ask for this.

Ultimately, each side must be prepared to invest time up front to ensure a good outcome for the client, but this sort of investment only makes sense if the customer offers potential for a pleasant and lucrative long-term business relationship.

FA & WB

Q *For the first time in 12 years as a freelance, an agency has gone into liquidation owing me money. I was alerted too late by a kind former employee who gave me the address of the liquidator and I duly sent in my claim (€4,500). But when I telephoned the lawyer to see if she'd received my dossier, I couldn't get hold of her, although I did speak to her before I put my claim in.*

Something tells me things are not looking too good.

Since the translation was for a large automotive company, can I assume that the agency got paid, or would it be safe to contact this company directly to see if they could help? Or would I be contravening some law if I did? I believe I am known to the end client's translation department because I have been translating their stuff for 12 years through this agency.

Revving Up

A Dear Revving,

We figure your money is gone and you can count yourself lucky if you see ten cents on the dollar.

You might check with a legal adviser, but we also figure that the rule about not poaching business is voided when the agency fails to uphold its end of the deal (payment for services rendered). So don't be shy about contacting the end customer, but do think carefully through the points you want to make before picking up the phone.

The aim is not to have a good moan about the deadbeats at Agency XYZ (although it will be satisfying to let the end client know that they have screwed their own suppliers around, since this may blacken the principals' reputation should they arise, Phoenix-like, from the ashes and start trading under another name).

The real point of your call is to leave the end client with your name and contact details for future work.

You can thus use a rueful "I'm checking up on XYZ; I'm afraid I'm out some money on their account for work I did for you" as a hook, but should move quickly on to a few comments on your indirect link to their department for over a decade—you might cite a few of the carmaker's current projects, to indicate in passing your familiarity with their products—and the fact that you are available for direct assignments.

Good luck!

FA & WB

LEARN FROM YOUR MISTAKES

Q *How come I never see an interpreter question in here? Anyway, here is mine. Last month, a businessman who had booked my services for three days called a week before the assignment. The conversation went more or less like this: "I wonder if I could ask your advice on a local question?"*

"Certainly."

"You know, I reserved a couple of rooms at Le Grand Hotel in your town for foreign participants in the seminar. Now they have decided they won't be coming after all. Do you think the hotel will give me a hard time if I cancel the reservations?"

"I don't think so—there is a major trade show next week, and I'm sure they'll be able to find other guests to take the rooms. Just tell them nicely; I'm sure they will understand."

"You are right, that's just what I'll do. Of course, without foreign participants I won't be needing an interpreter after all. I take it, then, that you will also be agreeable if I don't use you this time. Thank you very much for your help, and let's stay in touch."

When I reran the conversation in my mind afterward, I began to feel upset. Do you think I got taken advantage of?

Esprit d'Escalier in France

A Dear Esprit,
At the very least, your client was being disingenuous. Perhaps a hotel with fifty rooms or more can afford to be gracious about cancelling a few overnight stays—we can't really say, since hotel economics is not our field.

But you were being asked to forego not a small fraction but 100 percent of your revenue for the three days for which you had been contracted to work. That's a huge difference. Yet since you had agreed to his first question, it was difficult for you to assert your rights.

Two suggestions:

Be more wary in the future. For instance, in response to the first question, you could truthfully have said that you had no idea, depriving your counterpart of the advantage from his opening gambit.

It is also a good idea to write a clear cancellation policy into your contract. Cancellation policies employed by different interpreters run the gamut, from non-existent to payment in full regardless of how far in advance an assignment is canceled. Ultimately it is up to you to determine your terms of business, but a cancellation policy is one of the bedrock components you should have. It will strengthen your hand enormously: even if you decide that a situation warrants taking a conciliatory approach—perhaps because your client is genuinely financially strapped, or because there is guaranteed repeat business—it will be your choice, not theirs.

FA & WB

Q *I have a 4-year experience in translating from Korean into English, although my native language is Russian (I am Russian-Korean), but I translate into English because not many English-native speakers understand Korean and dare to translate from it into English.*

I have been doing very well so far and received recognition in Korea, where I live.

But recently I had a very unpleasant incident: one of the Korean translation agencies for which I have been working for over a year and who ranked me as the best translator in their company, asked me to translate the website of the most renowned hotel in Korea; they said they wanted me to do it since it was a really "big client."

Before I started, I visited several of American and Canadian hotels' web sites to learn the style and hotel expressions, and did pretty much of research. So I did my best in carrying out this project, but when the work was finished and sent to the hotel, a hotel person called the agency saying that they had an American journalist there who said my translation was bad. The Korean guy from the hotel admitted that he himself did not know whether my translation was good or bad, but as a matter of fact the American journalist said my English was "not perfect."

The agency (who has no experience in dealing with such problems) called me immediately and complained about my work. I said "Just send me a 'visual proof' that shows how bad my work is." When the requested "proof" came, I found that the hotel people (probably the journalist) had corrected only a tiny part of my translation, while over 90 percent of the translated text remained in its original state. I was really infuriated and said to my agency that my work was not corrected that much. But since the hotel people kept on complaining, the agency sent my work for proofreading to two Korean-Americans, who instead of "improving" my work spoiled it! They corrected the right expressions and sentences into wrong, placed commas where commas are not used, and the whole thing looked really bad! I was mad for the third time again!

Now, when I have repeatedly demonstrated to my agency that I was right and that my work was 90 percent perfect, they treat me as if I have betrayed them and spoiled their reputation. In addition, they had to spend extra money on proofreading (the agency does not usually use proofreaders because of high costs and send translation orders unproofread!).

I am highly recognized in the translation business in Korea (another my agency—a 100% American-owned company—praises me and gives me credit for my work) and I know that my hotel translation was high class, but the first agency refuses to listen to me (and I have quit it, actually). But I feel so much betrayed!

The most ridiculous thing is that another jerk (sorry for obscene word) has made a "final proofreading" of my work and his version was the one that was posted on the hotel's web site, and if you take a look at it—it is a total mess! What should I normally do in this situation? What would you do to prove that I had been unfairly treated?

Seething in Seoul

A Dear Seething,
Nice language combination you've got there, and your decision to use your relative rarity in selling your services makes good sense. We'll look into some of the trickier sides of that in a minute.

First, however, a word on dealing with complaints.

At some point in every translator's career, a client (or acquaintance of a client, or client of a client or spouse of a client) will criticize a text you've produced. How you react in the very first minutes on the phone or at the keyboard will set the tone for the rest of your relationship, so it is worth thinking about this in advance.

There are plenty of options—a meeting in person to discuss the project; a revision or rewrite; an apology and waiver of your fee or part of it if you are at fault; arbitration through a third party; or simply standing firm and writing off this particular client. But to get that far you've got to keep the temperature down and the atmosphere businesslike: losing your temper is unproductive and unprofessional—as is groveling and caving in, of course.

So... you were absolutely right to keep your cool and ask very precise questions about (1) who was challenging your text and (2) exactly what he/she said, and in what context ("it was bad" doesn't make the grade).

But surely everything would have been a lot easier if somebody had established up front (with the agency and/or end client) who was doing the revising, editing and proofing, including such, er, "details" as what the hotel thought they were getting and who was carrying the can.

Promotional texts like websites are high-wire acts, challenging even for an expert native speaker. Operating in this segment of the market without a safety net is crazy—everyone trundles along happily until the shit hits the fan (pardon the obscene expression) and the finger-pointing begins.

In this case the agency was clearly at fault for not assigning an editor at the very beginning; by the time they started frantically incorporating changes from Korean-Americans with dubious credentials it was probably a lost cause. Call us cynical, but we bet they've got the Q word scattered throughout their glossy brochure (as you say, the client is not in a position to judge what has been delivered).

But to protect your own reputation and build your business, you, too, should draw some conclusions. While your command of English is impressive, your letter includes examples of non-idiomatic usage that are jarring to a native speaker, which is probably what set the American journalist off.

You already have a highly professional approach to researching your jobs, you've got a dynamite language combination and your language skills are strong.

Why not use this incident to rethink the text types you deal in? If you want to work at the for-publication end of the market—and it sounds like there is demand in your market—either locate agencies that employ editors and proofreaders, or consider linking up with a freelance editor who will provide the fine-tuning that demanding clients require.

In short, use this as an opportunity to detach yourself from the clutches of slap-dash agencies like this one and go after your own direct clients. Direct clients often are more appreciative of high-quality translation work and also tend to provide more feedback and interactive support. It's harder work for you as a translator (you'll have to aim for 100% accuracy) but the rewards—not just financial, but also personal—are also greater.

FA & WB

179

Q*Our three-person agency (Spanish and Portuguese to English) specializes in medical texts, and we have found a handful of demanding clients prepared to pay good rates for material that is technically challenging. Work ranges from massive texts on clinical trials to a few sentences here and there; in general, we log assignments as they come in and bill weekly.*

Last month a major client challenged us on a slogan we'd devised for an advertising campaign. True, it was only five words (their argument), but the three of us spent well over an hour googling, discussing, and testing alternatives before submitting four options. An advertising agency would have charged them tens of thousands of dollars; we'd charged just $400. We made that argument, but they still refused. Comments?

We're Worth More

ADear WWM,
In our experience it is unusual for a longstanding, quality-driven client to balk at a bill like this, particularly with the explanation you've given. Was this perhaps a blip on the screen, an underling attempting to throw his weight around, a new bean-counter or boss weighing in?

In any case, rather than haggle, you can use it as an opportunity to revisit your billing practices and raise this client's awareness of just how lucky they are to have you on their side.

Concretely:

• Waive this job on your invoice. That's right: include it as a line item (date, reference number, etc.) but charge zero dollars. You might put this in italics or otherwise flag it as an exceptional occurrence.

• Enclose with your invoice a short memo to the company setting out your policy on hourly rates. The tone must be friendly and informative, not plaintive. They are not unfair bullies; instead, you are remiss for not having made the billing system clear.

Content-wise, rather than cite what a more expensive provider might charge, remind them what an hour of your time represents—not just that hour then and there, but the skills you have built up over years of honing your expertise in their field. That is what they are paying for; it is why your services cost far more than those of a beginner.

• Clients—even demanding, happy ones—don't spend much time thinking about translation other than when they need you. This is only natural. But it can lead them to underestimate how much effort you put into serving them. Regular reminders that you are at the wordface on their behalf will help redress the balance. So don't hesitate to copy them in when you see an article in a specialized publication in your language combination that they might otherwise miss. Likewise, get into the habit of listing in your invoice the services you provide that are not necessarily billed per se (phone queries on term X, Y or Z from their various departments, for example). Client education starts with raising awareness of your added value.

FA & WB

Q *A client in Canada who sent me a job at CDN$ 0.14 a word and confirmed I'd be paid quickly (but with no specific date) announced after delivery that the payment would come in stages, starting today. But this morning he said I'd have to wait a week; his client "is in a tight spot." Maybe I should have smelled a rat when I sent the CDN$ 1600 bill two weeks ago and his immediate reaction was "whoa, this is more than I thought!"*

What should I do now? Insist that he pay one-quarter of the amount right away? (He must have CDN$ 400 tucked away somewhere).

Squeezed

A Dear Squeezed,
You're right: a client who changes terms of payment mid-stream sets warning lights flashing. But so does translator who fails to lock in terms of payment in a way that rules out mid-stream changes.

Next time you quote for a job, specify standard terms & conditions right up front, including a specific date by which payment must be made. For sample terms & conditions, check your national translators' association site.

For your current standoff, insist on the one-quarter right now and specify dates for payment of the outstanding amount.

FA & WB

Q *A middle manager at one of my (direct) clients quit to join another company about six months ago. We'd had a cordial working relationship over three years and I was sorry to see him go. But the new job didn't work out, and he is now unemployed. I found this out last week when he phoned to ask if I could translate his CV. I was happy to do so, but on delivery discovered that he was not expecting to pay; he'd assumed this was simply a favor. Things got awkward and in the end I waived my fee. But I am unhappy; it was only two pages but took me more than four hours. Should I have insisted on payment?*

Career Helper

Dear Helper,

A professionally translated CV is so essential to the international jobseeker's kit that you can easily make a case for payment, but only if you do so up front, as you have discovered.

Next time, you can clarify this by mentioning, as soon as the subject comes up, how challenging it is to find exact equivalents for job titles and the like, and how this requires massive interaction with the client. This is where you slip in "which is why CV translations are so expensive." In the exchange that follows you set out your terms and conditions.

That's option 1.

In option 2, you view the situation as a marketing opportunity: if your man lands a new job with responsibility for outsourcing translations—or even talks you up to friends and colleagues—you will quickly recoup the four hours you've logged.

So we advise playing it by ear. If your contact's career is going places, consider it an investment. If he comes back every three months for a CV update, start charging the second or third time around.

And if you're offering a freebie and he insists on paying, have a few alternatives up your sleeve: rather than protest and accept a cut-rate fee under pressure (tacky), simply say that payment is out of the question but note, with a laugh, that you and your partner enjoy champagne/chocolate/orchids/[fill in blank] and see what shows up on the doorstep. Or give him the website of a charity you support and suggest that he make their day.

FA & WB

PAYING SUB-CONTRACTORS

Q *I am not satisfied with the work another translator has done for me. I am committed to paying him. How can I get him to do a decent job within his abilities without giving the impression I'm trying to wriggle out of paying him?*

No Cheapskate

Dear No,

A Set up a meeting with the translator and explain that an independent editor on the project has objected to his work. You took the heat for him at a meeting with the client, but Howard is furious and insists on a rewrite. So does the client. And so, on reflection, do you.

Keep his first and second drafts as examples for the next time you commission work from another translator. Show these to candidates up front, before the project gets under way; make it clear that exhibit A will not do and explain why. Your client insists on better work. So does your independent editor. And so, on reflection, do you.

FA & WB

Q *My partner and I run a small agency in Western Europe. Last month we subcontracted a technical translation to a prominent linguist who is also a tenured professor at a high-profile translation school.*

The results were disappointing.

This person also holds himself out as a financial specialist, which is why we turned to him in the first place. Yet the text he delivered showed gaping holes in subject-matter knowledge. A number of standard technical terms were clearly (mis)culled from a dictionary, while some basic accounting terms were rendered as word-for-word equivalents.

In my seven years in the business, I have seen any number of translator spats escalate into public brawls that do no good to our industry's image, and I don't want to get into a big argument.

But I don't think anybody—especially someone this prominent—should be allowed to get away with such a non-professional approach when it comes to actual translation. The experience also has me wondering what is going on behind the doors of translation schools.

My partner says we shouldn't waste time. He says we should pay the man's bill, chalk it up to experience and steer clear of academics in the future.

But there's a side of me that is itching to lay it on the line. What do you think?

Ivory Tower Blues

A Dear Blues,

First things first. Forget tenure, forget academic publications. The only "guarantee" of translation skills we know is asking to see something that the person has actually produced. Even then, s/he may have a bad day when tackling your job. Scary, isn't it?

This risk is why top-notch translators known for producing smooth, stylish text to deadline can often set their own prices. It is also why agencies get a well-deserved cut of the action when, through revision and editing, they make good any shortfalls.

To return to your academic, are you sure he produced the work himself? We have seen a number of cases recently in which busy academics subcontracted freelance work to promising students without telling anyone. While their confidence in the next generation is, er, touching, such behavior is also totally unethical and only underscores how out of touch these particular individuals are with quality issues at the discriminating end of the market—closed doors indeed!

The man's age might also a factor. FA & WB know several older translators who are inclined to dabble across far too wide a range of fields. Ten or twenty years ago, they might have got away with it; today, good clients are far more demanding.

In any case, you are right to avoid a public dispute, not least because most of the academics we know can run circles around businesspeople when it comes to politicking, building and exploiting power bases, and the like. They also tend to have a lot more time for this sort of stuff.

The issue here is feedback, which all good translators welcome (even as many tremble inwardly at what it might reveal).

As commissioners of the work, your company should definitely return a corrected copy of the academic's submission to him. Select a bright color for revision mode and print out the results so that the many changes are extremely visible. Enclose a brief cover letter explaining that returning finalized text to translators for information is your agency policy (and make it your policy, for all of the work you broker; good translators appreciate feedback). Emphasize, too, the premium you place on research, specialization and writing skills. We assume you already have a clause in your job order form that forbids further subcontracting.

If you have the time and energy, you might also consider writing an article on the importance of specialization and/or feedback for an academic or professional journal that Big Name is likely to read. Be sure to use some of his mistakes as (anonymous) illustrations.

And the next time you peruse one of his articles or books, enjoy the warm glow inside that comes from knowing you helped him back onto the straight and narrow.

FA & WB

Q *Last year I saw some excellent work by a translator in my language pair and made a point of getting his details. But when I actually passed some work on to him he did a mediocre job. I said as much in my feedback, and asked him to take another look at the text he had delivered; I knew he could do much much better, I wrote.*

Imagine my surprise when he blasted back a nastygram: sarcastic and superior, he cited the poor quality of the client's source text and spoke of sow's ears and silk purses.

The cherry on the cake was that he threatened me with a lawsuit if I did not pay him immediately.

I was taken aback, and prepared a sharp email to put him in his place, but left it to decant overnight and the next day phoned him instead. Imagine my surprise when he turned out to be shy, pleasant and very conciliatory—oh, and he fixed the text.

Surely there is a lesson here. Would you care to comment?

Peace on Earth

Dear Peace,

Your contact sounds like a visceral cave dweller: quick to take offense, convinced that clients (or perhaps even the world) are out to get him, and deep down under, exceedingly insecure.

His first missive was a variation on the classic "garbage in, garbage out" defense, which is often trotted out—always after the fact—by translators who suspect they've goofed. Should you meet these folks in person you will notice that many walk with a limp. This comes from self-inflicted bullet wounds in feet.

More interesting is the excellent result you got by phoning him. With that simple gesture, you cut short an escalating flame war that might have left you feeling you'd put him in his place ("and rightfully so!" harrumph harrumph) but would ultimately have been far less productive.

Many thanks for this reminder of how easily words on the page can be misinterpreted, especially among correspondents who have not met in person.

Conclusion? If you sense a conflict brewing, be it with a fellow translator or a client, pick up the telephone.

Even better, make an effort to meet up beforehand with both by regularly attending networking events.

FA & WB

BEST PRACTICE

Q *I've been contacted by a private bank in Switzerland to do the non-accounting portion of their annual report. They found me via my website, so I was not referred to them nor they to me. They appear to be a reputable company, but I've never taken on an assignment this big that didn't come through word of mouth. I don't want to look nervous but should I ask for part of the payment up front?*

Cover Up Front

A Dear Cover,
In our experience upfront payment is unusual (we are talking about an assignment of under €10,000, right?). But for a first-time client on a project of this size and importance, you should definitely get the details nailed down in writing—a good idea regardless of your initial contact.

Concretely, set out your process and offer a provisional figure, basing your estimate on the previous year's text if necessary. Be sure to include compulsory revision of proofs by yourself. You might also want to specify a lump sum covering X hours for interaction and changes to the source text, after which the meter starts running. You can indicate to your new client that you will update them on the state of play once half of this stock of hours is used up; this helps concentrate the mind at both ends.

Time-wise, calculate at least two full hours per 250-word page, and line up an outside reviser/editor if you don't already have one.

Since an annual report often generates additional work during the year, you might want to absorb some of the additional costs this first time around as a sweetener. But whatever you do, don't skimp on style and subject-matter research—annual reports are by definition a premium area, and a lucrative one at that. It's worth getting your foot in this door.

FA & WB

Q *I've just found a new client in Belgium and I'd like to know whether they're creditworthy. Where can I check this out?*

Solid

A Dear Solid,
Your reflex is excellent: it's always a good idea to verify the finances of a new customer before taking on work.

In addition to payment practices lists, the Belgian National Bank has just decided to make all (mandatory) annual accounts of Belgian companies available for free on the net.

Go to www.nbb.be/pub/home.htm?l=en. Click on "Central Balance Sheet Office" then "Consultation of annual accounts."

An esteemed colleague has looked up a few agencies on this site and the results are fascinating: some have a steady flow of profits and acceptable balance sheets. But one is on the verge of bankruptcy: €700,000 total assets for (-2K) in equity—yes, that's €2,000 negative capital. (Uh-oh).

Another translation group in the register has a complex web of companies, one of which reports equity of €687,000, down from an initial €30 million after accumulated losses of €29.3 million. "Somebody has deep pockets, but for how long ?... " says our man.

Other countries also provide this type of information for free.

The big challenge for translators may be to acquire the skills needed to interpret financial statements: why not look for a crash course, if only to gear up for a pitch to clients in the financial services industry?

FA & WB

Q *I've been in business for three years and recently had my first bad payer. The amount was under €1,000, but the incident was maddening and made me aware that I must get a system in place for checking out new agencies. I belong to a translator elist where participants occasionally swap information about the good guys and bad guys, but I'm looking for a one-stop shop. I've heard of specialized lists. Can you suggest one?*

On Their Case

A Dear Case,

Bad payers are nothing new—even in 1950, who was going to travel from Paris to Los Angeles and back to collect USD 1,000?—but with a large percentage of all translation business now being commissioned and delivered online, client references are more essential than ever.

You'll be happy to know that a number of translators have set up structures to pool payment information, starting with the visionary Karin Adamczyk in the 90s. As you read through the list below, keep in mind:

• Size *is* important—a 100-member list will, by definition, generate less information than one with over 1,000 members/contributors.

• Traffic is another indicator. Some lists are very active, averaging 10-15 messages a day. While most of these messages will not be of interest to any particular individual, that goes with the territory when you are on an international list, so don't complain. (Although volume alone means it may be worth setting up a filter to keep these messages separate from your regular email.)

• Most lists forbid recycling of information to outside readers: you get it from the horse's mouth or not at all. More power to them. Ultimately, a list is only as good as its moderators' attention to detail and scrupulous checking, including a willingness to axe hearsay ("I've never worked for them, but I recall somebody telling a guy I used to work with that...")

With those rules of thumb out of the way, here goes:

Online databases/resources

- Payment Practices

www.paymentpractices.net

This is the granddaddy of all payment issues lists, founded as a Yahoo Groups list in 1999 and ported to an online subscription-based database in June 2007. 6,997 outsourcers, 5,838 responses (direct experience) and 776 "comments" (non-payment-related information or summary of reports from other lists). Outsourcers receive two scores: the PP Reliability Score, an objective rating based on adherence to agreed payment terms, and the Translator Approval Score, a subjective indication of the rater's willingness to work for that outsourcer again. The annual subscription fee is $19.99/€14.99. A free 7-day trial is available, plus a discounted rate for ATA members.

- Blue Board - ProZ

www.proz.com/blueboard/

Reserved to paying members, although there is also a pay-per-view option ($0.50 per consultation). The big one: 15,522 total outsourcers, searchable by name or country, as of 30 August 2010. Not all listings have scores. The LWA ("likelihood of working" again) is a subjective 1-5 score that is entered by service provider. While there are many rules governing Blue Board postings, there are no rules or guidelines on how to rate an outsourcer, e.g., what constitutes a 1 or a 5.

- Hall of Fame & Shame - TranslatorsCafé

www.translatorscafe.com

Reserved to "moderators, Master members, other paying members and all active participants on the site." Free access on a case-to-case basis. 5,726 rating records for 1,600 agencies of a total 4,906 agency profiles and 2,281 rating records for service providers.

- "Nigerian check scam alerts"

www.paymentpractices.net/Scams.aspx

A free database of names and email addresses of assumed "Nigerian check scams" directed specifically at translators and interpreters.

- The Black and White List

Registration with go-translators obligatory. First month free.

www.gotranslators.com/Engl/Reports.php

896 entries. Searchable by name, country, email or URL. Provides reported contact for outsourcer but no information about why, when, or how often the outsourcer was reported.

- Payment Practices Tools In The Translation World
www.gotranslators.com/Engl/BPTools.php
Free list of websites/lists concerning payment practices.

Mailing Lists

- Untrustworthy Translation Agencies
www.translationdirectory.com/non-payers.htm
New entries are listed in the free monthly newsletter. The full list of 400+ outsourcers (as of 31 Aug 2010) can be purchased for €47.

- The TCR List (Translator Client Review List)
www.tcrlist.com
Archived messages can be listed by subject line or date and then viewed individually. Approx. 7300 total emails as of 30 August 2010.

- Translation Agency Payment Practices
http://groups.google.co.uk/group/transpayment
Online message group, 393 members, 347 total messages, about 5/month.

- Translation Agency Payment
finance.groups.yahoo.com/group/translationagencypayment
As of 30 August 2010 – 1012 members and 1663 messages, about 15/ month.

- TradPayeur (French)
finance.groups.yahoo.com/group/tradpayeur
502 members, about 12 messages/month.

- WPPF (WorldPaymentPracticesFree)
tech.groups.yahoo.com/group/WPPF
1318 members, 4803 messages, about 84/month.

- Betaalmoraal (Dutch)
groups.yahoo.com/group/betaalmoraal
380 members, about 9 messages/month.

- Zahlungspraxis (German)
de.groups.yahoo.com/group/zahlungspraxis
2467 members, 19933 messages, about 175/month.

- the-checklist (Italian)
it.groups.yahoo.com/group/the-checklist/

887 members, 81 messages/month.
- WPPF (WorldPaymentPracticesFree)
http://tech.groups.yahoo.com/group/WPPF
1318 members, 4803 messages, about 84/month)
- TranslationPaymentsWhoWhenWhat
tech.groups.yahoo.com/group/TranslationPaymentsWhoWhenWhat/
423 members, 30 messages/month. Founded Aug 2008.
- translation-agencies
tech.groups.yahoo.com/group/translation-agencies/
Any issues connected with translation agencies, not just payment. 1354 members, 2 messages/month in 2010, topics seem to go in fits and starts.
- pp_brasil (Portugese)
tech.groups.yahoo.com/group/pp_brasil/
133 members, 5 messages/month.
- transpaybulletin
finance.groups.yahoo.com/group/transpaybulletin/
All spam. No legitimate mail since 2007.
- Translators-RedAlert-Hotline
tech.groups.yahoo.com/group/Translators-RedAlert-Hotline/
64 members, 13 messages total since 2005, basically moribund.
- huntransbiz (Hungarian)
finance.groups.yahoo.com/group/huntransbiz/
28 members, was somewhat active in 2003/2004 but basically moribund now (3 messages in 2010, 1 in 2009, 4 in 2008).

Other Resources
- EU Directive 20035 EC (late payment) www.europa.eu
- ATA Business Practices list (advice and tips, not payment issues per se)
groups.yahoo.com/group/ata_business_practices/
- FIT Europe
www.fit-europe.org/
Information on debt collection procedures in various countries. Go to site, then click on Bad Payments > Material Received in the left hand menu.

But don't forget other sources of information: BBB, Dun & Bradstreet, credit agency reports, court records and company registries.

Most of the information in this list was forwarded by Ted Wozniak (thanks!), who took over Karin Adamczyk's Payment Practices list several years ago.

FA & WB

8
Specializing

In many cases, translators start out as generalists and sharpen their focus as they gain experience. For most language combinations, specialization holds the key to building a practice that is both intellectually stimulating and lucrative.

CHOOSING YOUR SPECIALIZATION

Q *I want to specialize, how do I start?*

Focus

A Dear Focus,
What a nice short question.
May we ask a few back at you?

• Why do you want to specialize?

Because you're stressed about waking up and having to tackle a new subject every single day? To earn more money? Or have you seen the results of a major study showing that specialization leads to better digestion, greater personal happiness and an improved sex life?

Valid points all, and taken together a good argument for doing everything you can to achieve better focus. Which will also help you avoid a potentially fatal translator illness: cynicism and burnout.

• Got any particular areas you are thinking of specializing in?

As we regularly point out in this column, translators always produce better texts in fields they are passionate about. But loving a subject and mastering it won't guarantee jobs if the demand ain't there (this with a tip of the hat to a delightful British colleague who lives and breathes cricket but has so far been unable to drum up much specialized work in his language pair: Spanish to English).

At the same time, there are plenty of market segments with texts just aching to be translated and no genuine talent on hand.

Now for some concrete suggestions:

• Search this column's archives for previous advice on specialization, including our recommendation that translators sit back, assess their strengths and weaknesses, and take out a three-month subscription to a national business daily. This alone will let you see what's hot and identify promising matches.

• Once you have an idea of the area(s) in which you want to specialize—industries where you'll have some expertise to start, if possible, and where demand exists—contact people working in that field to describe your project and ask them which sub-specialties they, as subject-matter experts, are tracking.

We're not talking about translators here, rather business people, scientists, engineers, architects, medical experts and so on.

Make it clear that you are not looking for work: what you want is their view of trends in their specialty, including professional events to attend, looming cross-border issues and super-specialist niches worth developing.

Discovering where potential clients' heads are at can be incredibly illuminating.

• Once you've got a few leads, buckle down and do the heavy lifting: immerse yourself in the field, read-read-read and link up the dots. And practice the translator's craft, of course. Who knows, those early contacts might become mentors, or even your first clients!

FA & WB

Q *My partner and I manage a mid-size translation company that does technical translation. We are conscientious, very involved in our community, have a good reputation, and get along well with our freelance suppliers.*

Unfortunately price pressures are mounting—so much so that we recorded our first loss last year. We currently charge customers €0.15 a word and have seen our direct competitors edge down to €0.12 in the past six months, which means they can't be paying their suppliers more than about €0.06 or €0.07. No one in Germany can work at that rate, so we assume they are shopping abroad.

I know you recommend raising prices, but this is our reality and we are about to hit the wall.

Discussions with translators and translation companies in more lucrative niches have convinced me that we must either set up subsidiaries in India, Madagascar and Colombia or leave "general technical" translation and specialize. But how to start? We have offices, staff, overheads, a loyal client base (but for how much longer?) and a stable of competent freelancers.

Can we reasonably hope to upgrade our existing operation to demand higher prices? Even more important, how?

Pressure's On

A Dear Pressure,

A hard question, yours, and your concerns are well-founded.

As you note, the market has moved on and for lack of specialization you find yourself competing with suppliers who can charge far less than you. Your options will depend to a great extent on how genuinely skilled your suppliers are (regardless of how well you get on with them).

Here are two suggestions (and we invite readers to jump in with their thoughts/comments, too):

• Build/consolidate your reputation for specialization with your clients by organizing highly focused in-house training—making clients an integral part of the event.

Start by identifying fast-growing tech areas where you have particular strengths, even if you are not yet billing enough for them. The very next time a challenging text comes in, use one-on-one contacts during revision to ask if one of their technical experts might be available to give a talk on same to a core group of skilled translators who will ultimately be working on their texts. The freelance translators you want are generally enthusiastic about opportunities to specialize, and by promoting the event (allow a few outside folks in to benefit from the ripple effect) you can start nailing down your position as the employer/translation supplier of choice in this area ("Remember that talk on helicopter parts/tunnel boring/water filters at Acme Translations?").

• Another option is to split your company in two. Have one unit be the boutique outfit for the kind of jobs that absolutely must be done by top-tier translators and editors with the most experience and best track record (and price accordingly); have the second unit handle the "bulk" translation jobs. This is not a perfect solution; among other potential problems, there will always be discussions with clients who expect top quality but will say "surely your off-brand outfit can do a good job on it."

FA & WB

Q We are two students of English Philology in Poland. We are very interested in perfecting our skills as translators (Eng - Pol) but are a bit worried if there is any demand and what field we should specialize in. Could you give us any hints?

Two Poles

ADear Poles,
Talk about being in the right place at the right time! Follow the strategy we outlined for Diving Back In above, and—if you do nothing else this year—bone up on European Union terminology (if you can't see why, take out a 3-month subscription to the Financial Times and come back in September).

Now is also the time to arrange internships with foreign companies present in Poland, including stints at their head offices and subsidiaries in the rest of Europe. Two weeks, four weeks, four months—there is simply no better way to start building the network of contacts you need to break into the profession and prosper.

FA & WB

Q*I work in a "language of limited diffusion."*
When I started out as a freelance translator, I did mainly localisation of software and hardware. At some point a lot of that was taken in-house in Ireland, and at the same time more translators came along who did the same thing. So I switched to printers and fax machines for a while, then mobile phones. In the meantime I had diversified into teaching, exam work, subtitling, proofreading and advertising, and I was also learning about white goods and black goods.

But at that point I discovered that there still was a steady market for "old technology", hazardous chemicals, safety and so on, which was familiar to me. I also did quite a bit of insurance-related translation as I had people I could ask and learn from.

To cut a long story short, I now do a lot of medical translation (instruments, equipment — contains a lot of "old technology" like pumps and valves, plus the newer electronics).

I also do substantial medical-related sub-editing in-house, and oil-related stuff. My teaching has increased again (but that may be in part because I enjoy it; I also quite like it as it gets me out and about, even if the pay tends to be low).

My point?

If you translate into a "language of limited diffusion", you simply cannot stick to the same specialism all the time (unless you are very lucky), partly because there will always be limited demand, and partly because market focus changes. And even if you translate into a major language, some of the above still holds true, but you have more opportunity to specialise within a specific field, like law or finance.

My view is:

1. Always be on the lookout for new (viable) trends

2. Adapt and be willing to learn

3. Invest in yourself

The harsh reality is that you can make yourself totally indispensable to a company, but if that company goes under or cuts back, you will suffer unless you have other options already open.

You cannot specialise in translating typewriter manuals any more.

Northern Lights

A Dear Northern,
Thanks for your reminder of the flexibility that goes with the territory for LLDs—and even some major languages. Your comments on serial specializations are also well taken. Last but not least, your career path highlights the fact that an inquisitive mind and the genuine curiosity good translators bring to the job is one of their most appealing—and profitable—characteristics.

FA & WB

LAW

Q *Do you have any advice on translating foreign laws and regulations? It is obviously impossible to contact the "author" with questions, so my approach to date has been massive background reading, followed by checking with a US attorney. I enjoy the assignments and my customers seem happy, but I worry about getting out of my depth.*

Legal Eaglet

A Dear Eaglet,
While your safety net makes good sense (and we assume you are paying for this service and billing it on to the client, not just running the texts past your next-door neighbor), be sure to ask your customer the Primal Question: what will the document be used for? To get an idea of the foreign law? To find out once and for all what a foreign law says (scary)? To publish a collection of foreign laws in translation? To submit the translation as Plaintiff's Exhibit A in a lawsuit based on a contract governed by the law translated?

This basic question applies to every single translation, of course, and is all too often overlooked—sometimes with disastrous consequences. Asking it will help keep you from getting in over your head, or at least remind your customers (and you) of some of the risks. It may also give you a chance to sign your work.

A lawyer friend notes that law firms routinely include disclaimers in everything they publish, and suggests translators should, too, especially for work of this type—e.g. "This translation is not intended, and may not be interpreted, to constitute legal advice; only a lawyer admitted to practice in the jurisdiction in question can give advice about the meaning of this law." Or "Laws and regulations are subject to administrative and judicial interpretation and there can be no assurance that a regulatory agency or court of law has not construed, or will not construe, the original statute/regulation in a way inconsistent with this translation." Or both.

FA & WB

Q *I currently translate from French into English, mainly in the legal sector, and would be interested in your opinion on language combinations for English mother-tongue translators on a long-term basis.*

More specifically, I would like to learn a third language to be guaranteed work over the long term. At present I'm toying with the idea of either Chinese (given China's strong economic growth) or an "easier" European language, such as Spanish—or perhaps even a rarer European language such as Turkish, Czech or Dutch.

Could you comment on the potential advantages of learning Chinese? Do you think that there will be a significantly higher flow of Chinese to English translation in the future than, for instance, Spanish?

Multi-speak

A Dear Multi,
To be sure, China is an economic powerhouse worldwide.

But even if you start learning the language now, it will be years before you are capable of actually translating anything from Chinese to English. Ideally you would have to go and live in China for a while, and study Chinese law while there—is that part of your plan?

More to the point, there is already massive demand in your current language combination and specialization, but only for seriously expert practitioners. Make no mistake, lawyers regularly criticize the superficial nature of many would-be legal translations, even when performed by experienced translators claiming specialization who have been in the business for years.

So we think you've got the wrong end of the stick. Unless there are special personal circumstances—you see a move to China shaping up through a spousal transfer, or there is a devilishly attractive Chinese translator across the street and you're casting about for an ice-breaker—you are better off sticking to your current combination and deepening your specialization.

That might include developing your knowledge of legal systems in English and French-speaking countries, and selecting a few particularly promising areas to make your own, gradually becoming the translator of choice in those niches—the person that demanding clients turn to.

FA & WB

Q *I graduated with a Ph.D. in French literature from a US university in 1992, and decided to become a translator instead of staying in academia.*

I'm now based in Cape Town, South Africa, where there is not much demand for French to English translation, and have decided to specialize in legal translation.

This poses a problem since I haven't been formally trained in translation, but I've been seriously translating (very part-time) for about ten years and I'm sure I've improved my skills by taking the bull by the horns and translating anything not too technical. Of course, some clients are happier than others. I try my best and continue working for agencies, since I believe that this is the only way to go (self-education, self-training) for someone like me starting out. There is not much here in terms of training anyhow, let alone courses in legal translation. At the age of 38, I'm not considering doing a law degree. Is there any material out there you know of which could assist me in developing an expertise in legal translation?

Courting Career

A Dear Courting,
Not being a fully qualified lawyer, should you even attempt legal translation? Well, if there were enough lawyer-translators around to meet demand, the market would probably say "No." But there aren't, and this is unlikely to change soon. In international law firms, bilingual attorneys are frequently pressed into service as in-house translators, but many greatly resent this and leap at the earliest opportunity to escape.

So—as long as you are open and honest with your clients about your credentials, we see no reason in principle to dissuade you.

But as you are no doubt aware, even if you find a retired attorney to take over part of the workload by becoming your reviewer/editor—the ideal scenario—you are still taking on a major challenge.

Here are some points our legal advisers feel you should consider:

• Not only are French-English legal dictionaries scarce, but a dictionary can only help you to remember terminology that you already know and understand. Unlike a translator of, say, circuit-board layout software manuals, you will have to learn about your field not just once but twice, since the legal systems of France and the Commonwealth are independent of each other and look back on completely different histories. Leaving aside legal concepts, parsing some of the sentences found in a typical contract is a brain-busting exercise in and of itself.

Conclusion: there is no substitute for hitting the books and studying the French and UK (or US or Canadian or Swiss or Belgian or...) legal systems. Instead of attempting to read the textbooks assigned to law students in university courses, you might try looking for primers targeting other vocations, such as business administration students. Speaking of which....

• Thirty-eight is definitely not too old to study the law. Hell, a healthy and alert 65-year-old could do it! And it certainly won't be any harder than if you train on the job to become a successful translator. So take a good look at your priorities, and consider law school or paralegal studies. Even a stint as a bilingual secretary in a law firm would give you some direct experience of legal documents and procedures—an essential first step.

• Finally, you may currently be in a backwater for French-English legal translation, but that does not mean you have to work in a vacuum. Example: legal portal findlaw.com has a host of legal forms and sample contracts, in particular recent technology deals. Reading these can be helpful for understanding legal style. A number of firms—Freshfields is one—publish free brochures that explain various areas of French law (such as property or securitization) in English. These are all the more valuable in that many are drafted by expert bilingual lawyers. The Chambre de Commerce Internationale at Cours Albert Ier in Paris has published a number of useful documents in French and English, including certain model commercial agreements (distribution, etc.). Its Rules of Conciliation and Arbitration are available in French and in English; they are an essential reference for any person interested in translating in this field, say our contacts. [www.iccbooks.com/Product/CategoryInfo.aspx?cid=139]

There are also specialized mailing lists that provide a forum for exchanging information and advice, e.g. the LIFT network (Law, Insurance, Finance) of the UK's Institute of Translation and Interpreting. Check www.legal-translators.co.uk/ for details on how to sign up.

Information overload? Not really. What it all boils down to is one question: Why choose law as your translation specialty? If you picked it because of its potential for earning a healthy income, we approve. However, you should also develop a genuine interest in a number of legal issues—ranging from the history of common law to recent developments such as copyright protection on the Internet. Are you sure that you don't want to go to law school after all?

FA & WB

Q *I am an Argentine lawyer, 40 years old, and am moving with my family to the U.S. next year. As my law degree is useless in the U.S. I am trying to find a translation program in which my former degree could help me to get a job after I graduate. I would like to obtain your impression about the "FIU certificate in Legal Translation & Court Interpreting" offered by the Florida International University: is the certificate a good one, and will it allow me to get a good job?*

Heading North

A Dear Heading,
You go to the head of the class, sir, for realizing that a law degree on its own does not qualify anyone to translate legal documents. To succeed, translators must have a firm grasp of the many major and minor differences between legal systems, not to mention great linguistic sensitivity—writing skills in their native language, and awareness of nuance in their foreign language(s). They are judged on the work they produce, day in, day out.

FA & WB are not familiar with the course at Florida International University but suggest you consult the directory of translation programs in North America published by ATA (atanet.org). You might also drop an email to ATA members working in legal translation in your language pair for their opinion.

Keep in mind that while a good translation program can teach you a lot, no diploma will guarantee anyone a job. One option might be to study to become a court interpreter, not least because this is an area where jobs are not being moved/sourced abroad (for obvious reasons).

If you do take a one-year certificate course in translation, be sure to get out and network in bar association meetings to link up with people who need your services. Your Argentine degree should serve you well here.

We wish you and your family all the best as you settle into your new life in the US.

FA & WB

Q *Help! I need some career advice. With an M.A. from Middlebury, a law degree and a recent M.A. in translation, I planned to become a legal translator.*

However, I'm finding that my translation degree was heavy on theory and light on practicality, so it did not prepare me to work with real-world legal documents. The few contracts I've translated resulted in negative feedback from the agencies, and I'm now gun-shy of taking on another legal job.

How can I gain experience with common legal documents like employment contracts, wills, court rulings, divorce decrees or articles of incorporation? Without experience in these everyday legal documents, I'm afraid I'll never develop a legal translation business. Should I just stick with general translation, which I'm not having any problem with, and give up my specialization dream? Any suggestions?

Legal Beagle

A Dear Beagle,
You don't say which legal documents you are unfamiliar with—did your law degree not include exposure to contracts (gulp), or are you referring to your foreign-language courses?

If it was the latter, your experience merely confirms a certain gap between some academics' approach to translation and what the market demands. Specialization is definitely what you should be aiming for, so by all means look into legal translation courses at other universities (check the course catalog first to be sure you are getting the nuts and bolts) or—better yet—seek an internship with an established legal translator or law firm.

FA & WB

LITERATURE

Q *I graduated as a Sworn Translator in English and Spanish in 1996 and since then have been working as a translator in my native country, Guatemala. I translate all sorts of documents—legal, technical, news articles, insurance adjuster reports, tourism articles and more—and really enjoy my job. I also have a degree in communications and in literature and would some day love to translate novels and short stories, but feel that I need to practice in this area to get a better grip. Do you know of any relevant study programs that I could take "at a distance," or could you advise me as to how to proceed to slowly begin specializing in this field—translating literature?*

Eager to Study

A Dear Eager,

Your question gave us an opportunity to revisit the informative and immensely readable web sites of the PEN American Center and ALTA, the American Literary Translators Association. While you will be working into Spanish, we recommend that you—indeed, anyone interested in literary translation—start there, with, respectively, PEN's translation homepage www.pen.org/page.php/prmID/154 and ALTA's "Breaking into Print" as well as other helpful guides https://www.utdallas.edu/alta/publications/alta-guides

The disappointing news is that distance courses in literary translation appear to be fairly thin on the ground, although we would be delighted to forward readers' recommendations.

In the meantime, an editor whose company specializes in publishing literature in translation suggests the following:

1. Try translating a few texts that have already been translated by a top-notch translator. The aim is not to see whether you've done it "right," but rather to analyze how the experienced translator made his or her decisions.

2. Read articles and books about literary translation. One we enjoyed was Robert Wechsler's "Performing Without a Stage / The Art of Literary Translation" Catbird Press 1998, ISBN 0-945774-38-9.

3. Select a writer you like who has not been translated into your language. Translate a few stories or poems, get the author's permission (the PEN and ALTA sites have a lot more to say on this critical point), and submit these short pieces for publication in literary magazines.

4. Go to translator conferences/events and network; get out there and build yourself a reputation. In literary as in technical translation, never underestimate the power of word of mouth—especially once you've got some work to show.

FA & WB

FINANCE

Q I have been a generalist translator for two years, and at the beginning of this year I decided to focus my energy on training to be a financial translator. Despite my lack of experience in the field, it's a subject that has always fascinated me, and so it was with pleasure and enthusiasm that I hit the books.

Over the past months, I have studied all sorts of material on corporate finance and *the financial markets, and I feel fairly confident of my newly acquired knowledge. I now subscribe to two financial dailies to keep abreast of economic developments, and I've compiled a solid financial glossary.*

However, when I try to market myself as a financial translator, I come across the same stumbling block every time. I have no experience, and agencies only want to collaborate with translators who have a minimum of 5 years' experience and/or a professional background in finance. I've offered to do tests but they are not biting.

I'm nervous about approaching direct clients at this stage. I lack experience in the field of financial translation, and I don't believe I should be approaching direct clients until I have translated financial material for agencies and received feedback on my work.

I don't want to throw in the towel just yet, but my plan to reposition myself at the top-end of the market is starting to seem more like a pipe dream than an achievable goal. Any suggestions?

A frustrated financier

A Dear Frustrated,
Your enthusiasm and preparation are great, and your reluctance to work for direct clients without initial feedback is a sign that you're taking this seriously. Good!

But as you point out, it's vicious circle time: without experience, you're a pig in a poke.

One promising vector that newcomers often forget is fellow translators. Ask around: many practicing linguists got their big break when a swamped colleague asked for help, and in our experience an increasing number of translators are interested in cross-revision.

So step one is to get yourself along to a translators' meeting in your city or region.

• Go equipped with proper business cards and some short samples of your work.

• Use the face time to network, demonstrating not only awareness of arcane concepts in finance but also your even-tempered and pleasant personality.

• Follow up with a personalized email to the financial (or other) translators you found particularly congenial; point out that you are available to help them with proofreading and other tasks, even—especially!—over normal vacation periods.

• Remind them at regular intervals of your existence and availability; no groveling, just that you'd be happy to help meet deadlines as Thanksgiving, the ATA conference or winter holidays approach.

Second, if you have not already done so, join the Financial Translators' e-list—no charge and open to all freelance translators. Advertising is not allowed, but it's a good place to seek out likely partners. Contact: dominique.jonkers@skynet.be. Finally, consider signing up for workshops and training courses where individuals and agencies known to specialize in finance will be teaching or otherwise on hand. Swiss association ASTTI's summer university for financial translators is one, and the French association SFT holds its *université d'été* for financial translators in alternate years.

Advantage: you'll learn more about your new specialism, even as you get a chance to step into the spotlight by asking informed questions of speakers.

Good luck!

FA & WB

Q *I'm a freelance translator, now a generalist (English>German), but keen to specialize in financial translation. OK, my degree is in literature (I understand that is one strike against me), but I am numerate, I've been reading about economics all summer, and I'm prepared to roll up my sleeves and work.*

That said, right now I'm overwhelmed by the sheer number of areas that I'll have to master to get anywhere. I feel I should start focusing, but I haven't even got the big picture straight yet. Is there any short course you can recommend?

Lost in London

A Dear Lost,
If English is one of your languages and finance your goal, you're certainly in the right place. One of the best general courses we know of is an introduction to financial markets offered by the Financial Times—not cheap, but it will give you a good overview. And you'll be studying alongside businesspeople who are potential clients for your services. For more information, contact The Learning & Development unit at the FT on +44 2078733000.

FA & WB

Q *I live and work in Rwanda. After getting a Bachelor's Degree in Translation and Interpreting from the Université Nationale du Rwanda in 2003, I moved into the freelance market, specializing in banking.*

It was a struggle to start, but I ended up translating memos, correspondence, central bank regulations, agreements, leaflets and so on. Two years later I applied to the Office of the Auditor General of State Finances, where I now work as an in-house translator.

Can you recommend any websites that might be of use to me? I am particularly interested in banking terminology and related areas.

African Banker

Dear Banker,
Your letter is a reminder of just how profoundly the internet has revolutionized the profession. Not only are there dozens of excellent websites out there (plus hundreds of mediocre multilingual ones—great fodder for the free trial offer approach for freelance translators looking for new clients—there are also virtual watering holes where like-minded professional translators get together to bounce ideas on terminology and other issues off each other.

For finance and banking, the discussion list par excellence is (surprise, surprise) the Financial Translators Forum. Registration is free, but limited to freelance and salaried translators; agencies are not welcome.

Focus is the watchword (don't start telling these guys about your summer holidays). To sign up, contact Dominique Jonkers at dominique.jonkers@skynet.be.

FA & WB

THE PRICE OF SUCCESS

I am if not the best, at least right up there among the top specialized translators in my field. I love that little surge of power that comes when a client has written something that is technically wrong and I can correct it (an error another translator might not even notice). I love knowing that, when the pressure is on, only I can deliver.

So what's the problem?

Recently three of my loyal clients have confirmed that I am their preferred supplier, only to volunteer that because of this they save all the really challenging texts for me and send the easier ones to less experienced, less qualified colleagues. They sincerely thought this would make me happy.

It is flattering, but also confirms that the swings and roundabouts that normally kick in with pricing-per-word are now working against me, since I get none of the easy texts. Every job is Everest. I don't even want to think about my per-hour earnings.

Where did I go wrong?

Pride Before Fall

A Dear Pride,

If you are the best you should be charging top dollar/euro/yen—and not necessarily by the word. An apple is an apple and an orange an orange; why should hard texts cost the same as easy ones? And why should your (expert) time be worth the same as that of an earnest beginner?

Your clients' admission that you are their gold standard is invaluable—a platinum bargaining chip.

Build on it by setting up a lunch or other meeting so that you can tell them in person how fascinating their field and texts are, citing cutting-edge articles from industry journals that they have not had time to read themselves. Exude passion and technical expertise from the first course through to, say, the cheese.

As dessert is served, explain that having re-evaluated your business model, you are switching to a different pricing scheme, namely charging by the time it takes you to do a translation to your exacting standards. To a degree, this avoids the sticker shock triggered by the dreaded words "price increase," since charging by the word and charging by the hour are not immediately commensurable.

You might point out that it will make sense at their end to sort their texts up front, deciding which require your bullet-proof care and which are "less important." Making this explicit is a good move, especially when you are also giving them useful best-practice advice.

To dispel any fears that you are asking for a blank check to dawdle on translation jobs and then hit up your client for the cost, note that you will be pleased in future to provide an estimate, free of charge, on reception of the source text, and that your client retains the option not to place the order with you.

Most important of all, make this explanation matter-of-fact, not pleading: the client needs you, and is lucky to have you on their side.

Tackle one client at a time, with a one-month lag between lunches so that you can tally up who of your loyal supporters remains on board and adjust your strategy if necessary.

Onwards and upwards, and report back please.

FA & WB

Q *I gather from the archives of this column that top-notch writing skills are a must for translators who want to be successful at the upper end of the market, and I'm concerned that my writing style is not quite as fluid and elegant as I would like it to be. I've also identified a mild but lingering case of translationese in my work, which undoubtedly comes a fear of breaking away from the original* structure in French and daring to produce a smooth, seamless piece of writing in English. I know I'm capable of it, I'm just not sure how to overcome the mental obstacle that is stopping me from doing it.

Do you have any good tips on honing writing skills and thereby eliminating the translationitis my current work is suffering from?

Budding writer

A Dear Writer,
We're glad you asked. Here are our top ten:
1. Read a lot. A word person should have at least one book on the go at all times.
2. Periodicals? Yes, them too. Stretch yourself with titles that are known for stylish writing (in English, try the Economist, for example).
3. If you run across interesting words in your reading, try to find a way to place them in your current translations. A fun source of these is www.savethewords. org (but don't overdo the placement business).
4. Take a course in creative writing. Or read a book on same. One we particularly like is William Zinsser's "On Writing Well."
5. Take a course in journalism.
6. Brush up on your grammar, punctuation and all that jazz. There are some amazing websites out there, and you can always peruse Strunk & White's classic "The Elements of Style," which has the advantage of being only 95 pages long.
7. Urge your local translators' association to organize training focusing on this specific problem: there are more people interested than you'd think.
8. Find some texts in your specialty area that have been translated well. Put the existing translation aside, and try your hand. Compare your output to the official translation, and note where you slip and slide. Note how the other translator solved tricky passages.
9. Arrange with a fellow translator to cross-revise the texts you produce; there is no better way of improving your style than through feedback of this type.
10. Write a lot. Start a blog, or pen articles for your local newspaper or professional association journal.

For a bonus point, have your articles translated into your source language (by a professional, of course). This is one of the best ways we know to become aware of what authors want from a translator, while heightening your own awareness of the importance of flow.

FA & WB

Q With all the festive spirit and good feeling around at this time of year, I thought it would be a suitable time to send you a thank-you letter for writing such an inspirational column.

I have read and made a searchable archive of all "The Bottom Line" columns, and have eagerly adopted all the advice you have given over the years.

I recently attended a training course in my specialist subject, have subscribed to two trade journals in both my source and target language, and have forged relationships over the past few months with expert translators in my specialist field, for whom I proofread in exchange for their advice on my work. I've also bought a few text books in my specialist subject, which I work on evenings in order to deepen my knowledge in the field, and I'm really embracing the possibilities of having the high-flying career that I have always dreamed of!

In fact, through these actions alone (and not necessarily marketing) I have already managed to convince several translation agencies to give me high-profile translation projects, and I'm now getting paid, hands-on experience. The pay may be minimal, and my translations are probably still of the kind that would have you two grabbing for a red pen to use as part of your pitch to the client in question (all beginners make mistakes! I just hope the agencies are proofreading my work before it goes out!)

But I'm not letting this deter me, because I'm only at the beginning of the long journey I have mapped out for myself based on the advice you have given. I have been building up a library of bilingual documents that I use to compile my subject-specific glossary, and I'm getting to the (very satisfying) point where everything is starting to gel and make sense. What a refreshing change to come into the office with a real sense of purpose, unlimited enthusiasm and a will to succeed!

Roadmap in Hand

A Thanks for your thanks.
We like feedback, too!

FA & WB

9
Ethics

Business sense, best practice and ethics: how reassuring that these generally dovetail for translators who are in it for the long haul.

THE BOTTOM LINE

Q *How can translators get the respect they deserve?*

Looking for Attitude

A Dear Looking,
By delivering impeccable work, on time, to discerning clients. By saying "no." By not undercharging. By signing their work. By using a whole string of tactics to remind clients just how hard it is to be an expert translator, and by demonstrating conclusively that the texts they produce will make a big difference to clients' image and, ultimately, bottom line.

Of course, if translators don't do this they also "get the respect they deserve"—but that's not what you are talking about, right?

FA & WB

SUB-CONTRACTING

Q *I head the translation department of a large bank. I think I can confidently say that we are good customers: when we commission outside work we plan ahead, we provide glossaries, we make it clear that we are available to field questions, and we pay promptly.*

In the past two months we have nonetheless been seriously burned three times. In one case a trusted freelancer subcontracted the job to a student, with catastrophic results; twice translation agencies did the same thing, passing our work on to less qualified people without telling anyone.

In all three cases we ended up with bad texts, and while our in-house reviewers caught the problems before publication, I was and am furious at what I consider unethical behavior. After all, no one forced these suppliers to take on our work, yet not one bothered to tell us that our jobs were being passed on to an unknown quantity.

I should add that I alerted our national translators' association (the suppliers were members), and there was a round of finger-wagging, but little more.

What can I do to make sure this never happens again?

Still Fuming

A Dear Fuming,
Some things are just not done, and in our opinion, subcontracting work on the sly while holding yourself out as a hands-on, first-person proprietor is on a par with poisoning the neighbor's cat and pissing in the town well. You will note that it is also strictly forbidden in the model terms of business published by at least one national translators' association.

In the case of translation companies, subcontracting is usually part of the package, but these suppliers earn their cut by thoroughly reviewing the work they deliver. If they fail to do so, they should pay a penalty.

To punish your less-than-ethical suppliers, simply withdraw your custom from them. And with the new translators you choose, state your expectations regarding subcontracting up front and in writing: do you want to be told in advance, do you never accept it under any circumstances, what safeguards would you consider adequate to maintain quality? Write these conditions into your contract with your suppliers, including a financial penalty for non-compliance.

If you feel strongly enough about this issue, consider offering a short account of your experiences to the translator association's journal. Raising the subject in public will clear the air and be a salutary reminder that clients deserve better.

FA & WB

Q *I am a freelance translator. For some time I have been working through an agency that has assigned me to do in-house translation for one of their industrial customers.*

The very day I arrived on site, the end customer made it perfectly clear that they would be interested in working with me directly. I consider it would be unethical (if not suicidal) to take up their so far veiled offers, but they are getting more insistent, and I am confident that if I don't agree to work with them directly, they will look for someone else who will. Then the agency and I would both lose out.

I have mentioned this to the head of the agency. I suggested that I should accept the offer and pay the agency a commission for, say, two years, or as long as the assignment lasts, to compensate them for their investment in seeking out the work. He is not interested; in fact I don't think he even believes my story.

What should I do? There is no way I could prove that the customer is looking for a direct contact and that the agency will lose the contract in any case, so if I were to "steal" the agency's client, I fear my reputation would be tarnished. However the end customer is a big concern, and there could be a lot of work in it, so financially the risk might be worth it. What do you advise?

Twixt the Devil and the Deep Blue Sea

Dear Twixt,

On-site assignments for an agency can be tricky and your dilemma demonstrates why.

A few general issues first:

Normally each link in the chain adds value. Here your end client views the agency's input as nil now that it has recruited you for them. This sounds to us like a naive client or naive agency or both. You are right not to add a naive translator to the equation by assuming you can have your cake and eat it, too.

So your reflex—reporting the exchange to your employer and offering to make good his investment—was the right one. We know of similar situations where translator and agency have agreed to part ways on mutually acceptable terms that keep the agency in the loop for future work with the translator's new employer. That's the best-case scenario.

Here we suggest you look harder at why this job is being offered to you— after first checking your existing contract to make sure you are not opening yourself (and the industrial customer) up to a lawsuit. That is time-wasting of the highest order, and in no one's interest.

• The more clients pay for services, the more they are likely to value them. If, as you seem to imply, the industrial customer's chief concern is price—your services are cheaper without the agency's margin on top—their offer may not be all that attractive. Price-driven clients can be more trouble than they are worth in the long term.

• If, however, the industrial customer is bowled over by your subject-matter expertise, writing skills and team spirit, and wants you on staff at any price, Fire Ant advises you to go for it—especially since you have already offered to compensate the agency for its loss of the customer (and very generously, in our opinion).

But in this case you must also make sure the price is right.

• You already know what this customer is willing (or apparently not too willing) to pay the agency for your services, so keep that in mind in your negotiations. If you don't know, find out!

• If the industrial customer's offer is to work with you not as a staff member with full employee benefits but as a freelance supplier, be sure to weigh up the cost of any additional services your agency is currently providing, including in particular revision. You will have to finance this yourself once the agency is out of the picture.

Beyond these immediate concerns, your question highlights the familiar agency/ freelance divide.

On the one hand, Fire Ant & Worker Bee are amazed at the number of skilled translators who assume there is no alternative to working through an intermediary.

Many "So you want to be a translator?"-type publications mention the direct client route only as a second thought. Let's be clear: a thriving market exists for translators with top-level writing skills, specialist knowledge and the energy to get out and link up with direct clients.

Good translation companies/agencies bring different skills to the table. They earn their piece of the cake through their ability to coordinate multilingual projects, locate the right talent for each job, provide resources and editing, assume financial risk and, in general, offer a timely response to a broader range of language needs. If they are not adding value, it is hardly surprising that they find their role (and margin) threatened.

FA & WB

FEEDBACK ON WORK

Q *This year a good (but minor) client of mine received four letters criticizing the English version of their annual report—not my work, nor do I know the translator who produced it. But the criticism has really set them on edge. Two of the critics were in the UK, one in Sweden and one in the US.*

I agreed to give the company an opinion. Now, having examined the text thoroughly, I think the translation is pretty good. Should I simply tell them as much?

No Whistle Blower

A Dear Whistle,

Amazing, isn't it? Feedback on translations is still so rare that four (4) letters are enough to set off a full-fledged attack of the corporate heebie-jeebies.

If the texts pass muster—and you might ask a trusted colleague for a second opinion just to be on the safe side—the challenge facing you and your client is to work out precisely what upset the letter-writers. Were British readers put off by US spelling? Was the text simply too long? Did both authors and translator stumble over a vital national statistic? Was the style too formal? Too relaxed?

Comments on language (mis)use can also reflect deeper misunderstandings: has the company had bad press on issues dear to critics' hearts? Has its share price plummeted? (Is its home country testing nuclear devices in nearby waters?).

If your clients are not fluent in English, their reluctance to pursue the investigation directly is only natural. This is your cue. Ask to see the original letters and help them read between the lines. You might even offer to phone the writers on the company's behalf, or help script a call by someone on the corporate communications team. This is good PR for them (and you), since personal attention will generate more specific information and prove to writers that the company cares. As always, feedback—good or bad—gives everyone a better understanding of requirements for future translations.

If you are feeling particularly energetic, consider launching a new trend: write a letter praising a good corporate translation you've seen recently, and post it to the CEO today.

FA & WB

Q *I am a translator waiting anxiously for the Diploma in Translation result, due in March. Last week I watched a recent British film in the original version with Spanish subtitles and noted some serious errors in translation. These completely changed the meaning and the Spanish version did not make much sense. I thought that I had to tell someone, but I do not know who is responsible for hiring the film's translators.*

Any ideas? This may not be the best place to ask but I am at a loss as to who to contact.

Film Freak

A Dear Film,
This spilling of the beans business gets many people's back up—all translators live in glass houses, says one of our contacts, while another muttered something about spitting in the soup.

Yet we can see where you are coming from: a good film may lose out on foreign markets due to sloppy subtitling. Unfair! Language itself deserves better. Yes! And your own critical sense has surely been sharpened by your course. So do speak up, but remember the ground rules:

• Assume that whoever is in charge is simply unaware of the problem, and will want to correct things once the issue has been brought to their attention. Well, perhaps not for this film, but for future releases. Your tone must imply as much.

• Be specific. "The subtitles were appalling" is little help; so is "your subtitler is hopeless." Go back and see the film again, and this time take notes.

• Cut the original translator some slack, if only to ensure that you are not dismissed as the smartass in the back row. Concretely, mention a few factors that may be responsible for the problems ("I realize the Spanish version was released just two months after the original, so I imagine things were pretty hectic"; "Perhaps the translator was working from a faulty transcript".)

And keep in mind that most films contain about 1200 subtitles. An error or two, especially in a film with a lot of regional accents and dialect, is not such a high failure rate, especially in view of time pressures as release dates loom. In cases of blatant incompetence, the local distributor (whose name will be on the poster) is the party to write to, since they have the largest stake in the commercial success of the film.

FA & WB

Q *Some friends of mine have a translation company in Northern Europe. They've recently put up a multilingual web site and both the Spanish and French are pretty poor. I think I understand the problem (and the problem is very typical for many well-intentioned translation teams). How would you go about discussing it in such a way that everybody learns something useful?*

Bean Spiller

A Dear Spiller,
Who is "everybody"? Does it include buyers? They have already learned something very useful about this company.

Forgive us for questioning your angle here, but we have recently done a 180° turn on this one, not least because of the sheer number of translation provider sites that correspond to your description. Sad, perhaps. Downright comical at times. But transparent in any case, and that we welcome. Surely it is far healthier for potential clients to see what they are likely to get if they shop in a given emporium.

If you really want to help your friends out, you will have to bite the bullet and tell them that their translations simply do not make the grade as promotional copy. Soften the blow by noting that their technical texts or patents may be top-notch; perhaps it's only websites and sales documents they should steer clear of in these language combinations. But do remind them that if they could not even commission top-quality work for their own purposes, something is seriously wrong.

To bring your points home, mark up or, better yet, retranslate a few paragraphs, or have them retranslated by a trusted supplier. This concrete input will give your friends and the translators from whom they bought the text a better idea of what to aim for.

A translation company that advertises its own services through poorly translated texts—on the web, no less—reminds us of a top-class caterer putting on a gala dinner to promote its services, only to serve up burnt burgers and greasy fries on paper plates. Caveat emptor.

FA & WB

Q *My company recently had a really bad translation experience with a translator of an Eastern European language who is a member of a national translators' association. Despite sterling credentials on paper, the quality of the translation she delivered was unacceptable (confirmed by a review the client had done and another review that we commissioned). I don't want to cause trouble for her but although she was very nice throughout the whole project, she was completely oblivious about her lack of translation and language skills, even when directly confronted with examples of mistranslation.*

We lost the client as a result (mainly our own fault since our project manager had not gotten an independent proofreader).

I now have two questions:

1. Should we tell the association? It does not offer certification in this particular language and obviously, it can't vouch for the quality of all translators who are members, but it does talk about its skilled and professional members on its website.

2. Secondly, how can I get an accurate and reliable idea of someone's qualifications if I don't speak the target language at all? References and sample translations are pretty futile, in my opinion, since these are bound to be good. Recommendations from other translators (which is actually my preferred way of finding new translators) are unavailable if it's a language you haven't worked with before. Requesting a free sample translation is something I hesitate to do. And since we're a small, non-profit agency we don't really have the funds to pay for a sample translation and review by a second translator.

Unhappy Buyer

Dear Buyer,
One of the reasons poor, sloppy and clueless translators chug along, dragging the entire profession down, is that unhappy clients don't take the time to flag their substandard work. Many customers don't even consider filing an official complaint since the effort is out of proportion to the amount involved—another reason why low prices are bad news all around.

Here you've told your supplier where her work fell short and she doesn't seem to have taken the comments on board. So we say yes, you should let the association know, if only to remind them that clients do notice and do care (and to lend support to anyone thinking of setting up a certification program in that particular language—why not?).

To avoid sterile he-said/she-said/no-I-didn't/yes-you-did exchanges, stick to the facts and enclose a copy of the review you commissioned.

As for locating skilled translation resources in a language you cannot judge yourself, this is precisely the type of added value that top-end translation intermediaries provide. They have put in place revision structures and invested the time and effort needed to sort the wheat from the chaff before letting clients into the room. Not surprisingly, their added value comes at a price, which is their margin.

In today's world of instant google searches and online databases of self-proclaimed "experts" of all types, from sex workers to Jell-o mavens, anybody can call herself a skilled Czech or Tagalog or German or English translator. To reduce the risk of commissioning poor work and losing a client, translator referrals are a good starting point, but there is no magic bullet: you either invest time and effort up front to identify top talent or you hire somebody who has already made that investment.

FA & WB

PROFESSIONAL IS AS PROFESSIONAL DOES

Q *I have a client—a European businessman—who travels extensively in the developing world. Over the past five years, he has had me translate personal correspondence, mainly letters from women he has picked up, used and professed undying love to before heading back home (the exchanges usually continue for a month or two after his return).*

Until now the moral side hasn't really troubled me. As far as I can tell, his lady friends are all of age and street-wise. They have no hang-ups about asking him for money, for example; in fact, that seems to be part of the deal.

Last month a new lady appeared. A young college student in a desperately poor country, she expresses affection for him and even suggests marriage. Unlike the others, she is genuinely articulate and seems, well, nice: what she is doing with this pot-bellied, wattle-necked pig is beyond me. I feel like clueing her in. The whole situation has got me depressed. What should I do?

Moral Dilemma

A Dear Postillon D'amour,
What is this—have you suddenly got religion? You happily took Pigman's money for five years, so spare us the rending of garments.

But to answer your question: one of the advantages of being self-employed is that you and only you decide who you work for.

If you have personal no-go areas, by all means say so up front in your terms of business (e.g., "I do not work on military contracts for religious reasons"). If for whatever reason you decide that an existing client is not—or is no longer—your cup of tea, there are at least two foolproof ways to get him off your customer roster.

1. Announce a steep (100-500%) rise in price.

2. Be busy every time he calls; he'll get the picture sooner or later.

If you opt for 1 and he accepts anyway, fall back on 2.

If he's still there, try 1 again.

Then 2.

In fact, a steady stream of 1-2-1-2-1-2 before caving in ("one last time") might solve all your problems, allowing you to retire with enough money to pay for a shrink to talk through your current and other moral dilemmas.

FA & WB

Q *Here's a hot potato—translating into non-native languages. We all know that a good professional should not do that. But where I live there are not many quality-conscious customers, and it is always cheaper to have an Ecuadorian translate into English than an American. Well, that's life.*

What amazes me is professional translators, even "model ones," bragging about it. What do you think?

Into the Fire

A **Fire Ant says:** If you like Mozart, do you like his music because he started composing operas as early as five? If you like Wagner or Verdi, does it matter to you that they did not start writing music of lasting significance until they were in their late twenties? Or where they acquired their skills—at their father's knee or in a conservatory?

Perhaps it does, if you habitually collect such information the way some people collect transformer plaques or 19th-century stock certificates.

More likely, your appreciation of the music depends little on the circumstances of its creation, but instead on its qualities.

Just so with translation.

Any translator who does not personally know at least one colleague producing top-notch work in a language acquired after childhood is either blinkered by prejudice or needs to get out more.

If there is no natural law prohibiting this empirical fact, then isn't it time to acknowledge that translators are not born, which is what advertisements touting "native speakers" imply, but made (and largely self-made, too)?

The emphasis on "native speakerhood" as a criterion of competence has the fatal effect of perpetuating the wrong idea of translators as globetrotting drifters—individuals who would lack marketable skills if not for the fact that the first language they learned happens to be in demand.

The ability to write well in the target language is only one of many skills that translators must possess, and like others it can be learned by talented adults. Translation, like music, is an art and a craft.

Results count, not the history of how you acquired a particular set of skills. Good translators are identifiable not from first principles but by what they put on the page, one job at a time.

Worker Bee disagrees but hedges: We have read and heard articulate folk claiming, sometimes emphatically, that the Golden Rule—translators work only into their own native language—does not apply in their case. Some base their argument on in-depth knowledge of a specialty subject or an obscure dialect/language combination, or both. Others cite a shortage of native-speaker talent in their language combination/subject. Still others describe their output as "native-speaker equivalent," and point to a satisfied, loyal client base.

If these intrepid transgressors are prepared to sign their work, taking responsibility in public—in front of both native-speaker readers and peers— well, why not? Likewise, let's assume they regularly remind their clients of the risks involved: as we all know, translation buyers are particularly vulnerable in that they can rarely judge the quality of texts delivered to them.

But there is an acid test, and this is where things get trickier.

Ninety-eight times out of a hundred Worker Bee can identify— immediately—work produced by non-native translators, through syntax, choice of prepositions, collocations, etc. Other reliable, non-twitchy sources report the same thing. This may or may not be important, depending on target readers and document type, but both translators and clients should keep it in mind.

• We agree that there is a shortage of qualified translation suppliers—people with specialist subject knowledge, linguistic skills in the source language, and writing ability in the target language. Stir in tight deadlines and/or budget limitations, and many clients will quite naturally settle for a less-than-ideal solution. Again, fine—as long as everything is out in the open. Transparency, please.

• By the same token, non-native translators who opine (or brag) that their own work is very good may be pushing it. Surely that judgment is for their native-speaker clients/readers/peers to make (blind spots are a terrible disease, sometimes fatal). Just as accepting on faith anybody's claim of producing excellent work is a recipe for trouble—a point that applies to established professionals, beginners, academics, you name it.

Conclusion? Samples, please. Make any claims you like, but put your signature where your mouth is.

• Market conditions aside, one sign that a translator is heading down a slippery slope is a defensive (or earnest) "Well, it's better than the junk that native-speaker language teacher down at the local school produces/d!" or variations thereupon. If you compare yourself with a non-professional producing substandard work, you are more than likely to end up with clients who pay non-professional prices. Which is OK, too, but rules out whining about exploitation, doesn't it?

Worker Bee far prefers to see suppliers aiming for the top end of the market. That means comparing yourself to the best—including texts written directly in your target language by professional copywriters, rocket scientists and other experts—instead of claiming to be a notch or two above the more dubious suppliers.

FA & WB

Q *In your response to Workaholic (page 226), you gave three options for what to do when one can't accept a job.*

When you write "Say No, and find an alternative," am I correct in figuring you meant to write "Say Yes but don't tell them that someone else is actually going to translate/revise"?

Also, can I ask which of the three you use? (I'm guessing that it depends on the subject of the text.)

Curious

A Dear Curious,
Thanks for asking.

We meant "Say No, and find an alternative and make sure you let the client know it's an alternative, that is, specify that you are not doing the translation yourself."

As a matter of principle, it is never a good idea to pass someone else's work off as your own. Taking that one step further, it is in your interest to remind clients at every opportunity just how complex translating is.

This is not to suggest you should fuss, split hairs and pick nits, which gets tiresome fast and drives clients away. Instead take every opportunity to remind non-linguists of a basic truth or two (e.g., professional translators work into their native language only; project management adds value and is not free), even as you position yourself as the problem-solver who smoothes the path.

In response to your second question, we have successfully used (1) Just Say No and occasionally (2) Say No, but suggest an alternative, the latter with mixed results (never underestimate the time involved in locating an alternative to pass the client on to).

Option (3), in which you locate the supplier and take full responsibility for his or her work in exchange for a cut of the action, is another matter altogether, with scope for severe stress and enduring bad vibes with former friends.

FA & WB

Q *I know you are not big believers in brochures, but in my case they work well. This, I believe, is for a specific reason: two of the four sides of my brochure are taken up by testimonials, including a number from well-known firms.*

Having said that, I'm constantly asking myself "How can I do even better?" (in selling myself to prospects).

You've suggested doing a free short sample and encouraging the client to compare your translation and the existing translation. This probably works well for marketing materials, speeches and anything that is published, but much of what I translate is confidential (legal documents), which in most cases are NOT posted on a web site or floating around the Internet.

Any thoughts as to what approach you'd take (besides your usual suggestion to attend business events attended by people from companies you'd like to have as clients) if you mostly translated documents that are NOT published?

Yours in Confidence

A Dear Confidence,
It sounds like you are doing just the right thing by using testimonials to link your name and services to the decision-makers in your market. That and getting out to bar association and other events, as you/we say.

The aim is to establish yourself—pleasantly, professionally, discreetly—as the go-to person in subject/service X. Testimonials do this very effectively, even for (especially for) confidential documents; they are also far more effective and credible than flabby lists of past and current clients.

Speaking of credibility, a word of warning on artificially crafted testimonials and other inaccurate claims. We are sure that your own brochure contains none of these, but in a world of anonymous and geographically remote suppliers, many would-be top players have no such scruples.

Examples have recently have come our way indicating that some suppliers figure the more high-powered the (fake) names and the more prestigious the (pseudo) addresses the better, apparently on the grounds that nobody's checkin'.

Readers, it's a bad idea to make stuff up. The translation world is a much smaller place than you'd imagine. Truth-calisthenics will and do catch up with abusers, and drive off the very customers they'd love to count in their client portfolio.

Thanks to Yours in Confidence for giving us an opportunity to address this important issue.

FA & WB

Q *I am deeply shocked when I see Internet sites of certain translators stating outright that "only people with translation degrees are genuine professionals." This, in my opinion, is contrary to CEN 15038 [the European standard for translation services] as well as to professional ethics, and might even be construed as unfair competition, especially when the authors of such statements make a big deal of their professional memberships on the same site. You guessed it: I do not have a diploma in translation but have been working since 1996 in the industry (and none of my clients seem to mind).*

What do you think?

No Sheepskin

A Dear Sheep,
There's little anybody can do about translators making claims like this on their websites or in advertising materials. But as a translator yourself, surely you are aware that they are only advertising their own cluelessness (or pomposity or navel-gazing or substance abuse).

Strictly speaking, such statements are also untrue: to be a professional you must be working legally (which involves paying taxes and the like) even as you generate enough income to pay your living expenses.

Plenty of translators with diplomas are not in that category.

Any translator who starts carrying on as you describe in person with other professionals would get laughed out of the room.

On a website? Let them rant: these guys are not a threat, rather comic relief. Loosen up!

FA & WB

STUDENTS & INTERNS

Q *Two summers ago we employed an intern and were under-impressed—the guy was a clock-watcher who never bothered to read the background material we recommended, left out bits and pieces of text, wrote poorly, etc., etc.*

Our assessment of his internship was tepid, although we did not blow him out of the water.

Last week a potential employer called for an opinion. They passed on the CV he is circulating and I was taken aback by what he claims he did during his stint with us. It goes well beyond stretching the truth. I should know: I was the one who had to rewrite every single sentence he produced.

I spluttered as much to the potential employer.

Should I raise this directly with the ex-intern or let him continue on his merry way and react only when asked?

Whistle Blower

A Dear Whistle Blower,
One option would have been to tell the potential new employer—in neutral language—what your intern actually did, and leave her to draw a comparison with the claims in his CV.

As things stand, the ex-intern has overstepped the line and needs a reminder of how small the (translation) world is.

Call him and express your surprise. Better yet, mail him a copy of his CV with the inaccurate part circled in red and marked "?". Enclose your business card.

If you are feeling particularly evil, you might make this anonymous.

FA & WB

Q *The university I work at has been getting an increasing number of requests from local businesses for translations of their manuals, websites and the like. They want these documents to be translated by our students.*

Our students are hard-working and dedicated, and we think they are destined for great things. But we also know how demanding professional translation is, and we think these businesses are very ill-informed if they imagine that professional work can be produced by students.

Can you suggest a response that informs the businesses of this, and if possible keeps the door open for internships (which our students have a hard time finding in this backwater)?

Academic

A Dear Academic,
Three cheers for you! Backwater or not, you've identified a slippery slope that many of the most prestigious translation schools have yet to acknowledge. A number even slither gleefully down the incline and off the precipice by passing such queries on to their student association or adopting them as class projects.

This genuinely touching but utterly unrealistic faith in their students' abilities has nothing to do with their teaching (well, maybe it does if the point is to impart information on how the translation market works out there in the real world).

As you so aptly note, the real point is that student work is not professional work.

To quote a colleague: "How many businesspeople would ask a law student to handle a major litigation? How many patients would go to a medical student for open-heart surgery, and how many medical school instructors would enthusiastically endorse the practice so that the student could 'get some professional experience'? It's fine to go to the local dental school if all you want is a cleaning, but if you need a root canal, the risks far outweigh the benefits."

In our view, a commercial website or a safety manual is a root canal job.

It gets worse: aside from the risk on this particular job, suggesting (or confirming) that the first port of call for a translation buyer should be students ends up working against translation schools' own graduates once they get out in the world: translation is something students do (at student prices), right?

Forgive the rant, you asked for advice. Here's what we recommend:

• Thank the companies for their enquiries and give them a copy of "Translation, Getting it Right", a brochure available in a number of languages and downloadable for free from the FIT-Europe site at www.fit-europe.org (look under "brochures"). It is also distributed in paper format by many professional associations. If you send a paper copy, you might fold it open to the page entitled "Teachers & academics: at your peril"; this discusses student work, too.

• Recommend that these businesses contact your country's national translators' association to find a qualified translator (most associations have online directories).

• Suggest that your establishment would very much like to assign a student to track the project, write up a report, and perhaps develop a glossary for the company as part of the assignment.

There is no better way for learners to dip a toe into the working world, and this is far less risky for clients.

FA & WB

10
Quality of life

Get your priorities right: if you are an excellent (or even good) translator, you should be enjoying yourself, your family and your job. If you are a mediocre (or even poor) translator, you will probably be better off doing something else.

LEARNING TO SAY NO

Q *I became a freelance translator three years ago, and took my first vacation last summer. It was immensely gratifying that all my clients came back after the break, even though they got good results from the colleague I referred them to.*

I know I work too much, but as a single parent and our family's sole breadwinner I worry about earning enough to raise my two small children. There's also another reason: even though my only contacts with clients are by phone and email, I've come to really like most of them. I don't like to disappoint people I like, so I end up taking on more work than is good for me. How can I learn to say no?

Killer Pace

A Dear Killer,
Congratulations on getting your business off to such a strong start!

However, neither your clients nor your kids will be well served if you collapse from exhaustion. If your clients have all come back to the fold, they clearly value your input, so maybe it's time to ease off a bit on the workload. Remember, it's a marathon, not a sprint.

To improve your quality of life, the most promising option we see involves building on your links with the colleague who took on your clients last summer. Why not approach her and suggest an overflow arrangement? Having a reliable back-up allows you to give out a phone number rather than disappoint with a flat no—or set yourself up for a heart attack with a friendly but reluctant yes. And yes. And yes.

Another option that works for some people is booking time for your family—actually blocking off afternoons or evenings in your agenda, as if you were reserving time for a job. This can help keep work from encroaching on the rest of your life.

To reduce worries about money, chart your income and expenditures, and identify where your most lucrative and enjoyable work comes from. Focus on those clients, and pass overflow on to your colleague. And—no doubt you were expecting this—raise your prices. Your workload alone means you are charging too little.

FA & WB

Q *Over the years, I have built up a loyal client base. But it is often difficult to satisfy the demands of all of my clients single-handedly.*

I don't like to say no and risk losing a client, so I momentarily forget my vow never to subcontract. Then I end up redoing entirely what I have subcontracted— to avoid the risk of losing a client! Then I ask myself what on earth I was thinking when I decided to subcontract in the first place. Then I make another vow never to do it again. Then the next volume crisis arrives.

Is there any way out of this trap?

Hard to Just Say No

A Dear Hard,
Freelance translators have a vested interest in reminding clients of at least two things: (1) translators are not interchangeable and (2) there are only 24 hours in a day.

There's no need to boast shamelessly or blast other suppliers' services (avoid the latter, it's counterproductive). But your decision to eschew subcontracting makes good sense in your situation—rest assured that many other expert freelancers have done the same.

Aside from printing out copies of your letter and sticking them on your bathroom mirror, refrigerator door and the wall behind your screen as reminders, we see three ways to avoid backsliding:
• Forward planning.

Look back over the past three years and identify when your peak periods fall. Choose a strategic off-peak date—January 1 or mid-year might be good—and write a short but pleasant reminder to all clients, making your no-subcontracting decision explicit.

The content might be that you enjoy working with them, you know they appreciate your work, and you are confident they will want to take steps at

225

their end to secure access to your services. Tell them you are a victim of your own success—a reminder that others recognize and appreciate the quality of your work, too (always flattering). Identify your peak periods clearly, and indicate that in those periods in particular you will only be able to accept work on a first come/booked, first served basis.

• Filtering by price.

If demand is too high, your prices are definitely too low. One way to find out—and defuse a looming volume crisis—is to test deadlines with a three-tier offer.

For obvious reasons you should do this before the assignment starts.

Here's how it works: if a client phones when you are operating at or near capacity, explain the situation and announce a 100% premium for next-morning delivery, 50% for next afternoon, and "my normal price if you can wait til next Wednesday. Listen, why don't you think about it and get back to me this afternoon?"

Be sure to give them a few hours to consider; that's the time it takes for the price differential to sink in. More often than you'd think, the deadline will be extended.

• Use slack periods to network and draw up a list of possible stand-ins.

These are not subcontractors, but freelance translators who seem to have a good grip on your subject areas. Note that contributions to elists are revealing but not bulletproof indicators of skill in translation. A first step might be to exchange review services with somebody whose style and approach you like, so you can build up a rapport and see where their strengths and weaknesses lie.

Make it absolutely clear to your client that they will be dealing directly with another supplier who is fully responsible for all work delivered this time around. This is win/win, incidentally: if things don't work out, your stand-in's screw-ups will consolidate the customer's ties to you.

We are all for freelance translators teaming up, but as you rightly observe one-off ventures formed when the pressure is on are rarely satisfactory—especially if you are the one carrying the can.

FA & WB

Q *Is it necessary to accept all job offers from direct clients, or can one occasionally say no?*

Workaholic

A Dear Workaho,
Of course you can turn down work—unless you have managed to clone yourself, in which case we hope you have been farsighted enough to patent the

process since it is likely to pay far more than even premium translation.

In the meantime, since you need time to eat, sleep, enjoy your family, take vacations and otherwise recharge your batteries, the question is not whether you can say no but rather how to do so—how to best deal with queries and offers that come at inconvenient or downright impossible times.

We see three options:

• Just say no.

Reply (regretfully of course) that you are fully booked and cannot take on any more work at this time. This confirms that there are other clients out there who value your services (good). At the same time it leaves your client in the lurch (bad). If they then make a terrible decision and the project blows up in their face, they will come back to you singed and reeling (good). But they may also find a white knight/perfect match to replace you, in which case they may never come back (bad).

• Say no, but suggest an alternative.

See our advice to Stuck in the Middle (page 231). The aim is not to lay your own reputation on the line, since Gloria (or her clone) may screw up. Instead, you offer the client an option or two to follow up on—being helpful, but keeping your distance. Ideally there will be increased stress at their end, which will make them all the happier to come back home to you next time around.

• Say no, and find an alternative.

In this case you are taking on the stress and responsibility of finding a suitable supplier and reviser, and ensuring that the job goes smoothly. Should you think this is a piece of cake, ask any serious translation agency about the challenges involved. Don't even consider it unless you have a pool of tried and tested suppliers to draw from, and experience in project management. In which case, be sure build in a margin for yourself, of course.

FA & WB

Q *I am a freelance translator living some sixty miles to the north of Paris in a little town that must remain nameless for reasons that will become clear as my story unfolds. The events I am about to narrate were set in motion on a summer's day in 2002.*

I was about to dive into the local swimming pool when I spotted our amiable lifeguard Laurent in uncharacteristically animated conversation with a pair of middle-aged gentlemen sporting the knee-length shorts so favoured across the Channel for reasons of modesty but banned in most French establishments on grounds of hygiene. My language skills saved the day, and our English friends soon returned wearing the required V-shaped trunks.

Indeed, so taken were they with Laurent that they signed up for private swimming lessons, and here again I was able to help out with some of the trickier technical terms like "dos crawlé", "le crawl" and "la brasse."

Laurent's gratitude knew no bounds and he has been coaching me for free ever since. He also took to singing my praises, and soon I was being asked to help out in all manner of language situations and receiving favours in return.

For instance, I have been writing CVs for various members of our fishmonger's family (thanks to me, his son now works as a waiter in a well-known London restaurant) and have also helped his daughter write a successful application to an American university, so now he keeps me supplied with prize oysters and home-cured salmon...

My girlfriend and I have become frequent and honoured guests at the Michelin-starred restaurant down the road ever since I rescued their menu (which they change twice a year) from the jaws of Babelfish. And I receive inexpensive treatment from our local dentist (dentures at cost price, fillings on the house) in return for regular summaries of articles from The Lancet and The American Journal of Dentistry.

An idyllic situation you might say but only other day, finding myself at a loose end between one job and another, I thought to put a value on all these gifts and services and discovered to my consternation that I have been earning an unofficial income of approximately €20,000 a year in return for informal translation work—enough to move me into a tax bracket where I should have been paying an extra €2,000 yearly or €10,000 over the last five years.

So what shall I do? Let sleeping dogs lie as my girlfriend suggests? Fling myself before the Hotel des Impôts and confess to my sins as her father (who has been peeking at my papers) obviously hopes? Or leave the country in a hurry?

Sick with Worry

A Dear Sick,
It is clear that you are essentially a Nice Guy and, just as importantly, recognized as such in your town. In fact, lots of translators are Nice Guys—and as long as they are getting enough business in their day jobs, what's the big deal?

The problem arises when Nice Guy reflexes get out of hand—when you are evicted for not paying your rent or mortgage and die on a park bench one cold winter morning, or when you collapse from exhaustion for that midnight to 3 a.m. session translating a local tourist brochure, a deserving immigrant's high-school diploma or a free-press article for the middle-school fête.

The cherry on the cake might be a future in-law's concern that his daughter is involved with someone whose grasp of economics stops at barter.

Our advice: Forget the tax people. They're unlikely to get on your case as long as you are paying a reasonable amount into the collective kitty.

Instead think quality of life.

If for you that means walking down the street with an entourage of monolingual admirers thrusting flyers, reports and signs at you for expert input, that's terrific. And if this opens other doors in your community, why not?

But if the time you invest in such endeavors is getting out of hand, the best solution is to have a phrase or two up your sleeve to indicate your unavailability and/or steer the conversation over into the realm of commerce. This is far easier than you'd think. E.g.:

• What a fascinating brochure! I'd love to translate it but I'm booked solid—yes, clear through to Christmas.

• Your wife's insurance claim? I'd translate it in a minute, but... my tax situation is iffy right now; it would be too risky for both of us.

• Ah, a CV! They are so tricky to translate—in fact that's why they are so expensive. Shall I look at it and give you a quote? What's your deadline?

Deliver these phrases with a Nice Guy smile, of course.

FA & WB

WHEN TO SAY YES

Q *Just before Christmas I received a translation representing 50,000 words to be completed for January 3—big rush!*

But on the purchase order, the translation agency marked "Our offices will be closed from December 25 through January 1." In other words, the agency brigade was off work partying for an entire week, while the poor translator (me) was working his rear end off and (yes) sacrificing his own new year's celebration just to be able to deliver on time.

Is it any wonder freelance translators get ticked off at agency arrogance?

Bah Humbug

A Dear H-Bug,
Congratulations on meeting the deadline, but why get all steamed up? Are you suggesting that a Santa-suited agency rep broke into your office and held a gun to your head?

Let's repeat that: nobody forced you to take on this job. And rush jobs at holiday periods are an ideal opportunity to double or triple your standard fees (agencies know about this, too).

Depending on your family obligations, such sweeteners can be downright festive and help get the new year off to a good start. Stop grumbling, be merry and start making money.

FA & WB

Q *I'm a successful patent translator but have long wanted to shift my focus back over into history and the social sciences—fields where I used to translate research and books to good reviews, and which I find more intellectually stimulating.*

Yet each time I gear myself up to make the break, I get sucked back into my current specialty.

Example: just today a patent agent from the past got back in touch, praising work I did a decade ago. He is keen to put more work my way. I want to say "No", but at another level feel I can't afford to refuse, so will probably say "yes"—and postpone my "new me" program yet again.

How do I break this cycle (and perhaps more to the point: should I even be contemplating such a move)?

Ditherer

A Dear Ditherer,
We're convinced that translators produce better work when they are passionate about their subject, so if you feel you are getting into a rut it makes sense to seek new pastures.

That said, unless you have (1) confirmation that new contracts will materialize quickly, (2) a pile of patent-translation-generated savings in the bank, (3) a trust-fund income, (4) a wealthy spouse or (5) a perverse yen to be independently poor, why burn your bridges?

Consider: quoting 25% higher to your new (old) patent client will allow you to either cut back your volume in this area (freeing time for new ventures) or build up a nest egg to finance the outreach you'll need to secure a new client base in the social sciences. No apologies, simply announce and apply your new fee scale; if a former client has taken the trouble to look you up ten years on, you must be doing something right.

But don't kid yourself. Developing your new clientele will take time and effort. Start by reading up on all the work done by the authors you used to translate, beginning with those who are still productive. Then pick up your phone and get back into direct touch with them. If they are impecunious university folk, however prominent in their field of research, this is where a wining & dining budget comes in—but only assuming monies are available somewhere, somehow, to pay for the translations that you hope will follow.

Good luck!

FA & WB

PEOPLE SKILLS

Q *I agree wholeheartedly with your advice to Hard to Just Say No (page 225). These days I do no subcontracting at all. Instead I refer clients to other translators when I am unable to do a job.*

Yet on more than one occasion, the client has complained, not about the quality of the work, but about the translator's customer relationship skills. It seems that some translators demand that referrals pay up front, on delivery or within two weeks. As if that weren't bad enough, they hound the client if the check is a day late, or call me to complain about the client! Is there some way, other than going back to subcontracting, that I can nip this one in the bud?

Stuck in the Middle

A Dear Stuck,

Are we correct in assuming that your translator contacts do provide good quality and that the clients are generally pleasant? Good, that makes it simpler.

1. Send translators to whom you might refer clients a short memo summarizing your view of useful people skills, including acceptable and unacceptable behavior, and who does what in referrals. Writing things down does help. Really.

2. Eccentric as some translators may be, your own reputation will suffer if you point their oddities out to clients too frequently or vehemently. So do avoid pigeonholing people as misfits from the git-go: keep "She's got a terrible temper, but her work is fine" and "Don't mind his bizarre telephone manner, he's a damn good translator" up your sleeve for extreme cases.

3. Try the arm's-length-with-feedback ploy: "I've heard quite good things about Gloria Mucklewitt; here are her contact details. Oh, and I'd be very interested in hearing how your project goes; I want to be sure I can refer clients to her in the future. Could you let me know? Thanks!"

You say this even if—hey, especially if—Gloria has been on the phone for the past ten days yapping about hopeless clients or tearing down fellow translators. (Again, we're assuming her work is good and that she is stepping into the breach because you are swamped).

By taking this approach, you will have passed on essential contact information and ensured you get a report, distancing yourself from the job and translator without voicing any particular opinion except that their work has been said to be good.

If Gloria does go twitchy on this customer, too, proper behavior is to chuckle about it with the client the first time, directing their attention back to the fine work produced. The second time you are free to revert to the Extreme Case phrasebook above. By the third time you may well have decided to do what many translators do from the start and refer clients politely to the directory of your national or regional translators' association.

With Gloria's help, they will in any case be all the happier when your backlog clears and they can return to your congenial fold.

FA & WB

Q *Last month I attended a translator workshop focused on fine points of electronic subassemblies for the automotive industry. I had been looking forward to the event, not least because it took place in one of the sunnier locales of the Iberian subcontinent. Good food, a pool and a civil starting time for the workshop after an evening sampling local viticulture—what more could you ask for?*

Yet when I joined my fellow participants for lunch, a polyphony of grievances began as soon as participants sat down around the table.

To my right, a bearded gentleman began jabbing his finger in my face while recounting some unforgivable wrong another translator had done him. To my left, a heavyset lady shouting in my ear swore eternal vengeance to an absent colleague who had besmirched her reputation. And so on.

I am mystified. I didn't know any of these people at all. What made them think that I had nothing better to do than listen to their bitching and backbiting? They don't behave that way when they are around clients, or do they?

Bemused in Brussels

A Dear Bemused,
Maybe they do. Keep in mind that many translators never see a live client, preferring to e-mail their work to translation companies instead.

If they don't share an office, employ clerical help or train a junior translator they may not see anyone in their work setting. That leaves the family or the dog as counterparts for social interaction, and the family soon tires of hearing

Daddy or Mommy talk shop. Some people lack even a dog.

Where can they go then to let off steam? You guessed it—a translator meeting!

Isolation breeds resentment, which eventually turns into a festering sore and undermines social skills. It's an occupational hazard, like black lung for coal miners.

FA & WB

Q *The other day, I was at a party and saw this blonde bombshell wearing a very tight-fitting sweater flash me an enticing smile. I sauntered over, drink in hand, and said hi. Man oh man, what a looker! And brains, too: an investment analyst with an MBA. When I told her that I am a translator, her smile kind of froze and she got this glassy look in her eyes. "So... can you make a living doing that?" she asked, craning her neck to see who else was in the room.*

Now why would she be like that to me? Also, this is not the first time this has happened.

Low on the Party Ladder

A **Fire Ant rasps:** On the face of it, the lady was simply rude, and bad manners should be laughed off. It's not the rudeness, though, that's really bugging you, right? BB was on to something deeper, and like the cruel child telling everyone that you just sat down in the puddle of beer, she put her finger on something real.

Nubile human females choosing a mating partner are no different from females in the rest of the animal kingdom. They expect the male to engage in some kind of display of strength and superiority that will hold their interest. Okay, we haven't got plumage to spread, or jackhammer beaks for drilling a tattoo into a redwood tree. But human culture—and female ingenuity—have developed ways to ferret out the alpha males from the chaff.

Money, status, and power still top the list as attention-getters. Unfortunately for you, translators can lay claim to none of these. And if you believe that women's lib means bodacious female MBAs welcome a partner who makes a fraction of their own income, think again.

Being the stronger sex, men of course are not so shallow. I have been known to say that it's personality, not physical beauty, that makes a woman attractive. (I also buy Penthouse magazine for the thoughtful articles only, not the pictures.)

Read Seneca, take cold showers, and comfort yourself with the thought that by the time you are fifty, many of your currently more successful rivals will be hemorrhaging money in alimony to their ex-wives.

Worker Bee buzzes: A "blonde bombshell," eh?

Who "flashed" you "an enticing smile"?

Give us a break.

Saunter, schmaunter: what you did was shuffle over, eyes averted, give her a goofy leer, blush, hike up your army surplus pants (revealing tube socks and sneakers) and dribble red wine down the front of your Voulez-Vous Coucher Avec Moi? Tee shirt as you toyed nervously with the cellophane tape holding your broken glasses together.

Forget the power/money/status argument altogether. Pure puffery. By the time your MBA babe issued her income query, you'd already missed the cut.

Where did you slip up? Easy. Through your dress and demeanor, you came across as weird rather than creative. This was a serious mistake, since your trump card, sir, is something few Porsche-driving options traders can fall back on.

You are a word artist (or should be), and in the right hands there is absolutely nothing more seductive than language and wordplay. The trick is to breathe life into the words, to lift them up off the page. Well, not all the words. "Man oh man, what a looker" is a non-starter, for example.

But to get even that far you will have to pull yourself together. This is easier than you might think. For one thing, translators have a distinct advantage over bankers wardrobe-wise, since you can take a cue from the creative talent on communications teams and dress casual. Just remember: creative casual, not weird casual.

With the economy faltering, snotty MBAs can be pink-slipped any time. At which point a free-thinking, witty, well-read and creative man of words could be just the ticket.

If you want to pursue this option, invest in a black turtleneck. Cultivate a soulful gaze. And get a new pair of glasses, for heaven's sake.

CLIENT EDUCATION

Q *Lately, I am running more and more into the following problems:*
1. Time constraints. Everything has to be done very fast—even if the client took lots of care and months to write the source document. In a rush, it's very difficult to do accurate work—let alone a good style. And by now, most of my jobs

have very short turnaround times.

2. Money. We are supposed to do better and better work for less and less money. ALSO, and that is a main issue, the client often just wants "updates," pieces documents together from segments done by different translation agencies, does his own formatting (with a HUGE potential of introducing mistakes), tries to get by as cheaply as possible.

3. Lack of understanding on the client's side. Unfortunately, very often the client isn't willing to listen or learn. He wants to have it his way, even if you explain to him time and time again that it's impossible or not recommendable.

4. Sub-standard quality of the source text.

5. The clients (especially their reviewers) expect the translator to deliver a product that is far superior to the source text. I'm running into that a lot lately—and aside from the fact that this is not appropriate in my opinion, it is also not possible: a translator or translation agency not employed by the client does not have the necessary resources to deliver such a product! (Yet, many times the translation is an improvement on the source text anyway, because translators ask questions and correct errors and/or ambiguities.)

6. The in-country reviewers will often hold the translator responsible for everything, including technical content (such as the ubiquitous redundance and lack of specific technical information in US English marketing texts). Even if the translator points out to the client in the U.S. that the text should be modified for the target market, the answer usually is to translate exactly what the source text says. And the reviewer often does not like it and thinks the translator should have changed it.

7. After all, translating the exact content of the source text IS our job. Or should be. Ideally, there is close cooperation between client, their reviewer, and the translation agency/translators. In that case, it might be ok to sign a name. The next question is though: WHOSE name? A translation, in most cases, is not the product of one person's work, but a cooperation of several people: translator, editor, proofreader, DTP staff, reviewer and possibly a technical writer who corrected some errors in the source language.

In most cases however, I would not care to sign my name to a product that I don't have control over!

First of all, we need to educate the clients so they cooperate with us. (An agency I work with told me that they lost a lot of clients, because this agency asks too many questions! The clients just wanted to get the job done fast and cheap and easy, without having to answer questions.)

Also, it might be nice to provide the clients and their reviewers with a list of indicators for good and bad translations. Many reviewers seem to think if they change on key term, the whole translation is bad (even if the term chosen by the translator is perfectly correct, just not used by this particular company). Or they make stylistic changes and claim that the whole translation is bad. It is very difficult for the clients to figure out what a good translation should look like—and in fact, this is true for many other industries. How do we know, for instance, whether the new roof put on our house will actually last? We don't find out until the warranty has expired! Just some ideas... And I also wanted to be sure that [our professional association for translators] is not expecting us to deliver all kinds of value-added services we cannot provide (due to a variety of factors).

Overwhelmed

A Dear Overwhelmed,
Congratulations, your letter sums up every query FA & WB have dealt with since the column's launch in 1998. No respect, no control, no power—and certainly no money. Excuse us while we go lie down in a darkened room with a cool damp cloth on our insect brows.

Yet a close re-reading suggests that many of your own practices place you squarely in the part-of-the-problem box. What is this about working more for less and less money? Accepting insane turnarounds? Working with agencies that refuse to deal with questions? Worst of all, are you seriously suggesting, madam, that "it is not appropriate" to deliver translations that are superior to the source text? Excuse us while we go lie down in a darkened room with a cool damp cloth on our insect brows.

Agreed, client education is a long slog. But rather than throw up your hands in dismay, we suggest you try to break the process down into do-able, concrete stages. Download "Translation, getting it right" from www.iti.org.uk, www.atanet.org or www.sft.fr, in English and French this instant and start distributing it to your clients (you'll find German, Dutch, Romanian, Italian and Czech versions at www.fit-europe.org).

Take a hard look at your client base and weed out the most obnoxious and clueless now.

Hone your writing skills, specialize in a subject area where demand is on the rise, and get out and start pitching your services. Network with fellow translators to share resources and ideas.

Above all, start saying "no." You owe it to yourself and the profession as a whole.

FA & WB

Q *My father-in-law is an architect in France, and occasionally does work for an American company's subsidiary in his area. He speaks very little English, and when he needs to provide a translation of his reports and/or correspondence, he generally either a) has one of his supposedly "English-speaking" colleagues or secretaries do them or b) asks me to do them.*

Like many people, he seems to think that anybody with a passable knowledge of English can translate. Last year he sent me a document produced by his secretary that was so badly mangled I told him it would be easier to just re-do it (example: "Nous n'avons pas été mis au courant du seuil significatif" rendered as "No one tell us the meaningful doorway.")

Now he wants me to evaluate one of his other colleagues' work.

How can I tell him in a tactful way that this stuff should be left to professionals, not self-proclaimed bilinguals or worse?

I should add that though I like and respect my father-in-law, we are not exactly close and he is a reserved person by nature; most of our conversations concern the weather and, lately, his new grandson. So I don't exactly have the kind of relationship where I could just call him up to chat.

Daughter-in-Law

A Dear Daughter,
In a few years you can broach the subject when discussing your son's language skills—bilingualism is a subject many families warm to, and a good opportunity to contrast oral and written fluency using concrete examples.

But that is many meaningful doorways down the road, so you'll probably want to act earlier.

Why not download "Traduction/Faire les bons choix" from the French translators' association at www.sft.fr and send it on to him? You can also ask the SFT to send him a dozen paper copies directly for distribution to his co-workers.

Written especially for non-linguists, this client education brochure is based on real-life examples of good and bad translations. It's short and readable. And endorsement by PricewaterhouseCoopers and the Paris stock exchange give its best-practice message extra credibility with people like your father-in-law.

FA & WB

11
Professional associations

E pluribus unum: onwards and upwards!

BENEFITS

Q *What guarantees does membership of a professional translators' association bring companies who buy the work produced by the association's members?*
Careful Buyer

A Dear Buyer,
In absolute terms, and assuming you are a buyer prepared to invest good money in exchange for a red-hot translation: none. Zero.

A translator is only as good as the last job turned in, and anyone can have a bad day.

Scary, eh? It's a jungle out there, and only the very naïve believe that membership of a professional association is a bulletproof guarantee.

True, some translator associations have certification processes, which may screen out the utterly incompetent and unacceptably dire. But you may still find yourself dealing with the moderately competent and bad-dayers, not only the highly skilled professionals you want and need.

So why do FA & WB tend to be boosters of professional associations?

First, because jumping through the membership hoops set by most translator associations generally does indicate that your supplier is at the very least exposed to professional discussions of quality and client service. This is surely a step in the right direction.

The translator training programs offered by many associations—including continuing education requirements or recommendations in an increasing number of countries—are another plus.

Finally, most professional associations have an arbitration body. So the chickens will come home to roost, even though these entities' rulings only kick in after the fact—when suspicious buyers challenge a poor job done, delivered and already used.

Note that the frustrating quest for quality is not limited to association directories. As you have no doubt discovered, any number of translation providers claim to deliver extraordinarily high quality work as a result of highly skilled teams, stringent process control and so on. Some do. Yet experience shows that the best intentions (and processes) can be short-circuited once constraints start piling up—tight deadlines, sloppy or committee writing of source text, non-availability of authors to answer questions, young or inexperienced project managers and revisers, etc.

For the record, Fire Ant & Worker Bee belong to the healthy-dose-of-skepticism school. We encourage translators to join professional associations and clients to turn first to said associations for advice on getting the job done right. But for the foreseeable future we will continue to urge both buyers and suppliers of translation to print supplier details—a.k.a. whodunit (literally)—on all published translations, including commercial and technical documentation. There is simply no better way to temper the bullshit factor and ensure that all parties have a vested interest in getting it right.

FA & WB

Q *I've noticed that the glossary of translation and interpreting terminology on my website has been reproduced in part or in its entirety on several commercial websites of other translators or agencies. This bugs me since it is out of order not to ask first and not to give due credit. It also contravenes copyright law. Finally, this website is my main (and very successful) means of attracting new customers.*

I've so far written to the offending webmasters, citing my conditions for using excerpts from the glossary (basically clearly visible credit to me with a URL to my website). But in my experience, that doesn't usually yield a response. Any suggestions?

Sweat of My Brow

A Dear Sweat,
This is where membership of your national translators' association pays off.

Let headquarters know of the problem and copy them in when you first write to offenders; this reminds the culprits that you are not alone—that the translation industry really is a village.

If a second reminder is needed, ask the association to do it on your behalf (be sure to give them all the information they need).

239

You don't belong to a national association? Consider an entirely different approach: email the guilty party a bare-bones "Dear [offender's name], I'm glad you liked my text. Did you know it was copyright? Sincerely, [your name]."

The advantage here is that you've provided factual information (you exist, you own the text and you are aware of the offense) without showing your hand. The word "copyright" plants an ominous seed, we're told, and the laconic style elicits contrition and compliance more readily than a threat. Is a lawsuit in the making? Will you be waiting outside their office tonight, baseball bat in hand? Or might things be put right by a sincere apology and immediate removal of the material or inclusion of credits and URL?

FA & WB

Q *I joined our national translators' association last year but will not renew my membership this year because their website is awful, incompetent, impossible to update and (above all) not productive financially.*

I have no way of knowing, but are all the other translators in this group bachelors/old maids with no children (I have three to support) or metrosexuals (I can't afford that luxury) or gay? (Don't get me wrong, this is perfectly respectable, my bro is.) Fact is, I have zero time, zero interest and zero budget for their dinners and get-togethers, my rare outings are to the supermarket around the corner.

A few statistics say it all:

Contacts from commercial website ProZ over a period of 3 years: 143. Of which 84 contracts.

Contacts from the professional association over 18 months: 1. Zero contracts.

From what I see guys like me don't exist in most translators mindsets.

Get Down to Business

A Dear Down,

We think your mismatch with your (ex-)professional association results from a basic misunderstanding of how such associations differ from commercial platforms.

For a start, most associations require proof that you are indeed a professional translator before they let you in. On commercial platforms you pays your money and gets your access. You may be able to participate for free in activities such as forums, but any structured input you provide is a gift to a commercial entity. And why not, say some. Indeed. To their credit, most platforms are very clear about this.

So what are professional associations for?

They are one or more steps back from the market: they facilitate contacts among professionals, raise awareness of best professional practices among translators and clients both, offer guidance in ethical and professional matters, organize training courses, and promote the profession as a whole to outside world.

What they are not is mega-translation agencies dedicated to placing jobs. This is true even if they display your contact details for potential clients, or give you an opportunity to meet like-minded professionals with whom you might decide to work on large projects. By networking in a professional association, you will often pick up business tips, too. (Here's one: if you ever do rejoin and decide to participate actively, don't try to get the conversational ball rolling with your second sentence.)

To address your closing comment, guys like you not only exist in translator mindsets, you populate entire neighborhoods of the translator world. You're at the wordface from dawn to dusk, with no time to network or socialize with clients or your peers, so busy are you making the next deadline to pay the rent and put food on the table.

Don't get us wrong. It's good to have your eye on the bottom line. In fact our main objective in writing this column is to get translators to reflect more about business matters. But ProZ and other commercial platforms, while entertaining forums for social exchange, are not the best place to build up a client base of demanding, well-heeled direct customers who are passionate about their texts. The reason is simple: this buyer profile does not fish in pools of anonymous self-proclaimed professionals. Of course if you're happy with the clients, friends and prices you find on ProZ, that's fine too.

If your national association is really that bad, we suggest you find another vector for networking. Just remember that you get out of any networking opportunity what you put into it. And to pull in the truly lucrative jobs, you must get out to venues other than supermarkets on a regular basis.

FA & WB

Q *Your long-time reader and fan needs your wise words again. After a seven-month wait on the edge of my seat, I have just received my ATA certification as English into Spanish translator.*

I feel happy, and my question to you is: what now?

That is, how am I going to take advantage of my certification? Experience and advice from the trenches most welcome!

Certified

A Dear Certified,
Congratulations! One immensely appealing aspect of taking and passing a test of this type is the personal satisfaction of measuring your skills against an industry benchmark.

In concrete terms, there are markets where a qualification of this type makes no difference at all, but if you've got it, hey, why not flaunt it: add "ATA certified, Eng>Spanish" to your business card, website and advertising materials immediately. Depending on your home country you might also want to expand ATA into "American Translators Association."

And be sure to look into the many membership benefits offered by ATA, as these may be as useful in the immediate future as any direct payoff in marketing terms.

FA & WB

Q *As an ex-pat Australian, living in Chile for the past 13 years, I have become proficient in Spanish. In fact, I worked for ten of those 13 years as a bilingual tour guide and interpreter and for the last three years have been working full time as a translator, English/Spanish/English.*

I now have confidence in my abilities to translate a wide range of subjects in both directions and am interested in looking for more work outside of Chile, however it has been made clear to me that some sort of certification is frequently required.

Looking at the fees for this with both ATA and NAATI (Australia) I realize that these two at least are well above the economic possibilities of a Chile-based translator.

My question then is whether you have any knowledge of certifying bodies in countries with somewhat more affordable fees. Any advice you can offer on this would be greatly appreciated.

Ex-Pat Australian

A Dear Ex-Pat,
The American Translators Association (ATA) states on its website "The fee of $300 includes all administrative and grading expenses." According to NAATI's site, the fee for certification is well over AUD 1,000 for non-resident candidates. But there are other options now, too: in recent years at least one commercial platform has launched its own certification system.

As a business expense for a full-time professional translator, three hundred dollars is hardly exorbitant, even in Chile.

But would certification with ATA or any other body be a wise investment?

We don't want to slight the efforts of the colleagues in translator associations around the world who have given countless hours of their time in efforts to establish recognized "brands of quality."

But we are not aware of hard evidence that the *direct-client* market perceives accredited translators as superior to non-accredited ones. (Agencies yes, perhaps.) And if certified translators do tend to earn more than non-certified or accredited ones (hard figures please, someone?) we think this might have more to do with their greater commitment to the profession. For the same reason, translators who are simply members of professional associations also tend to earn more than the great unwashed masses of self-proclaimed professional translators.

Perhaps the idea that certification is required comes from reading the application forms that some translation companies mail out to people seeking assignments. Forms chock full of questions in 6-point type, inquiring about your shoe size, the number of Albanian dwarves in your household, your social security number (especially if you are *not* a US citizen), and an appropriately fantastic number of words that you claim to have already translated.

But as others have already pointed out, filling out these forms generally does not appear to be the best avenue leading to well-paid work.

In our opinion, getting business has not changed much in the age of the Internet. The most lucrative work continues to come mainly from direct clients in markets where demand outstrips supply (sellers' markets), through word-of-mouth referrals. Certification is not an issue because direct clients hardly ever ask for it. Of course, zeroing in on these assignments is like squeezing through the eye of a needle. Again in our opinion, and with the caveat that, as always, our perspective is a limited and personal one, you get such work if you:

• set up your business when you feel confident that you are as well prepared as you can be, and have a sizable nest egg in the bank
• acquire and maintain specialist knowledge in a small number of fields
• exploit existing knowledge from a previous career
• hone your writing skills continuously
• relocate to a sellers' market, or travel there regularly to call on prospects and clients
• don't wait for the work to find you
• persevere with your networking: get out to client events and trade shows, buttonhole people; be persistent (and pleasant)
• sign your name to work that will be published

• join translator associations, regularly attend workshops, maximize your exposure to increase the chances of getting referrals.

Again, there may be all sorts of good reasons for seeking certification by translator associations, but as an experienced freelance translator hunting for direct business you should not expect too much from it.

FA & WB

MOVING & SHAKING

Q *I live in a country many people see as a translation backwater—but things are moving!*

About a hundred translators here are in the process of creating order out of chaos by setting up a national translators' association. We've made a lot of progress in establishing our structure and organization, and are working on a code of ethics and other projects. Would you have any input on client education and the like? Actually, any tips at all on stumbling blocks facing new associations would be most welcome. (It sounds like you've been there before.)

Meeting Man

A Meeting Man,
What terrific news!

One hundred people may be a nightmare to organize, but think of all the energy and good will you can tap into, gushes Worker Bee. Think of how you can advance together, promoting greater awareness of translation and better working conditions for one and all! Think, too, mutters Fire Ant, about the near certainty of dysfunctional loners and government-issue gasbags in your midst, and act now to ensure that your fledgling group does not get sidetracked by them.

No sooner said than done: below are our tips on what to focus on, what to watch out for, projects that will get everyone on board, and heads to knock together preemptively. (Readers' comments welcome.)

• Some translator associations admit agencies and companies, while others are limited to individuals, either freelance or salaried (company owners can nonetheless join as individuals if they are themselves translators). We can see pros and cons for both models, but is important to settle this early on, as there may be bad blood between freelancers and agencies. Your new association will need all its energy for moving ahead on concrete projects, not for squabbles.

• Given the surge in online marketplaces (ProZ, gotranslators, etc.) where "membership" is as easy as clicking, paying your money (in some cases) and posting a self-drafted and edited "professional profile," you should also decide whether your group is focusing on promoting the profession or promoting the services of individual members. If you opt to do both (why not), decide precisely where the line lies and plan ahead to avoid conflict-of-interest situations (e.g., if volunteers are manning your association phone line, they should not be siphoning off prospective clients for their own business).

• Translators attending your meetings should go away with more energy than they had when they arrived. Full stop. This means that if ever a negative, nasty or simply needy individual or group of individuals starts transforming your get-togethers into moan & groan sessions or food fights, you must rethink the whole set-up. It is worth stating this explicitly right up front: meetings must generate energy, not sap it.

• Training (1): Win-win! Training is one of the most constructive options around, and something a national association can do very effectively. Demand is absolutely enormous, perhaps because translation can be such a solitary job: most people are eager to get out and interact with others. Just as importantly, specialized knowledge helps translators produce better quality work and charge higher rates. We repeat: win-win!

• Training (2): By all means invite expert colleagues to contribute to your training sessions, but it's also important to bring in speakers from outside the language services industry. At one blow, your training becomes client education, since a scientist, patent agent or finance director who has spoken to a group of translators in a training session usually goes back to his or her own industry with a new awareness of what professional translators can do for that industry.

• A listserve/discussion group (yahoo, gmail or other) is free and a great way to get the flow going. Here colleagues remind us that most existing associations have gone through ups and downs when aggressive individuals or small groups have hijacked discussion lists with flames and rants, chasing the rank and file away. The solution is have list members sign an agreement setting out basic netiquette up front. You must also have a moderator.

• Money (1): In a general way, tread carefully on "money issues" (perceptions and reality), which can be a catalyst for all sorts of disputes and time-wasting.

• Money (2): Some members/potential members will complain about the cost of whatever you plan to do, whether their contribution be $1, $10, $20 or $250 (refreshments at meetings, room rental for training, chipping in to finance a website, etc.). Let such comments go by with a smile. Base your priorities on what the most dynamic, professional people want, and don't worry if there is not 100% agreement. Let us repeat that: the poverty cultists must not be allowed to set the agenda. They can climb on board later if the spirit moves them. Or drop out altogether.

• Money (3): Even the most dedicated volunteers can get discouraged if they lose too much business through the time they invest in the association. So decide together, from the start, what is reasonable "volunteer" work and what should be bought in. If your whole structure is financed by motivated people donating "free work," there will be burnout at some point—perhaps even bitterness and martyrdom (loudly proclaimed or suffered in silence). Both are to be avoided.

• Networking opportunities of all types are important, and work best if there is a specific timeline and objective. How about a joint writing project, such as an adaptation into your language of the excellent client-education brochure "Translation, Getting it Right"? (We admit to a vested interest in this particular venture).

• Re codes of ethics, a few years back FIT-Europe asked its member associations to contribute theirs to a central repository, now online at www.fit-europe.org. There may be some ideas to recycle there—why re-invent the wheel?

• At one of your meetings, create sub-groups and go around the table having each person describe how he/she sees the association "in ten years' time." This (1) helps get everyone thinking beyond immediate issues (where you might not all agree) and (2) creates a positive atmosphere as people realize that what they are doing now will have an impact in ten years. Finally, (3) it helps people get to know each other better.

We wish you the best of luck as you advance with your new association. And we'd be delighted to hear from readers with hands-on experience in this area.

FA & WB

Q *I've just returned from a local translator association's event on war-zone interpreting. To their enormous credit, the organizers of the meeting had arranged for two Iraqi interpreters to speak at the meeting and answer questions. Both had had to flee Iraq amid death threats, and one of them left the Middle East only 90 days ago. Fascinating!*

Alas, as soon as the Q&A period began, one of the Iraqis—a professional translator even before the Iraq war began—mentioned that many of his peers were not adequately trained as interpreters. That opened the floodgates, and the rest of the meeting degenerated into the Eternal Refrain. Our competitors are incompetent. Rates are too low. Computer translation is undermining us. Globalization is killing us. The Iraqis sat largely forgotten amid the collective kvetching.

What a squandered opportunity!

I don't hold office in the group, and I hadn't organized the meeting. I joined a few other dissident voices in pointing out the benefits of CAT tools and the upside of globalization—but the negativity in the room swept us aside. How can I help change the dynamic and make future meetings worth my time?

Fed Up

A Dear Fed Up,
It sounds you and the other dissidents stepped in too late—after all, the theme was topical, the speakers unique and potentially riveting.

What the organizers needed was a SWAT unit in the wings or (better yet) strategically positioned throughout the room. Experience shows that three or four well-prepared people can and will turn the tide, provided they move in quickly and ruthlessly. But they must do so in formation, and they must be suitably armed, with microphones and a string of pertinent, upbeat questions addressed to the speaker to get things back on track. Organizers should ask for volunteers in advance and have them write up questions ahead of time; these will be fired into the fray as needed.

Your moderator also plays a key role, putting her foot down pleasantly but firmly if ever a complainer starts getting out of hand or refuses to relinquish the microphone.

At some point it might be worth explaining to the group that the priority for every translator gathering is that participants exit with more energy than they had on arrival—reinvigorated, recharged with the buzz that comes from networking and exposure to new ideas.

Collective hand-wringing doesn't do this. True, it may encourage audience participation (hey, everybody has something to complain about), but it drives away translators with energy and ideas who, like you, have better things to do.

At a very basic level, formulating themes for meetings in a positive mode is another way to throw the negative navel-gazers off balance.

Example: not "Who will survive the financial crisis?" but "How to use market turmoil to build your practice." Not "Globalization means pressure on prices" but "Three ways to harness global markets for your business." Not

"Interpreters deserve more respect!" but "Adrenalin plus: one of the most exciting jobs in the world."

You get the picture. The point is not to squelch democratic exchange, but to thwart the Rodney Dangerfields.

FA & WB

Q *I've just become head of my local translator group. Members seem really interested in meeting up, so with our board (three people) we've thought of having evening events with a speaker four times a year. We don't want to reinvent the wheel. Do you have a list of do's and don'ts? Thank you.*

Out & About

A Dear Out,
No sooner said than done:
• Identify good dates (avoid clashes with school vacations, national sports events, etc.). You can use www.doodle.ch for this.
• Reserve a room, which should be central and convenient for good public transport/parking. A restaurant? Why not. But be sure your room is separate from other diners or the noise level will get out of hand.
• Book your speaker/guest, focusing on topical issues and/or outreach (non-linguists are often a good choice; since they return to their natural habitat afterwards this can be a good vector for getting word out about how professional your group is, and what translators do). But do check to make sure your candidate is a good public speaker (ask around). Include a blurb on him/her in your program so that participants can read up on him/her/the topic.
• If not in a restaurant, plan refreshments & catering: who will bring what/serve? Who will clean up? Don't forget the bottle opener.
• Publicize your event as early as possible, but do send a reminder out two weeks ahead, too. Some people need that extra push.
• Send a short email reminder to everybody two days before.
• Make sure the address, neighborhood map and an on-site phone number appear in several places (including the flyer that participants will print out at the last minute, as they dash out of their home or office).
• Get there early to put up signs to guide attendees to the room.
• Networking (1): as the date approaches, send a list of those who have signed up out to everyone. Do this in advance so that people can see who will be there and plan who they want to speak to.
• Networking (2): have name tags (inexpensive stickers & a felt-tip pen are

fine) on site so attendees know who is who.

• Networking (3): have more copies of the attendance list to hand out on the day itself, including contact details to facilitate exchanges.

• Depending on group size, arrange for a sound system. Test it; make sure you know how to use it.

• If you are using a microphone for Q&A, assign an imposing older member of your group to be mic-handler; youngsters may be more agile, but they are also more vulnerable to the antics of bullies, neurotics and nut cases in the room (see Fed Up above). Make it very clear that the mic-handler takes orders from the moderator, and the moderator only (e.g., "next question?", change in topic, close, etc.)

• Thank everybody involved profusely, in public and in private, at the end, and announce that suggestions for future speakers are very welcome.

FA & WB

MOVERS & SHAKERS (NOT)

Q *I have just become head of our local translators' group and am being driven nuts—we all are—by a know-it-all with vast amounts of time who joins every committee, bosses everyone around, and generally doesn't let anyone else get a word in.*

This person is retired with a comfortable pension; we are all hardworking, full-time translators.

We appreciate the help (sort of), but are being driven slowly (some of us quickly) crazy by the attitude. Worse, we have had direct feedback suggesting that this omnipresent soul is in fact alienating potential new members. What to do?

Helmsperson

A Dear Helm,
You may take some comfort in knowing that many associations have one of these, er, difficult people.

Most are well intentioned and genuinely unaware of what a turn-off their pushiness is. Usually they are in desperate need of recognition, perhaps floundering in a retirement vacuum after a busy working life at the wordface.

Solution: shower them with praise, up to and including an awards ceremony with engraved plastic fork, if that is all your budget can stretch to.

249

Then entrust them, with great solemnity, with a Major Task, e.g., writing the history of the association (since they alone have all the information needed to serve as Living Memories). Or a biography of the group's founder.

In short, get them out of your (and the association's) hair by giving them something non-strategic and extremely time-consuming to do.

But remember that you and the frazzled others will then have to pick up the slack on your committees. It's surprising how much even the most irritating organizer can accomplish.

FA & WB

Q *My professional association recently got an internet forum going, and debate heated up pretty quickly. In a spirit of good fun (but also irritation at the pomposity of some participants) I did, I admit, engage in a few flame wars. Things escalated and two months ago I unsubscribed.*

The association is organizing a get-together this summer in a city not far from here.

At one level I would like to meet (or examine from a safe distance) various people I've crossed verbs with on the net. Yet some pretty harsh words were said, and seen from here the event has all the ingredients of something particularly violent that should take place in a misty castle in Ruritania.

Should I give it a miss or go along anyway? If I do attend, what are some good opening lines?

W. Mitty

A Dear Walt,
By all means attend. Nobody holds a grudge (or should do) where forum debates are concerned. We have a sneaking suspicion that on-line belligerence may be all the greater in fields like translation, where many practitioners work in isolation and let their people skills go cold. Some of the fiercest on-line opponents we know of are drinking buddies in real life (take that, cyberspace!).

Why not break the ice with a friendly "Can I get you a beer/glass of warm milk?"

FA & WB

Q *I work for a translators' association in a small country, but from exchanges with my counterparts in larger associations, I think my problem is a general one.*

Here in [country deleted] we have a few utterly dysfunctional members who pipe up at every occasion to complain and fuss. The general consensus is that they waste everyone's time.

    How can we best deal with this? (Hiring a hit man is not an option.)

Undercover

A Dear Undercover,
   Drowning them in love might work—and as such folks tend to be needy, this may be exactly what they are looking for. It can also be an entertaining way to destabilize blustering timewasters. But it is time-consuming. After all, you are a professional association, not a psychotherapy unit (although you might consider adding such a service to your member benefits).

    Points to keep in mind:

1. In any job that deals with the public, handling complaints with a smile goes with the territory. (Could you imagine working at an airline ticket counter?)
2. You don't mention whether these fussbudgets are volunteering time on a committee or other association body, or simply calling headquarters out of the blue to kvetch. If they are volunteers, it becomes a personnel management problem and a peer should be asked to step in. Perhaps the association president could ask them to put the lid on.
3. Slow down your response time. Some of these people seem to be looking for pen pals. If you don't respond, they may move on to the next target.

But face it, at some point you will have to cut your losses. You cannot please all of the people all of the time, and you should accept that you will have to write off a certain percentage of complainers. It's just not worth it to you and your staff, or fair to the other members. So past a certain point "Thank you for your comments" is a more than adequate reply, whatever their complaint.

FA & WB

Q *A common phenomenon at translator associations around the world is that translators who don't have enough work, or who feel threatened by competition from translators in other countries, or who are simply disgruntled with their own feelings of being underappreciated, start attacking their association, accusing it of being the source of all their woes, and espousing anti-foreigner policies that are the very antithesis of what one would expect from folks who make their living from the communication between peoples and cultures.*

    Why do they waste so much energy fighting their association instead of working to improve their own lots, e.g. by marketing, networking, improving their skills, going where the clients are, etc. Any thoughts?

Puzzled in Peoria

251

A Dear Puzzled,

Peoria, eh? Well, we've observed this "our association is leading us all over the cliff, rise up fellow lemmings!" phenomenon on three continents since January. And before that just about every year for as long as we've been in the business, generally peaking as annual general meetings roll around. Which is only natural.

Assuming such campaigns are not somehow linked to sunspot activity or global warming, our first reaction is simply that change is a scary thing and all the scarier for people who feel they have little influence over trends shaping their lives.

So it's a lot easier to remain within your comfort zone—railing against the "translation industry big guys" as represented by regional or national translator associations—than it is to take a long, hard look at how individual behaviors contribute to the outside world's view of translation providers as a whole.

Well, we would say that, wouldn't we, since our niche is giving concrete advice to individual correspondents with specific queries. (Readers will note that we often recommend collective action through associations.)

All things considered, our main problem with single-issue militants is that however earnestly their case starts out, 99% of the time it ends up painting all opponents as either hopelessly naive or part of a global conspiracy. That is generally unproductive.

But you wanted our opinion, right? Two points:

• If critics' stated aim is to move the industry forward with idea A, B or C, they have a duty to do their research properly, set out their case clearly, and be scrupulously honest in citing statistics on membership support, however devious and addicted to smoke-filled back rooms they believe their target association's elected officials to be. For their own mental health, they should be prepared to step back, stand down and blog their case if necessary. They should avoid abusive language and naïve/conspiracy reasoning.

• Elected officials have a duty to respond point by point to the carefully researched issues raised, however strident or even unhinged they think the leaders of the peasants' revolt are. They, too, must be scrupulously honest in citing statistics on membership support should this issue arise. And for their own mental health, they should be prepared to step back and reexamine association policy at regular intervals. They must do this once. But in our opinion they need not respond further if their critics consistently misstate information that has been corrected already.

As one old-timer comments, "I have a soft spot for vocal gadflies as long as they are well-informed, intelligent and committed. But the license for criticism comes with the understanding that the gadfly must be willing and able to pick up the torch and show how it's properly carried."

FA & WB

Q *I've always been a supporter of professional associations, and joining our new national translators' group five years ago was a natural step. I became more active last summer, and in May was asked to serve as temporary head of a regional chapter while the official chair recovers from surgery. I accepted.*

I'm not in this for the long haul but want to make sure my tenure is constructive. Already a few people who seemed professional and friendly last year have launched petty attacks on others; clearly they've got some issues I knew nothing about before. How do I keep things on track?

Pitching In

A Dear Pitching,
Ah translators, bless their tetchy little hearts. Is it the solitary work that makes them so subject to mood swings, so quick to flare up at perceived slights, so eager to identify "plots" and ulterior motives... or was it an initial lack of people skills that lured them into a profession often one remove from the real world?

Who knows. All we can say is that the behavior you describe is the flip side of the passion and intensity that the best translators bring to their work on the page—qualities that generate infinitely greater rewards than the backbiting.

Short of loading everybody onto a chartered jet and whisking them off to a well-appointed resort for a weekend of team building with a facilitator, the only solution we know of is a thick skin, a ready smile, and a list of stimulating projects to divert some of that negative energy into constructive efforts.

You can top these up by:
• distributing praise generously, even lavishly, since one of the squabblers' problems is lack of recognition.
• avoiding conspiracy theories like the plague. Plotland is a bad place, and dividing the world into goodies and baddies is a staple prop of the relationally handicapped. Internet communications multiply opportunities for misunderstanding. This is where your ready smile comes into play, along with good-natured private appeals to well-intentioned but divisive committee members to pull together for the greater good.

FA & WB

12
Kitchen sink

A diverse community indeed.

COMPUTERS, COMPUTERS

Q *Does the evolution of machine translation mean that the death of the professional translator is nigh?*

Agent Provocateur

A Dear Agent,
Try again.

Computer translation is the "click! the penny dropped" mechanism that reveals to savvy clients (who are also the ones you want) why they absolutely must have an expert human translator. Someone who knows their industry and company inside out and who writes extremely well. Who can transform what they intended their glossy brochure to say (never mind what they actually wrote) into seamless prose that will get their message across to foreign readers.

For bottom-end translators (the plodders, the line-'em-up-word-by-worders) MT may represent a threat (some day). As the man said, who is going to pay money and wait around for a poor or approximate translation when they can get one instantaneously, for free, over the Internet?

FA & WB

Q *Here we go again. Both the New York Times and the Economist are waxing euphoric about how translation technology is going to change things radically and may even make us all redundant. These are very influential news media, and I bet other commentators will soon leap into the fray with the same message. As translators, we are small fry. How can we counter the trend?*

Drowning Fast

A Dear Drowning,
Step back and take a deep breath.

Now repeat after us: machine translation is here to stay. Really.

Even Fire Ant admits to using it off and on for press reports in non-European languages.

But unless you are a truly hopeless translator, it is not a threat. All-but-free translations where speed and price trump accuracy are not where any professional wants to be, so may we suggest that you don't go there—except to use Google Translate and other systems yourself to browse the world outside.

Should you need to explain the difference between these systems and what you do for a living, how about the chain saw analogy?

ATA used this in a letter to President Barack Obama last October: "The challenge for translation consumers lies in understanding the proper application of [human skills and technology]," [ATA media spokesperson Kevin] Hendzel noted. "Translation software is like a chain saw. It's an invaluable tool when you need to chop a lot of wood in a hurry—but you need skill to use it safely, and it's not recommended for surgery."

Nor will a chain saw get you far if you want to cut boards, paper, metal, textiles, a roast turkey, your fingernails, your hair or a steak at a business lunch.

At the same time, what would be the point of using human translators to gist huge quantities of material? Surgeons could also saw logs with their scalpels, say observers, but it would be an absurd waste of their talent and capabilities.

So here's an idea: rather than simply highlight the silly mistakes that machine translation makes, issue a friendly reminder to use the tool appropriately, taking care not lop off a finger (or a leg). And tell yourself that current media coverage is above all a testimony to the power and reach of the press and PR departments at Google and Asia Online.

FA & WB

INTERPRETERS

Q *I was at a friendly gathering of bilingual friends this weekend when one of them mentioned that she was being flown to a nearby military base this week to "interpret" for a foreign delegation visiting state-of-the-art aircraft and weapons there.*

Although I do not know the details (who these delegates are, the purpose of their visit, what exactly my friend is expected to do, etc.), I was nevertheless shocked when she started joking around about not knowing anything about the technical aspect of the visit, and hoping that they wouldn't start discussing anything too complicated. She then went on to boast about how she improvises, smoothes things over, and adds in her own explanations when she "interprets" for someone who says something inflammatory or unclear, or when she doesn't understand. She is obviously not a trained interpreter, although she is perfectly bilingual and a highly intelligent person. She is also a friend of mine, whom I've always liked and respected.

I don't want to offend her, nor do I know if there is anything that can or should be done about this situation. But I find it outrageous that military authorities are turning to untrained bilinguals as interpreters. Aren't they aware of the importance of hiring professionally trained and certified interpreters?

Down with Amateur Hour

Dear Down,

Military authorities are cleaning up their act, we're told, spurred by recent gaffes and media interest in same. But the behavior you describe—self-deprecation on the part of folks plying the cocktail circuit—is an enduring trait of linguists, be they untrained bilinguals or professional translators and interpreters.

Note that we are not recommending expert translators wade in trumpeting years of study and decades of experience in field X, Y or Z, reeling off high-profile assignments with captains of industry and government leaders. Arrogance is a turn-off, too, and many assignments are strictly confidential.

But if clients are to acknowledge professional skills and pay you properly, you can't hide your light under a bushel.

Quiet confidence with the occasional insightful yet discreet anecdote about saving the day is the way to go. A sense of humor won't go amiss either; perhaps that is what your friend was aiming for. Unfortunately, she simply underscored her amateur status—including her ignorance of the wee matter of confidentiality.

Should the opportunity arise again, you can help by countering amateur and even professional linguists' silly stories in public with some pithier ones of your own, weaving in the importance of training, experience and your role as solution provider.

FA & WB

Q *I have a very basic question about interpreting.*
I work in medical research and often attend international meetings. At the last one, two out of three of the interpreters' teams systematically (as in: every single time) pronounced "European" as "EuROPean" (as in "Fallopian") and "Europe" as "EuROPE." They also referred repeatedly to what sounded like "tardjet" which I realized belatedly must have been "target."

The delegates joked about this during coffee breaks, but we all found it jarring and distracting.

I found myself wondering why these highly skilled, intelligent people in the booth had such trouble with easy, common words when they were coping well with some of the more difficult terminology and concepts. I gather from the conference organizers that they were all "qualified interpreters." Can you explain?

White Coat

A Dear Coat,
Good question!

Unlike translation, where a flawed written phrase can come back to haunt the perpetrator, interpreting is oral and by nature ephemeral. Which means practitioners can genuinely lose touch with their output—out it goes into the black hole in space, never to be heard by them again.

Unlike translation, too, interpreters may not be working into their native language. In your case, it sounds like both odd pronouncers were not native English speakers; perhaps they were influencing each other in a booth-induced folie à deux?

In any case, in a work environment where stress levels approach those of an air traffic control tower, correcting a fellow interpreter's pronunciation can be tricky.

One expert compares a colleague in the booth to a "buddy" in diving—a potential life-saver if things ever go seriously wrong. Good interpreters don't work half an hour "on" and half an hour "off," says this source, since an energetic colleague will provide backup, writing down figures and names, and even checking terminology in the background while the partner is at the microphone. With that sort of constructive relationship, it is relatively easy, during a break, for a native speaker to say "by the way, I noticed that you pronounce 'European' in an interesting way…" But it doesn't always happen.

Then again, some interpreters become blasé, as if they have made it into an exclusive club and are somehow beyond reproach.

An obvious remedy is continuing education, but there are not many opportunities. Another is delegate feedback, which remains all too rare. So next time, why not step back to the booth yourself during a coffee break and try "Hi, I noticed that you pronounce 'European' in an interesting way." Report back, please!

FA & WB

ALL SHAPES AND SIZES

Q*I operate a translation business and regularly deal with suppliers I can only describe as social misfits.*

Right now I am being stalked by an American gentleman from Wisconsin who has come to see me four times this week, wearing lederhosen and misbuttoned shirts (my company is in the financial district of a major city on the East Coast of the US).

Wednesday it was a non-stop talker from southern California in sweats and bangles with a giant plastic flower (from a shower curtain?) clamped to the top of her chignon.

Thursday a trio of wispy things who mumbled and all but fainted as they thrust CVs at me, yet applauded when the lederhosen man burst in to berate anonymous "agency owners" (not me, as far as I could tell) for "exploiting translators."

What is wrong with these people, anyway? They are always bleating and whining about their low incomes, but practical marketing advice about approaching new prospects (e.g., acquire and wear business attire for strategic meetings; turn down the volume and listen to others; look at the person you are talking to if you hope to do business with them), either gives them the vapors or gets them stamping their feet.

I used to find this amusing, but lately am getting depressed at just how clueless they are.

Do they not realize that their own lack of basic business sense/social skills is a big part of their problem (and mine)? How can we get clients to take translation seriously when so many practitioners are this weird?

More to the point: my retirement is still 15 years off. How can I keep from sweeping into the office with the living-room drapes across my shoulders myself one fine day?

Checking the Mirror

A Dear Mirror,
You could always suggest that your local translators' association endorse

a professional dress code. Or issue T-shirts with your corporate logo and a hard-hitting tagline to promising but offbeat suppliers as a step up the ladder in dressing for success.

Which brings us to the most important issue, one you have delicately sidestepped: what kind of work do these people produce? If it is good to excellent, surely it is in your interest to encourage their wildest eccentricities in both dress and manner, since this will scare off competing agencies and consolidate your role and margin as go-between. Direct clients won't touch weirdoes with a barge pole, which is precisely what we want, right?

If your impecunious translators are also poor translators, consider a Trojan Horse ploy: act now to straighten out their wardrobes and manners as a prelude to unleashing them out on the market as direct suppliers. This could be the best investment you ever made; as everyone knows, clients recovered singed and reeling from translation disasters are some of the most loyal around.

A summer solstice drinks party with a fashion theme might be just the ticket. Book a speaker from Dale Carnegie, and announce up front that there will be plenty to drink and eat; this should bring in all the bottom-feeders.

In the meantime, take regular precautions—make sure nobody is packing a gun and don't take any of these guys to lunch with clients. And let us know how the party goes.

FA & WB

Q *I recently discovered that a person with whom I have exchanged various comments on an elist has been claiming to potential clients that he "has worked with me." This makes me very unhappy, since work-wise I am quite a stickler, and an independent stickler at that.*

I'm uncomfortable simply telling him that I want him to stop it, as this seems too aggressive (perhaps he didn't really mean it that way, perhaps he has personal problems that I am unaware of). But I want it to stop.

Have you got a good one-liner and/or hook to make this point succinctly, elegantly, not too unpleasantly?

Every Man for Himself

A Dear Every,
How, indeed, do you let indelicate/unaware/desperate individuals know they've stepped over the line?

The least painful option we've found is an email indicating you are aware of what is going on, yet providing a plausible excuse to let the guilty party off the hook (this first time).

Example: "Hi, I recently discovered that [fill in client name] has erroneously come to the conclusion that we work together—no doubt because our language combinations are similar. I've written them already to set them straight, but wanted to ask that you keep an eye out for it, too. Wouldn't want to tread on your toes. Thanks!"

FA & WB

Q*I find I translate much better in the nude. My style is far more flowing, the words much easier to find. Is this something to worry about?*

Baring Soul

A Dear Bare,
In general we are all in favor of adapting working conditions to maximize productivity, but we need more information. Do you work at home or in an office? Do you live in a temperate zone?

FA & WB

Q*Your opinion of anonymous bloggers and cyber-posters please. What do these people have to hide? Assuming they genuinely know something about the translation industry and are not just government-issue, garden-variety (or hybrid) ranters, bullshitters, nut cases or conspiracy theorists, why the cloak of invisibility?*

Spooky

A Dear Spooky,
We wondered the same thing—briefly—before recalling how many bona fide adult-age humans enjoy spicing up their otherwise bland existence with gossip-mongering, in-jokes, fantasy worlds, secret societies and the like. And as anyone who's had anything to do with translator associations knows, a passel of linguists seem positively driven by the plots-and-rumors brigade—resulting in massive time-wasting for all concerned.

So let's look at it another way: anonymous or not, well-written blogs are a constructive use of energy. Some are downright entertaining and insightful. (Anonymous attacks on individuals and groups being the exception; at best silly and childish, at worst cowardly).

In our opinion the real drawback with anonymous postings lies elsewhere.

Consider: a good blog is seriously time-consuming to maintain, but an excellent showcase for an individual translator's writing style. What better way to reinforce your brand in a sometimes crowded market?

But this only works if readers and potential buyers know who you are. People, this is a no-brainer. What's with the "I can't afford to let people know who I am"?

Seen in this light, writing under a pseudonym demonstrates twitchiness, but above all a poor grasp of business and marketing.

It is hardly surprising that familiar complaints of anonymous bloggers are "lack of recognition and respect for translation" and "stupid clients." We bet these guys don't sign their professional output either (see Just Passing It On, page 50-51). Now why would that be?

FA & WB (identified in the column on line and in this book)

Q *I have already started teaching translation. So far so good. But I don't know how to score my students' translations. Do you have any suggestions?*

I should add that they are working towards a BA in English literature. The courses I teach include "Theories of translation," "Translating simple texts," "Translating idioms and metaphorical expressions," and "Translating literary texts." Students are supposed to get a general idea of translation at the end of the curriculum.

Paper Chaser

A Dear Chaser,

It sounds like your courses discuss what translation is (or might be) rather than training people to actually do it. Well, why not? But keep the distinction clear in your mind. Your students will be learning new ways to listen to the voice of authors in translation, and, with luck, gaining some appreciation of the challenges facing literary translators. They are not training to become translators. The assignments they do for you—including graded work—should reflect that.

Concrete suggestions: have students annotate translation assignments, explaining their choices. This will allow you to check that they have identified problems, even if you don't agree with their solutions. Devise exercises to test their grasp of method, and let them demonstrate that they know how to use the resources at their disposal. Make sure that those resources are available; exams or classroom exercises without dictionaries and other reference works are pointless. (Ever see a surgeon operate without a scalpel?).

You might also consider inviting practicing literary translators in for interviews or Q&A. Translating is a demanding, exciting field, and you are in an excellent position to bring this home to students.

Whatever you do, keep in mind a comment by one industry specialist: a

90% grade is pretty good for students, but in real-world translation, it is a fail. You might even repeat it to your class at regular intervals to remind them (and yourself) that their experience of translation as an academic exercise is very different from what professional translators do.

FA & WB

Q *Browsing the web I found a "controversial" language column by Peter Newmark that makes me wonder: Do translation academics have anything to teach working translators?*

Wordface Worker

A Dear Wordface,
An intriguing example, although Peter Newmark is hardly your typical academic; some would even call him a maverick.

An academic of our acquaintance insists that it is important to develop an ability to self-monitor and see yourself (and your texts) from the outside. If well taught, says this gentleman, theory can provide the conceptual tools you need to do this. We agree 100%.

The trick is to select the right materials from the work of theoreticians. Why not start with the aptly titled Can Theory Help Translators? by Andrew Chesterman and Emma Wagner, in St Jerome Publishing's "Translation Theories Explained" series (ISBN 1-900650-49-5; ISSN: 1365-0513).

FA & WB

Q *Wordface's query didn't state what "something controversial" I'd written in my column. What was it?*

The correspondent sounded as vague as most of yours. I try to make concrete suggestions to translators—at present on rule-governed and expressive punctuation—usually with examples. Take it or leave it. Your Wordface Worker is being superior, above the conflict, a vague wistful wondering comment, and no point at all.

Why don't your correspondents state their names? What are they hiding? I'm neither a maverick nor a scholar, just a pathetically serious person.

Peter Newmark

A Dear Caterpillar,
There's a misunderstanding here—several, in fact, and we hope we haven't contributed to another one of those tiresome practice vs. theory skirmishes (which miss the main point, to wit: how, concretely, can one most effectively

teach or consolidate translation skills?).

With regard to Wordface Worker, here's the inside dope: in a 3-minute lull between coordinating a morning fax and revising the work of a close-knit team of six translators working for 15 financial analysts, themselves revising investment strategy hourly as equity markets plummeted, all the while tracking European Central Bank policy statements and interest-rate movements with one eye and the latest developments in Enron-land with the other, our intrepid translator correspondent stumbled on your "Translation Now" remarks to the effect that English is superior to all other languages and wondered if he was on the same planet.

As he moved on to your paragraph on slang ["Both literary and non-literary translators have the task of finding a modern language that is easy and natural and avoids the numerous vivid neologisms, formerly called slang (e.g. 'anorak', 'eye candy', 'road rage'), which are normally old words with new meanings, that are too closely bound up with the contemporary translator's culture but are not appropriate to the time setting of the SL text."], a big fat brokerage report hit his desk, chockablock with poison pills, triple witching, the infamous dead cat bounce, white knights and inverse head-and-shoulder chart patterns—all images that speak to readers in other world financial markets.

Mind you, the bit about commas (rule-governed or expressive) may have hit home.

But not to worry. We hear that Wordface Worker is reconciled following your latest comments that good writing is as important in non-literary as in literary translation. We enjoyed that one, too, although if you are exhorting translators to "rigorously exclud[e] the superfluous in information texts" we feel you should also remind them to use a source-text wordcount for their invoices.

FA & WB

P.S.: Notwithstanding our reply to Spooky (page 260), we dole out pseudonyms liberally, following in the footsteps of such American columnists as Dorothy Dix and Garrison Keillor (ah, the late lamented Mr. Blue!), all in a spirit of good fun.

OUTREACH

Q *My college alumnae magazine recently ran an obituary for Shulamith Nardi, a Hebrew-English translator, interpreter, and communications advisor for decades to prime ministers in Israel. I was delighted to see that the person who wrote the obit distinguished between "translator" and "interpreter." I'd like to write a letter to the editor and comment on that, but I'm not sure of the key points to make so that readers will be educated a bit (if my letter gets printed). Do you have any suggestions?*

Mile a Minute

Dear Minute,

An article on how to write letters to the editor that make the cut is available on ATA's website (atanet.org). You might add to that some of the tips offered by the ever erudite Neil Inglis that we've distilled below:

• Editors face huge space constraints, so keep your letter short and tailored to your audience, weaving in references to current events or issues as topical hooks.

• Avoid lengthy recitations of your professional qualifications: explain your connection to the translation & interpreting world adroitly and in passing, if at all.

• Be witty; hand-wringing and self-pity are huge turn-offs.

• Prune drafts ruthlessly to eliminate cherished insights that are not strictly relevant to the matter at hand.

• If you are going to criticize, try using the sandwich technique: (1) congratulate the journalist for an insight, any insight (even if s/he has written utter nonsense, you can always express thanks "for raising this important issue"); (2) set the record straight and/or stick the knife in; (3) end on a humorous or philosophical note.

So much for general suggestions.

But in this case your journalist got it right, right? So you might simply congratulate him or her on being so astute, pointing out how few people outside the language industry make this key distinction. Emphasize the different skills that practitioners of each of these challenging professions bring to the task. A quote or anecdote about Ms Nardi would be particularly apt, if you've got one handy.

Or you might say—and this is just an example—that a translator is to an interpreter as the late Michael Jackson was to a heart surgeon: translators and facial reconstruction addicts live with mistakes forever after, while heart surgeons quietly bury theirs and interpreters commit any errors to the wind.

FA & WB

Q *I have an idea for improving the exposure of translators to the public. What about a motion picture? I think translation lends itself pretty well for a conspiracy theme, where in the end a translator saves the world or civilization as we know it. There is lots of material from secret messages in the Bible, cryptography and spies, prophecies and lost treasures, etc. The modern touch would be something involving a financial translator going to an heroic end, a sort of "Independence Day" to save the world, or at least the stock exchange, by struggling with a translation.*

Don't you think a Hollywood production would help us gain public appreciation? Any ideas? Any script? On second thought, the book should be first; sort of a Michener saga spanning the whole world and all ages.

Lights! Camera! Action!

A Dear Action,
An intriguing option. We suggest you submit a detailed proposal to the Fédération Internationale des Traducteurs (www.fit-ift.org). Be sure to include information on funding. Tell them Fire Ant & Worker Bee have agreed to play bit roles (see our agent).

To arouse interest, you might suggest to your national translators' & interpreters' association that they organize a film festival featuring screen portrayals of linguists as part of their annual conference—an alternative offering of mid- to late-evening fare for delegates not into Slavic singalongs, poetry readings and clog dancing.

There are plenty of flicks to choose from. Sidney Pollack's "The Interpreter" with Nicole Kidman and Sean Penn is an obvious choice. But there are many many others. What about Peter Greenaway's "The Pillow Book"? In this adaptation of the erotic 10th century Japanese literary classic, the male lead is a bisexual translator named Jérome and the female lead, a model and aspiring writer named Nagiko (Vivian Wu) "attempts to win over her publisher by sending to his offices a series of men whose bodies she has covered from head to toe with exquisite calligraphy—a kind of sexually-charged, high-concept book proposal." Heady stuff.

Fire Ant & Worker Bee agree to sit on the jury if you get this one off the ground (see our agent).

FA & WB

Q *I am really interested in Translation. Could you please offer me some information about it? Thank you very much.*

Big Question

A Dear Big,
At last a succinct question!

The usual answer is that translation involves taking reams of paper with lettering on them and turning them into reams of paper with lettering in a different language. While true, this explanation misses the point.

What professional translation is really about is turning white rectangles of paper with lettering on them into smaller, usually colored rectangles with figures on them—the more colored rectangles and the larger the figures the better. That is the point of the entire exercise—to enrich you, the translator.

If you were not as crassly materialistic as Fire Ant and Worker Bee, you could also say that translation is the grandest, most foolhardy enterprise that humans can engage in on this planet.

Picture the body of human knowledge, encompassed in language, as the earth. Then translation collectively becomes the most insanely ambitious activity ever conceived, namely to draw a 1:1 scale map of the earth. Failure is certain, yet you will score many small successes. A mere ant toiling in an anthill, you are part of a glorious project that connects you with an unbroken line of workers from time immemorial.

Welcome to the hill!

FA & WB

WEB ADDRESS BOOK

American Foundation for Translating and Interpreting (AFTI)	**www.afti.org**
American Translators Association (ATA)	**www.atanet.org**
American Literary Translators Association (ALTA)	**www.literarytranslators.org**
Association Suisse des Traducteurs, Terminologues et Interprètes (ASTTI)	**www.astti.ch**
Conférence Internationale Permanente d'Instituts Universitaires de Traducteurs et Interprètes (CIUTI)	**www.ciuti.org**
Institute of Linguists (IOL)	**www.iol.org.uk**
Institute of Translation and Interpreting (ITI)	**www.iti.org.uk**
International Federation of Translators (FIT)	**www.fit-europe.org**
National Accreditation Authority for Translators and Interpreters (NAATI)	**www.naati.com.au**
National Council on Interpreting in Healthcare	**www.ncihc.org**
New York Circle of Translators	**www.nyctranslators.org**
PEN American Center—Translation	**www.pen.org/translation**
Société Française des Traducteurs (SFT)	**www.sft.fr**
Society for Technical Communication (STC)	**www.stc.org**

INDEX

ABOUT THE EDITOR AND CO-AUTHOR

Chris Durban is a freelance translator (French to English) based in Paris, where she specializes in publication-level texts for the foreign shareholders, clients and partners of a selection of corporations and institutions.

For years she wrote *The Onionskin*, a client education column in ITI Bulletin (UK) and the ATA Chronicle (US), and from this developed *Translation, Getting it Right*, a 30-page guide for translation buyers now available in eight languages. Well over 100,000 paper copies have been distributed worldwide to date. She is also co-author of *Translation, Buying a Non-Commodity*, a detailed look at how specifications can help buyers and translators work together successfully. A third brochure for buyers—*Interpreting, Getting it Right*—is forthcoming.

Chris regularly gives lectures/workshops on specialization and working with direct clients, and has published many articles. Most emphasize the benefits that accrue to translators and clients alike when linguists take a proactive approach.

Since 2007, she has been particularly interested in raising awareness of the importance of writing skills for translators. To this end, she has taught on training courses with Ros Schwartz and in 2009 organized *Translate in the Catskills*, a writing workshop for translators. She is also co-founder and co-organizer of the SFT's *Université d'été de la traduction financière*, held every two years in Europe.

A member of the American Translators Association (ATA) and the Société Française des Traducteurs (SFT), Chris is a Fellow of the UK's Institute of Translation and Interpreting (ITI). She has served on ATA's PR committee and was awarded the association's Gode Medal in 2001. She is a past president and board member of the SFT.

Of course she is also co-author, with Eugene Seidel, of the *Fire Ant & Worker Bee* advice column that has run in Translation Journal (www.translationjournal.net) since October 1998.

To order additional copies of *The Prosperous Translator, Advice from Fire Ant & Worker Bee* visit www.prosperoustranslator.com

For volume purchasing inquiries or to contact Chris Durban about a media or speaking engagement, email fa&wb@translationjournal.net

CPSIA information can be obtained at www.ICGtesting.com
Printed in the USA
LVOW132048301212

313811LV00001B/86/P